Connoisseur's Guide to Bordeaux Wines

Yves Durand

Sterling Publishing Co., Inc. New York

I look upon my wine cellar as a haven to which I can retreat and laugh at inflation, recession, and shortages.

— *Yves Durand*

Library of Congress Cataloging-in-Publication Data

Durand, Yves, 1939–
Connoisseur's guide to Bordeaux wine.

Includes index.
1. Wine and winemaking—France—Bordeaux. I. Title.
TP553.D82 1987 641.2'22'094471 87-10117

Published by Sterling Publishing Co., Inc.
Two Park Avenue, New York, NY 10016
Distributed in Canada by Oak Tree Press Ltd.
c/o Canadian Manda Group, P.O. Box 920, Station U
Toronto, Ontario, Canada M8Z 5P9
Distributed in the United Kingdom by Blandford Press
Link House, West Street, Poole, Dorset BH15 1LL, England
Distributed in Australia by Capricorn Ltd.
P.O. Box 665, Lane Cove, NSW 2066
Manufactured in the United States of America

Contents

Appendix

Introduction

Like all red-wine lovers, I have been wooed, seduced, and overwhelmingly satisfied by the great red wines of Bordeaux. No matter how delicious other red wines that I taste may be, I will gladly rendezvous anywhere at any time for another sip of charming, irresistible claret.

As a Frenchman, I am used to being in control of my loves—except with claret. The great château-bottled reds of Bordeaux are different. They have breeding and elegance; they command respect; their beauty withstands the test of time; their worth is not questioned; and they are in such demand that I consider it a privilege to know them. Even so, they have never taken advantage of this situation, and they have never disappointed me.

Do not think that this love of red Bordeaux wine comes from some ignorant partiality of mine to all things French. I judge all of them by international standards of consistency and quality. In so doing, I find that as a group the great red Bordeaux are truly exceptional and as yet unequaled in the world of wine.

In honor of these great red Bordeaux, I have compiled many tasting notes over the years and gathered those of what I consider the fifty-five best and most consistent properties into this unique reference book. Here are ratings and tasting notes for each of the top fifty-five châteaux in nearly every vintage year of consequence from 1945 onwards. Although 1945 was an outstanding vintage year, not all of the châteaux were lucky enough to make outstanding wines. Now you will know which ones did and which didn't produce outstanding wines, as well as which wines are still maintaining their character and elegance.

Perhaps this book will inspire you to organize your own Bordeaux tasting notes. In comparing your impressions with mine, let us agree to disagree as all wine experts do when they compare notes, but let us do so in a spirit of true brotherhood and our mutual love for the great reds of Bordeaux. When you have occasion to taste some of these remarkable wines from great vintages, remember to take good notes.

These ratings and tasting notes are, of course, subjective, but they have proved to be very helpful whenever my friends ask me what to buy and how long to keep the wine before it reaches its peak. Considering the costliness of these great Bordeaux, this information is very necessary before one decides to buy, age in a wine cellar, and drink.

All of the red wines reviewed here are from the best districts of Bordeaux: Haut-Médoc, Graves, St-Emilion, and Pomerol. For the Bordeaux bargain hunter, I have provided a list of the top Cru Bourgeois châteaux in the Médoc (see page 24). I have also indicated the names of good properties outside of the Médoc which I have not included in my classification (page 25). All of these châteaux produce very good red wines in a more moderate price range.

This book is the fruit of twenty years of tasting red Bordeaux wines. I began to appreciate claret almost as soon as I left my mother's bosom. I was born in 1939, on a farm close to Bordeaux. Pepe, my viticulturist grandfather, taught me at an early age to share his enthusiasm for well-made wines. I learned so well that on hot summer days, when I was no more than twelve years old, I would make the perilous descent through the trap door into an empty fermentation vat. I would pull myself up and over the edge of the vat and jump down onto the cool and musty dirt floor of the locked wine cellar. I would fight my way through spiderwebs, kneel down next to a barrel, and drink the heavenly nectar directly from the spigot. Unfortunately, on one of these expeditions my younger brother, Bernard, forgot to close the spigot tightly. For several hours, many gallons of the precious beverage trickled onto the ground. As you can imagine, I was severely reprimanded. No wine was served with my meals for a whole week.

As an adult, I worked for ten years in the best restaurants in seven different European countries. In 1965, I arrived in Atlanta, Georgia, determined to open a French restaurant and grow roots in this land of cotton (actually there is no more cotton around Atlanta than Château Pétrus in Burgundy). After a few years, the Rue de Paris restaurant opened.

At this time, my interest in the delicious nectar of Bacchus became more acute and my desire to learn about, compare, taste, and critique wines grew immense. I religiously and almost scientifically kept thousands and thousands of tasting notes that I acquired in my profession covering three decades. I also participated in or helped to organize a number of wine-tasting clubs in Atlanta. Allow me to take this opportunity to extend my appreciation, gratitude, and love to all of my friends in the following wine clubs: the Sommelier Guild of Atlanta, the Knights of the Vine, the Commanderie de Bordeaux, Vingarde (better known as the Atlanta Wine Hall of Fame), and the "nameless wine group of six," which meets every other week to assess fully mature French wines and to have just plain fun.

All of these various tastings have given me a unique opportunity to evaluate and compare all of the leading properties in Bordeaux, and to share with you my personal and professional experience on the subject with the affection of a true oenophile.

To your health and to my love— *Par Bordeaux, pour Bordeaux, toujours Bordeaux.* May this book bring you closer to fine wine and allow you to share my passion for the great reds of Bordeaux.

The Bordeaux Region

The Bordeaux region in the southwestern part of France has been famous for its elegant red wines since the twelfth century during the time of Henry II. The English coined the term "claret" for the red Bordeaux wines, and their preference for claret helped to popularize these wines throughout the civilized world. It is in Bordeaux that the noble Cabernet Sauvignon and Merlot grapes are combined to make the world's most aristocratic and sought-after red wines. However, these illustrious grapes are not the only reason for the success of the red Bordeaux. Climate, soil conditions (various combinations of gravel and limestone), and the exacting techniques of its winemakers with their centuries-old traditions also contribute to the end product.

Although one-third of Bordeaux's wines are white, its reputation, for the most part, rests with the great red wines produced in the districts of Médoc, Graves, St-Emilion, and Pomerol (with the exceptions of Sauternes and Barsac, which produce sweet white wines of outstanding quality and reputation). The Médoc, particularly the southern half of the district closest to the city of Bordeaux called the Haut-Médoc, is without doubt the most prestigious of the four districts. The glorious villages of the Appelation Contrôlées Margaux, St-Julien, Pauillac, and St-Estèphe (and to a lesser degree, Moulis and Listrac) are located in the Haut-Médoc. By an Appellation Contrôlée, the French government strictly controls the production of wine in a particular location. These laws concern defined areas, grape varieties, minimum alcohol content, maximum yields, methods of cultivation and vinification, and standard of quality.

Médoc

The red wines of the Médoc, the area slightly north of the city of Bordeaux along the western bank of the Gironde Estuary, were classified in 1855 because they were considered Bordeaux's finest. The classification of 1855 was realized for the benefit of the Paris World's Fair of that year. It was meant to classify not only the red wines of the Médoc, but all of the red wines made in the Bordeaux area more commonly known as the Gironde region. This 1855 classification contains only the wines of the Médoc, with the exception of one red wine of the Graves district, Château Haut-Brion. It is easy to understand why, after all these years, this classification of the Gironde's red wines became known as the classification of the Médoc.

The 1855 classification (see page 164) divided the very best of all of the châteaux among five classes called growths, or *crus* in French. Every château within a growth or cru is considered to be of equal quality with the others. Remember that for a property to even be classified as a fifth growth is quite an honor and accomplishment. The only official change that has ever been made in the 1855 classification was the promotion of Château Mouton-Rothschild from second to first growth, which occurred in 1973. Every château that appears in the 1855 classification is called Grand Cru Classé or Cru Classé. There are sixty-one châteaux listed in the classification, which is organized as follows:

5 First Growths (Premiers Crus)
14 Second Growths (Deuxièmes Crus)
14 Third Growths (Troisièmes Crus)
10 Fourth Growths (Quatrièmes Crus)
18 Fifth Growths (Cinquièmes Crus)

Many years after the 1855 classification was

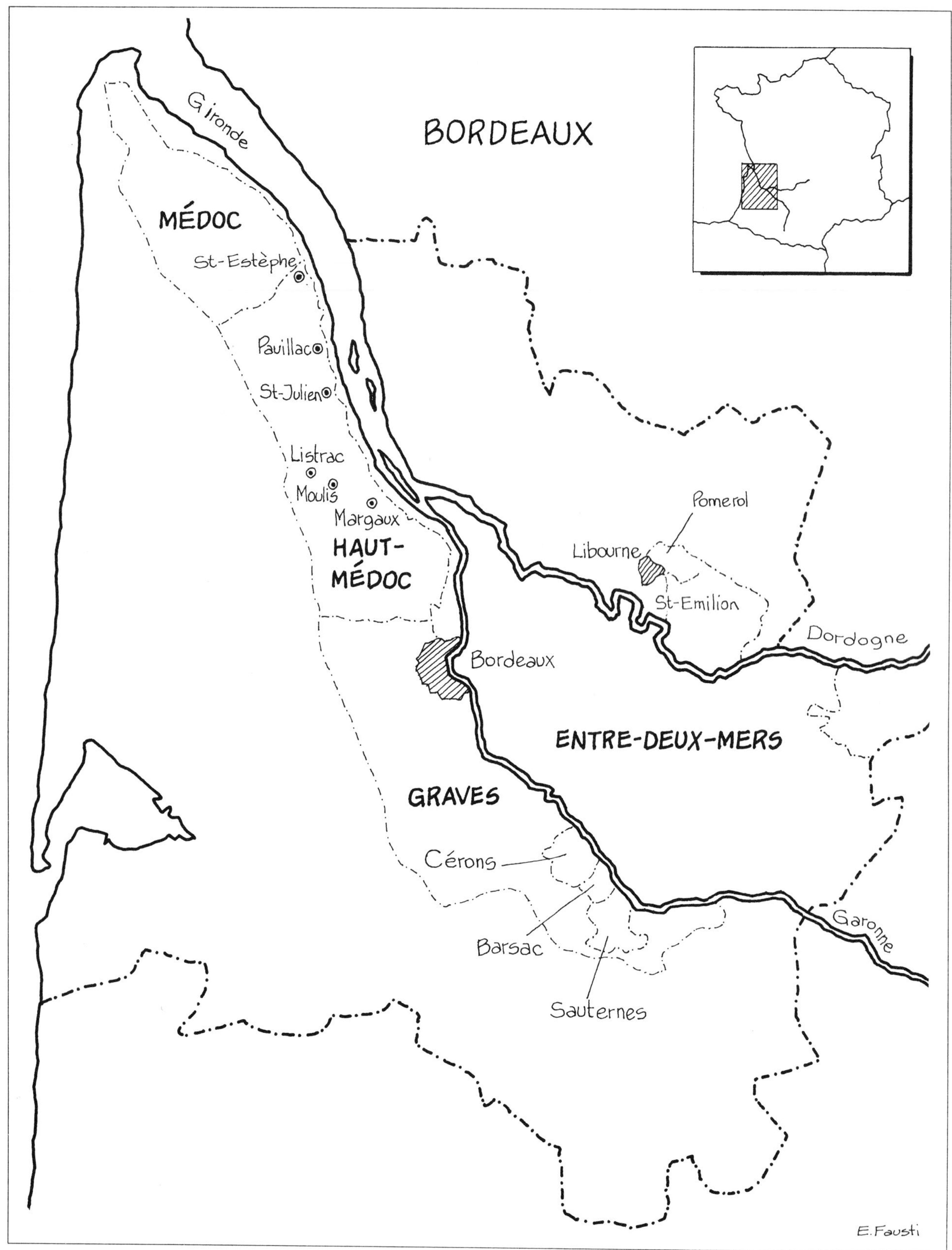
BORDEAUX
Gironde
MÉDOC
St-Estèphe
Pauillac
St-Julien
Listrac
Moulis
Margaux
HAUT-MÉDOC
Pomerol
Libourne
St-Emilion
Dordogne
Bordeaux
ENTRE-DEUX-MERS
GRAVES
Cérons
Barsac
Sauternes
Garonne
E. Fausti

made, five wine brokers (courtiers), under the authority of the Chamber of Commerce of Bordeaux and the Chamber of Agriculture of the Gironde, sought to give some recognition to the many hundreds of châteaux in the Médoc that produced superior wine but did not make it into one of the top five growths. In 1932, 444 châteaux were placed into the following three categories (see page 171):

Crus Bourgeois Superieurs Exceptionnels (6)
Crus Bourgeois Superieurs (99)
Crus Bourgeois (339)

Then in 1978, the *Syndicat des Crus Grands Bourgeois et Crus Bourgeois du Médoc* established a "*Palmares Syndical de 1978*" (honor list of 1978). Actually this list was first created in 1966 and revised in 1978. This 1978 honor list was composed of three categories. Politics prevailed, and only 123 wines were on this "honor list," since only the members of the syndicate were eligible for consideration. None of the Bourgeois classifications (1932 or 1978) were made official by the French government. The 1978 categories (see page 179) are:

Crus Grands Bourgeois Exceptionnels (18)
Crus Grands Bourgeois (41)
Crus Bourgeois (64)

From among the two classifications of Crus Bourgeois, I have chosen my own favorites for the Bordeaux bargain hunter, and I have compiled a small list in alphabetical order for your use (see page 24). These few Crus Bourgeois, 36 out of 251 in existence today, have provided me with much enjoyment. I have included them in this book because, in my experience, they have always been a very good value.

Graves

The red and white wines of the Graves district (see page 12 for a description of its location) were first classified in 1953 and then again in 1959 as follows:

Red Crus Classés (13)
White Crus Classés (9)

If the words "Grand Cru" or "Cru Exceptionnel" appear on wine labels from the Graves district, it does not signify that the wine is in a higher class. However, if the word "Superieur" is on a white Graves label, it indicates a higher minimum alcoholic content (12 percent instead of 11 percent for the regular white Graves).

A notable omission in the Graves classification is the great white wine of Château Haut-Brion, an omission that was never corrected. Wine writers David Peppercorn, Alexis Lichine, and Robert Parker all have said that it was corrected in 1960, but it is simply not true. White Château Haut-Brion is still an unclassified wine. The red Château Haut-Brion is the only Graves in the 1855 classification and today is considered one of the two (along with Château La Mission-Haut-Brion) very best red Graves wines, yet these two are not given any preference or superior rating among the red Graves of the 1959 classification (see page 170).

St-Emilion

This red-wine-producing region, which is slightly northeast of the city of Bordeaux on the bank of the Dordogne River, was classified, in 1955, 1969, and 1985. Each of its two categories lists the châteaux in alphabetical order, not in order of quality (see page 167). The two categories are as follows:

Premiers Grands Crus Classés (two first great growths classified in class A and nine in class B)
Grands Crus Classés (63 great growths classified)

In 1984, the laws for Appellation Contrôlées of St-Emilion changed. But this has nothing to do

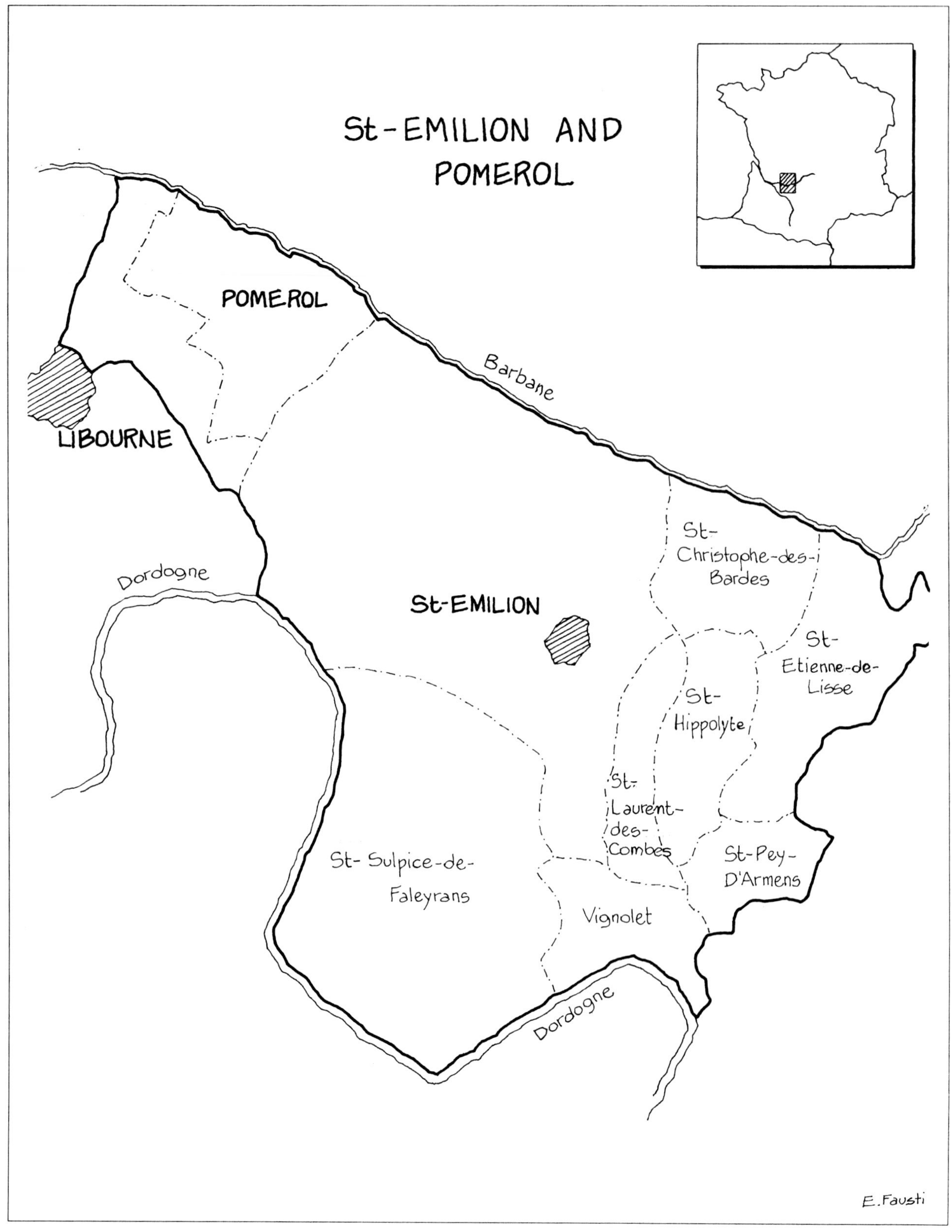
St-EMILION AND POMEROL
POMEROL
LIBOURNE
Barbane
Dordogne
St-EMILION
St-Christophe-des-Bardes
St-Etienne-de-Lisse
St-Hippolyte
St-Laurent-des-Combes
St-Pey-D'Armens
St-Sulpice-de-Faleyrans
Vignolet
Dordogne
E. Fausti

with the actual classification, which remains the same. Remember, Appellation Contrôlées are French laws governing the production and quality of wine within an area. A classification is an official ranking of the quality of the wine produced at each estate of that area.

Before 1984 the former St-Emilion Appellation Contrôlées were:

St-Emilion (11 percent minimum alcohol)
St-Emilion Grand Cru (11.5 percent minimum alcohol)
St-Emilion Grand Cru Classé (11.5 percent minimum alcohol)
St-Emilion Premier Grand Cru Classé (11.5 percent minimum alcohol)

As you can see, the former appellations were mixed up with the classification. This was not the practice in the rest of Bordeaux. For example, in Pauillac, a property qualifies for Pauillac's Appellation Contrôlée no matter how unknown or mediocre the wine is. It will enjoy the same Pauillac appellation as Château Lafite-Rothschild.

The new St-Emilion Appellation Contrôlées are:

St-Emilion
St-Emilion Grand Cru

In essence, the word "Classé" has been deleted. However, the meaning of Grand Cru Classé and Grand Cru in relation to wines from St-Emilion have no relationship to the Grand Cru Classés of the Médoc or Graves. They were not judged by the same standards and therefore cannot be compared.

Pomerol

Pomerol is the smallest red-wine-producing region in Bordeaux, bordering on the northwestern side of St-Emilion. None of the wines of Pomerol were ever officially classified, but many people consider Château Pétrus to be the equal of the first growths of the Médoc or the first great growths of St-Emilion.

LALANDE DE POMEROL AND NÉAC

These red-wine appellations are located north of Pomerol in the communes of Lalande and Néac. Like the previously mentioned appellations, they are authorized to use the Cabernet Sauvignon, Merlot, Cabernet Franc, and Malbec grape varietals (Médoc and Graves may add Petit Verdot as well). You probably will never encounter a bottle with the Néac A.O.C., because virtually all of the properties use the Lalande de Pomerol A.O.C.

FRONSAC AND CANON-FRONSAC

These two red-wine appellations are located west of Pomerol and the city of Libourne on the right bank of the Dordogne River. The wines from Canon-Fronsac are generally better than the ones from Fronsac since its grapes come from the best slopes in the area. Actually, only parts of two villages can claim the Canon-Fronsac A.O.C. The Fronsac A.O.C. can be claimed by six and one-half villages.

ST-EMILION SATELLITES

There are three red-wine appellations located north of St-Emilion, which are named Puisseguin-St-Emilion, Lussac-St-Emilion, and Montagne-St-Emilion, from east to west. Until 1973, there were two other satellites that have now merged with Montagne-St-Emilion: St-Georges-St-Emilion and Parsac-St-Emilion.

BORDEAUX-CÔTES DE CASTILLON

This rather new (1955) red-wine appellation is situated on the eastern border of the St-Emilion A.O.C. It comprises nine villages, which are authorized to use the Carmenère and Petit Verdot grape varietals in addition to the ones listed for Lalande de Pomerol.

Dry White Bordeaux Wines

Graves

This region of Bordeaux covers quite a distance: It is approximately 30 miles (50 kilometres) long, from the Médoc border in the north to the southern border near the Lot et Garonne region. On the east, it is limited by the plains running along the Garonne River; on the west, it borders the Landes National Forest. The Graves region totally surrounds the city of Bordeaux and encompasses three regions of Appellation d'Origine Contrôlées: Sauternes, Barsac, and Cérons.

White wines of Graves are primarily made from a combination of three grapes: Sauvignon Blanc, Sémillon, and Muscadelle. For the most part, they make wines that are dry to very dry in style. (The exception to this rule is moelleux, which is an aromatic, almost viscous white wine. Even though the residual sugar is low, one gets an impression of fruity sweetness. Many of these wines come from the region of Cérons, but they are atypical of Graves wines.

The white wines of Graves are the best dry whites in Bordeaux, but by no means can they be considered outstanding. I have not tasted the hundreds of properties and their different vintages. But of the approximately fifty I have followed through the years, few have made it on my list of favorites. The quality of most white classified wines from Graves is not better than many unclassified whites. The price is the only difference.

The best of the white Graves wines, which are very expensive and also rare, are:

Domaine de Chevalier (classified)
Château Haut-Brion Blanc (unclassified)
Château Laville-Haut-Brion (classified)

These three châteaux have one thing in common: They age very well for white wines—often from ten to fifteen years and in some vintages as long as twenty to thirty years. They are rich, opulent, and powerful. When mature, they acquire a delicious nutty taste without losing the freshness and liveliness of their crisp fruit. The hard decision is to choose whether or not to invest in these wines instead of, for instance, a Corton-Charlemagne. After all, Sauvignon Blanc will never be Chardonnay.

The following is a list of some very affordable white Graves that I recommend:

Château Couhins-Lurton (classified)
Château de Fieuzal (unclassified)
Château La Louvière (unclassified)
Château Le Reverdon (unclassified)
Château Pontac-Montplaisir (unclassified)

I will not bother to mention other classified growths of white Graves wines. There is no point in paying high prices for wines that are simply not worth it. Too many of these classified properties have been producing wines unworthy of their reputations.

Entre-deux-Mers

This very large wine-producing area lies between two rivers (not two seas)—the Garonne and the Dordogne rivers. By law, only the whites can bear the Entre-deux-Mers A.O.C.; the red wines of this region must bear the A.O.C. of Bordeaux. The whites are vinified in a very dry style, with no more than four grams of residual sugar per litre. Since the '80s, this region has improved its winemaking methods and now these very pale-colored white wines are clean, crisp, and dry, with an understated aroma. The grapes used are generally the same as for the rest of the Bordeaux region: Sauvignon Blanc, Sémillion, and Muscadelle. By law, 70 percent of these white varietals must be used, to which can be added a blend of the following additional grapes: Merlot Blanc (maximum 30 percent) and Colombard, Ugni Blanc, and Mauzac (maximum 10 percent). This is an unpretentious dry white wine with very good acidity, lean, and not opulently flavored. It makes a delightful complement with oysters on the half shell, grilled fresh sardines, and hors d'oeuvres.

Geographically speaking, this is one of the most charming regions of the Gironde with beautiful châteaux and old ruins. It is a hilly area flanked by vineyards, especially near the township of Monségur and the villages of Targon and Sauveterre. If you ever have the chance to drive from Bordeaux to St-Emilion, I recommend the following sightseeing trip, which should take approximately three hours. Drive along road D10, which follows the Garonne River. At Cadillac, make a left turn on D11 towards Targon. After Targon, turn right on D671 towards Sauveterre. Then follow D14 to Castelmoron, D139 to Saint-Ferme, D16 to Auriolles, and D126 to Blasimon. Visit the Moulin de Labarthe and also the old abbey of Blasimon. Take D127E to D670, then turn north on that road, and you should be in St-Emilion in fifteen minutes.

I almost forgot to mention a small bit of trivia about Entre-deux-Mers that Mr. Burton Hobson, my gracious publisher, would never forgive me for if I did not write about it. Within the A.O.C. Entre-deux-Mers and located north of Cadillac in the region of Haut-Benauge, there are nine communes that claim a dual appellation: Entre-deux-Mers or Entre-deux-Mers-Haut-Benauge.

However, the wines from these areas can only be white and the quality and conditions of production are exactly the same for both appellations. In this same mini-region there is also a dry white wine from the A.O.C. of Bordeaux-Haut-Benauge, which is made a little differently from that of an Entre-deux-Mers-Haut-Benauge or a simple white Bordeaux.

Graves de Vayres

This little-known A.O.C. is on the left bank of the Dordogne River, facing Libourne and surrounded by the Entre-deux-Mers region. Graves de Vayres has been decreasing its production of white wines, since reds are more profitable. The dry whites are very similar to those of Entre-deux-Mers. However, contrary to Entre-deux-Mers, the vintners of this area can legally make a moelleux-style white wine, which is mellow and rich. Its red wines—made from Cabernet Sauvignon, Cabernet Franc, and Merlot grapes—are entitled to the Graves de Vayres A.O.C. The best white or red wines of this region come from vineyards planted on gravelly soil. To give you an idea of how minuscule the production is: There are 2,500 acres of vineyards, but only 375 acres of red grapes and 750 acres of white grapes are declared as Graves de Vayres A.O.C. These produce about 140,000 cases of white (43 hectolitres per hectare maximum) and 66,000 cases of red (40 hectolitres per hectare maximum).

Sainte-Foy-Bordeaux

Sainte-Foy-Bordeaux is located in the northeast corner of Entre-deux-Mers, and sold its wines labelled Entre-deux-Mers until 1926. Today it has its own appellation and can make both white and red wines. Sainte-Foy-Bordeaux is known mostly for its white wines; however, more red wines have been produced in recent years due to their profitability. The white wines can be dry, moelleux, or very sweet (*liquoreux* in French).

The dry whites have a very subtle nose and a slight color. They are lean, crisp, and dry with very good acidity. Here again, the whites are made from Sémillon, Sauvignon Blanc, and Muscadelle. A combination of Merlot Blanc, Colombard, and Ugni Blanc can be added in proportion of no more than 10 percent total.

The production of the moelleux and the very sweet liquoreux wines have been cut back drastically since the consumer's demand has decreased. The liquoreux can have a beautiful yellow color, much finesse, and a very attractive floral bouquet. The moelleux resemble the taste and texture of the liquoreux, but with much less residual sugar.

Côtes de Bourg

This region is partly on the right bank of the Dordogne River and partly on the right bank of the Gironde Estuary. It is located directly across from Margaux. This A.O.C. can be Bourg, Bourgeais, or Côtes de Bourg (which appears the most often). Red and white wines are produced under this A.O.C.

White wines are produced mainly in the north and in the east of the area. The grapes used are Sémillon, Sauvignon Blanc, Muscadelle, Merlot Blanc, and Colombard. The wines are generally dry, but a few are made in the moelleux style. The dry ones are very pale in color, light, refreshing, uncomplicated, with a very characteristic but understated aroma and flavor.

The red wines are produced from Cabernet Sauvignon, Cabernet Franc, Malbec, and Merlot grapes. In good years, they acquire a lovely color and are high in alcohol, yet they remain supple and fresh with an aroma of their own imparted from the soil.

Premières Côtes de Bordeaux

The Premières Côtes de Bordeaux region is shaped like a corridor alongside the right bank of the Garonne River. It is about 40 miles (70 kilometres) long from the southeast to the northwest, and four miles (seven kilometres) wide. It starts north of Bordeaux in the commune of Bassens and ends south in Saint-Maixant. It totally surrounds the A.O.C.s of Loupiac and Sainte-Croix-du-Mont. The A.O.C. of Premières Côtes de Bordeaux applies to red and white wines. Thirty-seven communes are on the slopes and hilltops that dominate the Garonne River.

Since the 1981 harvest, the white wines of this region must have no less than four grams of residual sugar per litre. Therefore, dry white wines cannot be produced under this A.O.C. These white wines tend to have a pronounced aromatic bouquet with a certain finesse when backed by good acidity. They are sweet to very sweet, and some of them even have a tendency to become liquoreux, especially when they come from one of the 22 communes that can claim the A.O.C. of Cadillac. Drink and enjoy white Premières Côtes de Bordeaux as apéritifs or served with foie gras, since they retain an attractive floral dimension without overpowering the foie gras or one's taste buds.

The red wines are made from Cabernet Sauvignon, Cabernet Franc, Carmenère, Merlot, Malbec, and Petit-Verdot grapes. On the label, the name of the commune or village may be added to the words Premières Côtes de Bordeaux, but only for red wines reaching 11.5 percent of alcoholic content. The minimum alcoholic content required for the red A.O.C. Premières Côtes de Bordeaux is 10.5 percent. The best red wines of this region are generally produced in the northern part of this appellation.

Château Archambeau
Château de Cérons
Château Hillot
Château Mayne-Binet
Grand-Enclos du Château de Cérons

Sainte-Croix-du-Mont

Sainte-Croix-du-Mont is located on the right bank of the Garonne River across from Sauternes. The Sainte-Croix-du-Mont A.O.C. is only for their sweet white wines (liquoreux in French) produced from Sémillon, Sauvignon Blanc, and Muscadelle affected by the noble rot.

Generally speaking, the wines of Sainte-Croix-du-Mont have less breed than those across the Garonne in Sauternes. But they do possess charm and style made of high-quality fruit laced with honey and an aromatic floral component. They are mouth-filling, velvety, and long-lasting on the palate. And they can be very reasonably priced.

The quality of each individual growth can vary greatly with the nature of the soil and subsoil, the care of the vineyard, the picking of the grapes and the vinification procedures.

A few recommended properties are:

(!) Château Coulac
Château Grand-Peyrot
Château La Grave
(!) Château Lamarque
(!) Château Loubens
(!) Château Lousteau-Vieil
(!) Château du Mont
Château La Mouleyre
Château du Pavillon
Château La Rame
Domaine de Roustit
(!) Château de Tastes*

(!) My favorites.

(*) Uprooted in the early '80s by the city of Sainte-Croix-du-Mont (of all the people). Mr. Bruno Prats, the proprietor, kept only one hectare (2.5 acres) in the best possible location (the slope), from which he produces a Château de Tastes only in great years.

Loupiac

Loupiac is north of and contiguous to Sainte-Croix-du-Mont. Its wines can only be sweet and produced from Sémillon, Sauvignon Blanc, and Muscadelle grapes affected by the noble rot. Its maximum yield per hectare is 40 hectolitres.

The white wines of Loupiac have less breed than those of Sauternes and are very close to those of Sainte-Croix-du-Mont. They equally possess charm and style. They can be round and velvety on the palate with flavors reminiscent of apples and tropical fruits with perhaps less honey undertones. They are mouth-filling and long-lasting on the palate.

The quality of each individual growth can vary greatly with the nature of the soil and subsoil, the care of the vineyard, the picking of the grapes and the vinification process.

A few recommended properties are:

Château du Cros
Clos Jean
Château Loupiac-Gaudiet

Cadillac

This township is adjacent to Loupiac, but twenty-one other communes have the right to use this A.O.C. All twenty-two are in the Premières Côtes de Bordeaux territory and as such can claim either A.O.C.

The Cadillac A.O.C. was created on August 10,

1973, but on December 18, 1980, a decree greatly modified conditions of production in this area. The latter date is when Cadillac became an A.O.C. of sweet white wines. The decree specified that only Sémillon, Sauvignon Blanc, and Muscadelle grapes can be used. The must has to contain a minimum of 221 grams per litre of natural sugar. The alcoholic content must not be less than 12 percent, the yield not more than 40 hectolitres per hectare. But a new criterion required for a liquoreux wine is a minimum of residual sugar (18 grams per litre of fermented wine in this case). Only Côtes de Francs Liquoreux has a similar clause (27 grams). Sauternes, Barsac, Cerons, Sainte-Croix-du-Mont, and Loupiac do not have such precision to obtain their respective A.O.C.s.

I believe this welcome new clause is probably due to the relatively recent A.O.C. of Cadillac (1973, 1980) and Bordeaux-Côtes de Francs Liquoreux (1967). I wish that the other five liquoreux A.O.C.s would adopt similar criteria.

Cadillac is a very young A.O.C., but I expect that its wines will be very close in style to those of its neighbors, Loupiac and Sainte-Croix-du-Mont. The following are a few properties that already have made some very good quality liquoreux white wines in years when the climatic conditions lent themselves to the development of noble rot.

CRUS	**COMMUNES**
Château La Bertrande	Omet
Château Birot	Beyguey
Château Fayau	Cadillac
Château du Juge	Cadillac
Château Justa	Cadillac
Château Labatut	Saint-Maixant
Château Malagar	Saint-Maixant

Yves Durand's Classification

With so many Bordeaux classifications made by people at different times using variable criteria, it is almost impossible to make comparisons between them and establish a hierarchy among the properties of all the districts. That is why I propose to do what the Chamber of Commerce of Bordeaux cannot do—create my own red Bordeaux classification of all the châteaux over many vintages, so that we can compare Médocs with Graves, St-Emilions, and Pomerols.

I have kept the format of the 1855 classification and ranked the château into first through fifth growths, listing the individual châteaux alphabetically by district. Then I have put a plus or minus number next to a château to indicate that I have upgraded it or downgraded it from its original place in the 1855 classification. Some of the châteaux have so impressed me in recent years that I have given them an exclamation point (!). This means that I feel they are on their way up to a higher growth or level in my classification.

As you look through my classification, pay particular attention to the nine châteaux listed in the first growths, the nineteen châteaux listed in the second growths, and the twenty-seven châteaux listed in the third growths, because these are the fifty-five great red Bordeaux for which I have compiled tasting notes in the rest of this book.

Yves Durand's Classification of 135 Red Bordeaux Wines

PREMIERS CRUS (9 First Growths)	**Appellations Contrôlées**	
Château Lafite-Rothschild	Pauillac	Haut-Médoc
Château Latour	Pauillac	Haut-Médoc
Château Margaux	Margaux	Haut-Médoc
Château Mouton-Rothschild	Pauillac	Haut-Médoc
Château Haut-Brion	Graves	
Château La Mission-Haut-Brion	Graves	
Château Ausone	St-Emilion	
Château Cheval-Blanc	St. Emilion	
Château Pétrus	Pomerol	

(Yves Durand's Classification continued)

DEUXIÈMES CRUS (19 Second Growths)	**Appellations Contrôlées**		
Château Beychevelle	St-Julien	(+2)	Haut-Médoc
Château Cos-d'Estournel	St-Estèphe		Haut-Médoc
Château Ducru-Beaucaillou	St-Julien		Haut-Médoc
Château Gruaud-Larose	St-Julien		Haut-Médoc
Château Léoville-Barton	St-Julien		Haut-Médoc
Château Léoville-Las-Cases	St-Julien		Haut-Médoc
Château Léoville-Poyferré	St-Julien		Haut-Médoc
Château Lynch-Bages	Pauillac	(+3)	Haut-Médoc
Château Montrose	St-Estèphe		Haut-Médoc
Château Palmer	Margaux	(+1)	Haut-Médoc
(!) Château Pichon-Longueville, Comtesse de Lalande	Pauillac		Haut-Médoc
Domaine de Chevalier	Graves		
Château Figeac	St-Emilion		
Château Magdelaine	St-Emilion		
Château Certan de May	Pomerol		
Château La Conseillante	Pomerol		
Château L'Evangile	Pomerol		
Château Lafleur	Pomerol		
Château Trotanoy	Pomerol		

TROISIÈMES CRUS (27 Third Growths)			
Château Branaire-Ducru	St-Julien	(+1)	Haut-Médoc
Château Brane-Cantenac	Margaux	(-1)	Haut-Médoc
Château Calon-Ségur	St-Estèphe		Haut-Médoc
Château Cantemerle	Haut-Médoc	(+2)	Haut-Médoc
Château Duhart-Milon-Rothschild	Pauillac	(+1)	Haut-Médoc
Château Durfort-Vivens	Margaux	(-1)	Haut-Médoc
Château Giscours	Margaux		Haut-Médoc
Château Grand-Puy-Lacoste	Pauillac	(+2)	Haut-Médoc
Château d'Issan	Margaux		Haut-Médoc
Château La Lagune	Haut-Médoc		Haut-Médoc
Château Langoa-Barton	St-Julien		Haut-Médoc
Château Lascombes	Margaux	(-1)	Haut-Médoc
Château Pichon-Longueville-Baron	Pauillac	(-1)	Haut-Médoc
Château Pontet-Canet	Pauillac	(+2)	Haut-Médoc
Château Rausan-Ségla	Margaux	(-1)	Haut-Médoc
Château Rauzan-Gassies	Margaux	(-1)	Haut-Médoc
Château Talbot	St-Julien	(+1)	Haut-Médoc
Château Haut-Bailly	Graves		
Château Pape-Clément	Graves		
Château Canon	St-Emilion		
Clos Fourtet	St-Emilion		
Château La Gaffelière	St-Emilion		
Château Pavie	St-Emilion		
Château Gazin	Pomerol		
Château La Fleur-Pétrus	Pomerol		
Château Latour-à-Pomerol	Pomerol		
Vieux-Château-Certan	Pomerol		

(+1)—promoted one growth level in comparison to its 1855 Médoc classification
(-1)—demoted one growth level
(+2)—promoted two growth levels
(-2)—demoted two growth levels
(+3)—promoted three growth levels
(!)—wines that could eventually make it to a higher classification

(Yves Durand's Classification continued)

QUATRIÈMES CRUS (25 Fourth Growths)	Apellations Contrôlées		
Château Batailley	Pauillac	(+1)	
Château Cantenac-Brown	Margaux	(-1)	Haut-Médoc
(*) Château Chasse-Spleen	Moulis	(+2)	Haut-Médoc
(!) Château Les Forts de Latour (second label of Latour)	Pauillac		Haut-Médoc
(*) Château Gloria	St-Julien	(+4)	Haut-Médoc
Château Grand-Puy-Ducasse	Pauillac	(+1)	Haut-Médoc
Château Haut-Bages-Libéral	Pauillac	(+1)	Haut-Médoc
(!) Château Haut-Batailley	Pauillac	(+1)	Haut-Médoc
Château Lafon-Rochet	St-Estèphe		Haut-Médoc
(*) Château Lanessan	Haut-Médoc	(+3)	Haut-Médoc
Château Malescot-St-Exupery	Margaux	(-1)	Haut-Médoc
(*!) Château Meyney	St-Estèphe	(+2)	Haut-Médoc
Moulin des Carruades (formerly Carruades de Château Lafite) (second label of Lafite)	Pauillac		Haut-Médoc
(*) Château de Pez	St-Estèphe	(+3)	Haut-Médoc
Château Prieuré-Lichine	Margaux		Haut-Médoc
Château St-Pierre	St-Julien		Haut-Médoc
Château du Tertre	Margaux	(+1)	
(!) Château La Tour-Haut-Brion	Graves		
Château Belair	St-Emilion		
Château Grand-Pontet	St-Emilion		
(!) Château La Dominique	St-Emilion		
(!) Château Certan-Giraud	Pomerol		
Château L'Eglise-Clinet	Pomerol		
Château La Grave-Trigant-de-Boisset	Pomerol		
Château Petit-Village	Pomerol		

CINQUIÈMES CRUS (55 Fifth Growths)			
(*) Château d'Angludet	Margaux	(+1)	Haut-Médoc
Château Belgrave	Haut-Médoc		Haut-Médoc
Château Boyd-Cantenac	Margaux	(-2)	Haut-Médoc
Château de Camensac	Haut-Médoc		Haut-Médoc
Château Cos-Labory	St-Estèphe		Haut-Médoc
Château Clerc-Milon	Pauillac		Haut-Médoc
Château Croizet-Bages	Pauillac		Haut-Médoc
Château Dauzac	Margaux		Haut-Médoc
Château Ferrière	Margaux	(-2)	Haut-Médoc
(*) Château Fonbadet	Pauillac	(+2)	Haut-Médoc
Château Kirwan	Margaux	(-2)	Haut-Médoc
(*) Château Labégorce	Margaux	(+2)	Haut-Médoc
(*) Château Labégorce-Zédé	Margaux	(+2)	Haut-Médoc
Château Lagrange	St-Julien	(-2)	Haut-Médoc
Château Lynch-Moussas	Pauillac		Haut-Médoc
Château Marquis-d'Alesme-Becker	Margaux	(-2)	Haut-Médoc
Château Marquis-de-Terme	Margaux	(-1)	Haut-Médoc

(!)—wines that could eventually make it to a higher classification
(*)—These châteaux were not classified in the top five growths in 1855. In my opinion, they deserve to be in this classification because of their quality. Below fifth growth, there are three levels of "Cru Bourgeois." I treat these three levels as if they were sixth, seventh, and eighth growths.

(Yves Durand's Classification continued)

	Châteaux	Appellations Contrôlées		
(*)	Château Meaucaillou	Moulis	(+3)	Haut-Médoc
(!)	Château Mouton-Baronne-Philippe	Pauillac		Haut-Médoc
	Château Pédesclaux	Pauillac		Haut-Médoc
(*)	Château Pontensac	Médoc	(+3)	Haut-Médoc
	Château Pouget	Margaux	(-1)	Haut-Médoc
(*)	Château Poujeaux	Moulis	(+2)	Haut-Médoc
(*)	Château Siran	Margaux	(+2)	Haut-Médoc
(*)	Château Sociando-Mallet	Haut-Médoc	(+3)	Haut-Médoc
	Château La Tour-Carnet	Haut-Médoc	(-1)	Haut-Médoc
	Château de Fieuzal	Graves		
	Château La Louvière	Graves		
(!)	Château L'Arrosée	St-Emilion		
	Château Balestard-la-Tonnelle	St-Emilion		
	Château Beauséjour (Duffau-Lagarrosse)	St Emilion		
	Château Cadet-Piola	St-Emilion		
	Château Cap-de-Mourlin	St-Emilion		
	Château Corbin	St-Emilion		
	Château Croque-Michotte	St-Emilion		
	Château Curé-Bon-La-Madeleine	St-Emilion		
	Château Fonplégade	St-Emilion		
	Château Fonroque	St-Emilion		
	Clos des Jacobins	St-Emilion		
	Château Larmande	St-Emilion		
	Château Soutard	St-Emilion		
	Château Troplong-Mondot	St-Emilion		
	Château La Tour-du-Pin-Figeac-Moueix	St-Emilion		
	Château La Tour-Figeac	St-Emilion		
	Château Le Bon Pasteur	Pomerol		
	Château La Croix-de-Gay	Pomerol		
	Clos L'Eglise	Pomerol		
(!)	Château Le Gay	Pomerol		
	Château Lagrange	Pomerol		
	Château L'Enclos	Pomerol		
	Clos René	Pomerol		
(!)	Château Rouget	Pomerol		
	Château de Sales	Pomerol		
	Château Taillefer	Pomerol		
	Château La Violette	Pomerol		

Top Crus Bourgeois Châteaux of the Médoc

	Chateaux	Appellations Contrôlées
	Château d'Agassac	Haut-Médoc
	Château Belle-Rose (real property, but used as second label of Pédesclaux)	Pauillac
	Château Bel-Orme-Tronquoy-de-Lalande	Haut-Médoc
(!)	Château Brillette	Moulis
	Château le Bosq	St-Estèphe
	Château Capbern-Gasqueton	St-Estèphe
(!)	Château Cissac	Haut-Médoc
	Château la Couronne	Pauillac

(Yves Durand's Classification Continued)

	Châteaux	Appellations Contrôlées
	Château Clarke	Listrac
	Château le Crock (dangerously mortal)	St-Estèphe
	Château la Fleur-Milon	Pauillac
(!)	Château Fourcas-Hosten	Listrac
(!)	Château du Glana	St-Julien
	Château Gressac	Médoc
	Château La Gurgue	Margaux
(!)	Château Haut-Marbuzet	St-Estèphe
(!)	Château Hortevie	St-Julien
(!)	Château Lalande-Borie	St-Julien
	Château Larose-Trintaudon	Haut-Médoc
	Château Loudenne	Médoc
	Château de Marbuzet (real property, but used as second label of Cos d'Estournel)	St-Estèphe
	Château Moulin-de-la-Rose	St-Julien
(!)	Château les Ormes-de-Pez	St-Estèphe
	Château Patache d'Aux	Médoc
	Château Phélan-Ségur	St-Estèphe
(!)	Château Pichon	Haut-Médoc
	Château Pontac-Lynch	Margaux
	Château Pontoise-Cabarrus-Bronchon	Haut-Médoc
	Château Saint-Bonnet	Médoc
	Château Soudars	Haut-Médoc
	Château Tayac	Margaux
(!)	Château Terrey-Gros-Cailloux	St-Julien
	Château la Tour de By	Médoc
	Château La Tour St. Bonnet	Médoc
	Château Tour-du-Haut-Moulin	Haut-Médoc
	Château Verdignan	Haut-Médoc

Best Châteaux Outside the Médoc

GRAVES

Château Les Carmes-Haut-Brion
Château Ferrande

ST-EMILION

Château L'Angélus
Château La Grave Figeac
Château Haut-Sarpe
Château La Marzelle

POMEROL

Château La Croix
! Château Le Pin
Château La Pointe
Château Tailhas

MONTAGNE-ST-EMILION

Château Roudier
! Vieux-Château-Saint-André

CANON-FRONSAC

Château Canon (Christian Moueix)
(Not to be confused with the other Château Canon of the same A.O.C., but owned by Henriette Horeau)

FRONSAC

Château La Dauphine

LALANDE-DE-POMEROL

Château de Bel-Air
Château Belles-Graves
Château Grand-Ormeau
Château Tournefeuille

CÔTES DE BOURG

Château Tayac "Cuvée Prestige"

Tasting Notes Guidelines

Taste is a very individual and subjective sense. My reams of wine-tasting notes reflect that truth. For instance, many French people prefer their red Bordeaux wines on the young side with a fair amount of tannin. Others—myself included—like their wines older and mellower. I enjoy certain flavors more than others, which influences my judgment. The time of day, your mood, and the number of wines tasted can make a difference as well. To be as fair and objective as possible, care should be taken when assembling wines for a tasting. For example, I would not include a big wine that would completely overpower a subtle one.

Most of the wines described in these tasting notes were served in comparative double-blind tastings, which means that the identities of the wines are not known. In single-blind tastings, the people involved know what the wines are but do not know in which order or glass they will be poured. A few very old wines, those from the '40s and early '50s, were usually sampled with their true identities known by everyone present at the tasting. Horizontal tastings compare different châteaux of the same vintage year; vertical tastings examine different vintages of a particular château or property. Evaluation of younger vintages for purchase or cellaring was done in conjunction with various wine clubs or by myself alone.

After writing notes about my overall impression of a wine, I score it on a scale from 0 to 20. The rating of a wine that is older than 12 years can be subject to bottle variations due to size and shipping and storage conditions. I determine the final score after analyzing all of my notes, taking into account the date, place, and other wines present at the various tastings. Remember that ratings are approximations that should never be considered as hard facts. The points given to a bottle of wine are based on the quality of the wine when it has reached or will reach its maturity.

The following are the explanations of the symbols and abbreviations I use in my tasting notes:

[1975]	Drink now since it will not improve. It was at its peak in 1975.
[1996]	Start drinking now and enjoy it; it could improve or reach its peak by 1996.
	Not recommended.
[1990/1995]	Lay it down for aging; it should reach maturity around 1990 and peak by 1995.
20	Extraordinary
18½ to 19½	Outstanding
17½ to 18	Excellent
16 to 17	Very good
14 to 15	Fair to Good
12 to 13	Average
below 12	French market
CS	Cabernet Sauvignon
M	Merlot
CF	Cabernet Franc
PV	Petit Verdot

1945—Austere and lean with a wet-leaf aroma. Still rough with untamed tannins. Not easy sipping. Drink up! (1986).
[1975] 13

1952—Tasted in a vertical tasting, not one vintage would persuade me to break my piggy bank. Strange taste, unlike other clarets. I do not care for it (1976).
[1972] 13

1953—Better than the '52, but not great. Concentrated and beefy on the palate, but unbalanced. It should have a long life (1976).
[1983] 15

1959—The best Ausone of the '50s, but the least attractive of the first growths of this vintage. Strange bouquet, medium-to-light body and tannic. Lacks grace and suppleness (1976).
[1995] 16

1961—More advanced than the '59, it has more breed and elegance. I enjoyed sipping it, although it does not compare with its peers of this vintage (1976).
[1995] 17

1962—Beautiful bouquet. On the palate, very pleasant, light, and graceful (1980). In a comparative blind tasting of Ausone ('62, '64, '66, '67, and '71), the nose was not too forward, but pleasant with some cedary undertones. Medium-to-full body. It has a certain style, but was a bit unbalanced. Older-type wine, which is still astonishingly attractive (1983).
[1990] 16-1/2

1964—In a double-blind horizontal tasting, this wine fared very well against the august company of Figeac, Haut-Brion, and Palmer (1976). Big but restrained aroma. Medium full on the palate. Good flavors with cedar and fruit, some tannin. Will last long. Unimpressive finish— not short but not long either (1979). From a more recent vertical blind tasting, the wine is minty, delicate, and quite attractive on the nose. Harmonious and elegant on the palate. Medium-to-full body. Has good fruit and balance. The finish has improved— it is long, smooth, and graceful. Much better than expected (1983).
[1995] 17-1/2

1966—Very minty on the nose, but not offensively so. Soft and enjoyable on the palate with a minty overtone. Medium-to-light body. Weak finish (1983).
[1990] 16

1967—In a vertical tasting, our entire group scored it well. The nose was a little subdued and reminded me of the '74 Chappellet fragrance, although lighter in style. Medium to full on the palate. Good fruit with a hint of menthol flavor. Smooth, elegant, with breed. Good balance followed by some tannic backbone in the aftertaste (1983).
[1995] 16-1/2

1970—Light color and body. Some cedar laced with red fruit and a hint of herbal flavor. Elegant balance in this somewhat feather-weight-style wine (1986).
[1991] 14

1971—Delicate minty aroma. Soft and elegant on the palate. Medium-to-light body with good flavors. Smooth and graceful finish (1983).
[1990] 16-1/2

Ausone

CHATEAU AUSONE
SAINT-EMILION
APPELLATION SAINT-EMILION CONTRÔLÉE
1962
Vve C. VAUTHIER & J. DUBOIS-CHALLON
PROPRIÉTAIRES A SAINT-ÉMILION (GIRONDE)
MIS EN BOUTEILLES AU CHATEAU
DEPOSÉ

Appellation Contrôlée: St-Emilion Grand Cru

Principal Owner: Madame Dubois-Challon and Héritiers Vauthier

Administrator: Pascal Delbeck

Average Production: 2,000 cases

Vineyard Area: 7 hectares, 17 acres

Grape Varieties: 50% M, 50% CF

Average Vine Age: 47 years

Average Yield: 28 hectolitres per hectare

Classified First Great Growth "A"

Yves's Classification: First growth

Food Complements: (5 to 7 years old) leg of young wild boar St-Hubert, (10 years or older) roast chicken with dauphinoise potatoes

Ausone

1973—Spice and clove on the nose. It has the "weird" Ausone characteristic fragrance, quite different from other Bordeaux. Soft and round on the palate (1976).

🍷 [1981] 14

1975—Medium color. Perfumed nose. Medium body, not too open. Good underlying qualities, but not in the class of a premier cru, sorry! (1980). Medium-light amber color. Elusive aroma. On the palate, the wine lacks flesh and backbone for this vintage. Some fruity flavors, unfortunately overshadowed by a dry oakiness (1986).

🍷 [1990] 14-1/2

1976—This year things seem to have gone right at this property. Earthy, concentrated texture. Good fruit and flavor, fair amount of tannin, unyielding and firm. Very good prospects for the future (1981). Dark, brick color, with amber edge. Deep, powerful and rich bouquet of cassis, cedar and spice. Warm, mouth-filling entrance where the berry-like flavors are generous and bountiful. The wine is deep, very concentrated and stylish with a savory, multifaceted finish. Loaded with rounded tannin, a forceful wine for long aging (1986).

[1990/2010] 18

1978—A success! Bravo! A high-class wine. Do you remember that timid, light-weight Ausone style? Not any more. The 1978 is deep, concentrated, and earthy like a Graves. It has style, a lot of fruit, depth, and plenty of tannin. A great wine that we will have to wait to enjoy at its fullest (1982).

[1992/2020] 18

1979—They did it again! A bit less concentrated than the '78, will mature sooner. Distinctly a first-growth wine. Earthy, cedary aroma with lush ripe fruit. Attractive texture, well structured, subdued flavors of cedar and raspberry. Deep, tannic, and long in the mouth (1982).
[1989/2010] 17-1/2

1981—Dark color with amber edge. Lovely fragrance of ripe red fruit, mushrooms and vanilla. Medium-to-full body, well balanced, elegant structure, and good depth. Very attractive flavors of cherries and cedar that linger in the aftertaste backed up by some youthful tannin (1984).
[1989/2005] 17

1982—I almost had to take out a mortgage for this wine, and finding it was not an easy task either. The result was neither celestial nor tantalizing. It is at a very reserved stage of its life, backward to the point of being stern. On the positive side, it has a huge, powerful concentration, it is chewy and full of extract. For the moment, the rich flavors are prevented from blossoming and showing their attributes due to a robust load of tannin. A wine to lay down and forget until 1995 at least (1986).
[1995/2025] 18

1983—Medium-dark color. Most attractive soft cedar aroma. A very elegant and flattering wine. It has breed and is subtle. It is feminine and graceful. It has a beautiful cedary flavor with the most graceful and impeccable balance. I love it (1986).
[1992/2005] 18

1984—No wine was bottled under Ausone's label in this disastrous merlot year.

Beychevelle

MIS EN BOUTEILLE AU CHATEAU
CHÂTEAU BEYCHEVELLE
Grand Vin 1975
73 cl
APPELLATION SAINT-JULIEN CONTROLÉE
ACHILLE-FOULD PROPRIÉTAIRE A SAINT-JULIEN - MÉDOC
PRODUCT OF FRANCE

1945—Nice, attractive nose, yet not overwhelming. On the palate, it shows good concentration and flavor, but the wine is still austere and tannic. I do not think that more age will help (1975).
[1975] 16

1947—Served as a *bonne bouche* after a wine tasting in 1976. We were disappointed, expecting better. The wine lacked suppleness and length. Not much fruit or breed. Drink up (1976).
[1970] 12

1953—Beychevelle at its best! Long and rich on the palate with a cedary overtone. Medium body, extremely smooth and velvety. Very well balanced (1984).
[1990] 19

1955—Like the '53, another great Beychevelle! In double-blind comparative tastings held by Mr. Garland Duke, this wine showed at the top against other second growths. Rich and forward bouquet, but one-dimensional. Velvety and long on the palate. Elegant and flavorful. Medium body, balanced, and a long, lingering finish (1975).
[1985] 18

1961—Deep, rich aroma with sweet fruit and cedary bouquet. Huge, full body. Smooth and generous on the palate. Deep, soft, round and elegant. Long, lingering finish. A great bottle (1984).
[1995] 19

Beychevelle

1962—Nice, soft, fruity aroma. Light and appealing on the palate with good fruit. Faulty finish (1977).
[1977] 15

1964—In this year, most St. Juliens were harvested before the rains. Beychevelle made an excellent wine, rich and supple, with depth and character. Good cedar flavor. Exquisite balance and finish (1979).
[1990] 17 1/2

1966—Deep aroma of good cabernet yet still firm. Enormous on the palate. Very concentrated and of very good quality, but the wine needs more time to reach full development and enjoyment (1979). Medium brick color with advanced amber edge. Old wine cellar, mushroomy nose, with a hint of wood and spice rendering the aroma a bit austere. Medium-to-full body. Powerful yet round, deep, with a good backbone of tannin now tamed. Long and firm finish. At its peak, but with many more years of pleasure ahead (1986).
[1996] 17

lightful flavor of earth and ripe fruit followed by a delicious aftertaste (1981). Light brick red—the advanced color of old wine. Great, damp earth, mushroom aroma that is not complex, but very fragrant and forward. Medium-light body, rounded texture. Not much concentration, but very attractive flavor. Drink soon, the wine is fading (1985).

[1983] 17-1/2

1967—Medium brick color, amber edge. Deep, subdued, old-wine-cellar, mushroom and oaky aroma with a hint of unusual oriental spice. The flavors are of oak and coriander seeds with a remnant of dissipated berry fruit. The good news is that the wine is not stern, and it is still attractive. Medium-bodied, long on the palate, with a very subtle and delicate balance and style. Lacks depth and concentration. An interesting wine at this age for this vintage. Drink now (1987).

[1983] 15-1/2

1970—A few wine journalists gave this wine undeserved bad press. I challenge them to retaste the wine—we all make mistakes (thank God!). Medium-light ruby color with amber edge. Charming, subtle, old cabernet nose laced with oodles of berry fruit. Medium-bodied, the wine is at its peak. It is soft, elegant, even graceful. The aftertaste is woody and oaky with a hint of dried-out tannin, giving the wine a good backbone and a long oaky aftertaste. Drink now (1987).

[1985] 16-1/2

Brane-Cantenac

Appellation Contrôlée: Margaux

Principal Owner: Lucien Lurton

Average Production: 29,000 cases

Vineyard Area: 85 hectares, 210 acres

Grape Varieties: 70% CS, 13% CF, 15% M, 2% PV

Average Vine Age: 20 years

Average Yield: 31 hectolitres per hectare

Classified Second Growth in 1855

Yves's Classification: Third growth

Food Complements: (4 to 6 years old) calves liver with onions, (10 years or older) cornish hen Forestiere

Second Label: Domaine de Fontarney

1971—When young, this vintage had a powerful and elegant aroma of fruit. It had a medium body. Perhaps more concentration than the '70, but with a hole in the middle. When older, the wine showed a rich texture, but a dry, one-dimensional flavor. Good acid and fair balance (1980).

[1985] 15

1975—Look out for bottle variations. I had one mediocre tasting in 1985, but two enjoyable ones in 1986. On the positive side, it has a light, aromatic bouquet of cherries, mushrooms, and damp earth. Medium body, sweet cherry/earthy flavors. Nice wine with food, but lacks the charm and elegance to achieve greatness. Firm finish (1986).

[1993] 16

1976—This vintage was another great disappointment. While in France in 1981, however, one bottle I had was refined, harmonious, and elegant. It had breed, was long in the mouth, and medium-bodied. Did they keep the good stuff in France? (1981). In America, light and flabby, lacking structure and character, but some good redeeming fruity quality gives the wine some appeal (1985).

[1986] 14

1978—Dark color. The aroma is a bit herbaceous, but has plenty of fruit. Distinctive concentration on the palate, well built. It has balance and some charm. Fair amount of tannin and acid. Lay it down until the end of this decade but don't expect a miracle (1982). Medium color, advanced amber edge. Nice, simple cherry fruit on the nose with a hint of damp earth. Supple and delicate on the palate with a nice backbone with a hint of residual tannin. Fairly concentrated and in balance with all of its other components. Not great, but very charming (1986).

[1988/1998] 16

1979—Simple, fruity aroma laced with a spicy herbaceousness. Medium-light body and structure. Soft, mild, one-dimensional flavor. To be drunk over the next few years (1987).

[1991] 14

1980—I did not expect much from the vintage and I did not get much. Some fruit, lean and thin. Beaujolais-Nouveau style. A wine for picnics (1983).

[1983] 11-1/2

1981—Medium-light color. Light nose, soft, and bashful aroma. Medium body, round and silky texture. Pleasant vanillin, ripe fruit and cedary flavors. Supple and elegant finish. An easy-drinking wine. A good effort from this property (1984).

[1988/1999] 16-1/2

1982—The genteel and distinguished proprietor, Monsieur Lucien Lurton, can be very proud of this vintage. Medium ruby color. Generous, soft, and warm bouquet of cedar and ripe black currants. Most enjoyable! Full-bodied, deep concentration of flavors loaded with fruit. Outstanding texture, rich and round, yet well structured with plenty of soft tannin. Proverbial Margaux balance. The finish is soft and cedary (1985).

[1990/2005] 17-1/2

1983—Medium purple color. Deep cassis and cedar aroma that is quite forward and vivaciously young. The wine is full-bodied and concentrated, with robust, rounded tannin. Supple and well-balanced. The rich, complex and delicious cabernet fruit is already seductive and lingers in a long and harmonious finish (1987).

[1990/2001] 17

1984—Medium-light color. Lovely, soft, cedary/oaky aroma enhanced by a rich, fruity component. Uncharacteristic Margaux bouquet appearing closer to a Cordier wine in style. Exquisite flavors of blackberries, cassis, and oak. Soft, round, and supple texture. Long and harmoniously balanced. Not big in size but delicate and graceful (1987).
[1989/1994] 16

Calon-Ségur

Appellation Contrôlée: St-Estèphe
Principal Owner: Capbern-Gasqueton and Peyrelongue families
Administrator: Philippe Gasqueton
Average Production: 20,000 cases
Vineyard Area: 50 hectares, 124 acres
Grape Varieties: 50% CS, 25% CF, 25% M
Average Vine Age: 36 years
Average Yield: 36 hectolitres per hectare
Classified Third Growth in 1855
Yves's Classification: Third growth
Food Complements: (5 to 8 years old) pot roast, (12 years or older) paupiettes of veal
Second Label: Moulin de Calon

Grand Cru Classé

CHÂTEAU
Calon-Ségur
SAINT-ESTÈPHE
Récolte
1981
Mis en Bouteille au Château
Appellation Saint-Estèphe contrôlée
75 cl
HÉRITIERS GASQUETON PEYRELONGUE, PROPRIÉTAIRES A ST-ESTÈPHE (GIRONDE)
DÉPOSÉ
PRODUCE OF FRANCE

1955—Shared at lunch with John Lawless. Old wine-cellar aroma of mushrooms and earthiness. Medium to full on the palate, not at all austere. Excellent earthy/truffle flavors. Smooth old tannin. It has character and style with a chewy texture. A slightly rough aftertaste followed by a great finish. A very good wine which lacks complexity (1983).
🍷 [1995] 17-1/2+

1959—Brick color with amber edge. Deep tobacco bouquet. Medium-to-full body and nicely structured. Sweet ripe cabernet with a hint of cedar. Still some tannin, but not bothersome in the least. A long-lived wine (1979).
🍷 [1999] 16

1961—Dark color. Good fruity aroma. Austere on the palate and needs more time (1977). Dark ruby color. Small earthy and fruity bouquet. Tough and rough on the palate. Too much acid makes this powerful, virile wine out of balance and not too pleasant (1981).
🍷 [2005] 15

1962—Medium, faded red. Rich, soft, and delicate aroma. Medium body with nice texture and flavor. Off balance. Will not improve and should be consumed (1981).
🍷 [1980] 14

1966—Very good. It has depth and concentration, is loaded with tannin which makes it firm and austere. Needs more time, but great prospects (1979). Fully opened now, but will hold for many more years. Deep and concentrated, still a trifle austere. Damp earth, mushroom, and oak flavor. A typical St-Estèphe in style—not a generous, graceful wine, rather a powerful, robust, vigorous one (1986).
🍷 [2006] 17

1967—Surprisingly seductive, none of the '67s' dried-out characteristics are apparent here. Quite the contrary—the wine is fleshy, meaty, generous, with ample fruit. It has a mellow texture and a gentle lingering finish. At its peak (1985).
🍷 [1985] 16

1970—Nice fruity aroma. Medium body. Not much concentration for a '70, but it is loaded with fruit and has a trace of good, rounded tannin. This makes the wine charming and easy to drink (1979).
🍷 [1990] 16

1971—Light-to-medium brick red. The nose is closed and unimpressive. Light body, without class. Hot finish and indistinctive. Overall, not a success (1979).
🍷 [1977] 11

1973—Light in color. Elegant and attractive nose and taste. No depth or concentration. Lean and rather thin, but has more character and flavor than the '71. Drink now (1979).
🍷 [1979] 14

Calon-Ségur

1975—Beautiful, dark brick color with amber edge. Deep, mushroomy and damp earth aroma enhanced by oak. The nose is very forward. Mouth-filling, round, and supple with pronounced and appealing dry leaf/woody/leather/mushroomy flavors. Concentrated and very well balanced with good depth. An excellent example of this property (1987).
[1997] 17-1/2

1976—Medium-dark ruby color. Medium body, supple even though it has a good amount of tannin and acid. Nice with subdued fruity flavors. Should make an elegant and flavorful bottle in a few years (1980).
[1990] 16

1978—Very backward and unyielding (1981). Rather disappointing, simple nose. Superficial and innocuous on the palate (1986).
[1990] 13

1979—Dark color, a good sign for future drinking. Deep nose of cassis, cherries, and earthiness. Lean and austere on the palate. Very dry with a good amount of tannin. Shows some charming and attractive undeveloped fruity character. Will have a good future when it softens up (1982).
[1989/2000] 15

1980—Light color. Very spicy and stern nose. Light body. Straightforward with no complexity. Lacks fruit, suppleness, and length, but finishes with a strong backbone of tannin (1983).
[1990] 13-1/2

1981—Medium-light color. Unyielding and spicy nose with a light fruity aroma. Medium body. Woody and stemmy flavors. The wine is balanced and does not have much tannin. Lightly structured (1984).
[1989/1996] 14-1/2

1982—Medium-dark color. The nose is deep, spicy/fruity/oaky and a bit severe and tight. Full-bodied and mouth-filling with an excellent velvety texture. Very pleasant ripe fruit, cedar and oak flavors. Round and supple with good concentration. Well structured, good depth, and excellent rounded

tannin. Long finish. One of the best Calon-Ségurs in years! (1985)
[1992/2012] 18

1983—Medium-dark color. The nose is deep but restrained with a cherry/oaky aroma showing through. Medium body. Ripe red fruity flavor not too developed yet. A bit unbalanced, hot and alcoholic. Tannic finish (1986).
[1990/1996] 15

1984—A light, medium-bodied wine, still a bit reserved. Discreet oaky flavor and a mellow finish. Drink during the next few years (1987).
[1988/1993] 14

Canon

APPELLATION S^T-ÉMILION CONTROLÉE

Château Canon

1er Grand Crû Classé St Émilion

MIS EN BOUTEILLES AU CHATEAU

1967 *André Fournier*

Propriétaire
à Saint-Emilion (Gironde)

WETTERWALD BORDEAUX

Appellation Contrôlée: St-Emilion-Grand Cru

Principal Owner: Eric Fournier

Average Production: 8,000 cases

Vineyard Area: 18 hectares, 45 acres

Grape Varieties: 55% M, 40% CF, 2.5% CS, 2.5% Malbec

Average Vine Age: 32 years

Average Yield: 38 hectolitres per hectare

Classified First Great Growth "B" in 1969

Yves's Classification: Third growth

Food Complements: (3 to 6 years old) stuffed bell pepper, (8 years or older) roast veal soubise

1961—Last tasted against other '61s at Lee Kramer's home. Unfortunately, it did not fare too well when compared to Lynch-Bages, Rauzan-Gassies, and Ducru-Beaucaillou. Pleasant nose, but small and restrained. Rather nice on the palate but lacks the complexity and backbone of a great wine. Average-to-lean finish. Ready to drink (1983). Medium brick color, amber edge. Deep mushroom aroma and flavor, with some dry tannin. Medium body. The finish is a bit too dry and unbalanced. Drink up (1985).
[1983] 15-1/2

1962—Lean and dry without enough flesh and fruit (1976).
[1976] 14

1966—The nose is attractively perfumed. Rich and elegant on the palate with cedar and vanilla flavors. Well balanced and backed up by good amounts of tannin. Long in the mouth (1978).
[1990] 17

1967—Brick color. Light spicy nose. Lean and not much flavor with a short finish (1975).
[1977] 12-1/2

1970—A well-made wine. Very perfumy bouquet. Quite delicious on the palate with sweet ripe merlot and cedary undertones. It has a fairly good backbone of tannin (1980).
[1992] 16

1971—Good color. Rather light body. Vinous nose lacking amplitude. Subdued fruit and cedar flavors followed by a touch of bitterness in the finish (1976).
[1981] 14

1973—Light and a bit unbalanced by acid (1978). Should be drunk by now.
[1981] 12

1976—Light amber color. Strong woody scents laced with some fruity components followed by a tannic astringency on the palate. Here is a wine that has all of the components of its class and breed, yet it does not have them in harmony and is completely unbalanced. A very awkward, unpleasant wine (1986).
12

1978—Dark color. The nose exhibits a powerful, perfumy bouquet. Full-bodied, concentrated, and very well structured. Still firm and unopened due to good tannin and acid. Firm finish, but will round up. Wait and you will be rewarded (1982).
[1990/2008] 17 +

Canon

1979—Dark color. Very fruity, perfumy bouquet and flavor with roasted undertone. Mouth filling, long on the palate, it has depth and balance. Cedar, spice, and vanillin overtones. Long, firm finish. A wine that will develop harmoniously (1983).

[1989/2000] 17

1980—A mild and gentle little St-Emilion with an honest and attractive berry nose. On the palate, the wine is a bit stemmy, followed by a pleasant taste of red fruit laced with plenty of wood. The finish is light, but it is there (1986).

[1990] 13

1981—Assertive, tannic and unromantic. Lacks flesh and softness. Woody nose and taste. A difficult wine that will need a long time to mellow down, and by then the fruit will probably have disappeared. Presently unbalanced by an overdose of oak (1986).

[1991/2001] 13

1982—Tasted three times in 1985 and once at the château in the summer of 1984 with the handsome, young proprietor. I grant that this vintage is one of the better efforts since 1966, but it is not in the class in which many of the wine press rank it. Medium-dark ruby color. Restrained nose of black currant

and vanilla. The bouquet is bashfully piercing through. Medium-to-full body, mouth-filling, round and supple. Well structured with good rounded tannin. Exciting flavors of ripe fruit and oak. Agreeable finish (1985).
[1992/2010] 17-1/2

1983—I do not find in Canon what other people seem to see, although I admit that I enjoy the exquisite cedar and jasmine flavors. I find a little distracting herbaceousness in the nose. On the palate, it is supple, even velvety, backed by good young rounded tannin. It is very well made with a delicious creamy taste of cedar. It has character and style. The color of this wine is medium to light, indicating a rather precocious maturity (1986).
[1989/1998] 17

1984—No Canon was produced in 1984.

Cantemerle

Appellation Contrôlée: Haut-Médoc

Principal Owner: Société d'Assurances Mutuelles du Batiment et Travaux Publiques

Administrator: Jean Cordier

Average Production: 20,000 cases

Vineyard Area: 53 hectares, 132 acres

Grape Varieties: 45% CS, 10% CF, 40% M, 5% PV

Average Vine Age: 25 years

Average Yield: 34 hectolitres per hectare

Classified Fifth Growth in 1855

Yves's Classification: Third growth

Food Complements: (5 to 8 years old) chicken liver barley, (12 years or older) boureks stuffed with lamb and sweetbreads

1959—A flavorful, delightful wine! Not powerful, but offers elegance, charm, and *savoir faire*. Medium brick color with amber edge. Soft and round texture. Cedar flavors, with very ripe, almost sweet fruit. Long in the mouth and lingers with great distinction (1979).
[1989] 17

1961—Medium color. Huge bouquet with exciting ripe berries. Medium body. Long in the mouth with an outstanding, almost sweet flavor. Extremely well balanced. Great aftertaste and lingering finish. A great, complete wine, very elegant as well (1980).
[1995] 18-1/2

1962—A great wine that is little spoken about. Another very powerful bouquet like '61. Medium body, elegant, round and soft. Nicely textured, fleshy and extremely flavorful (1979).
[1986] 17-1/2

1964—A very well-made wine; they must have harvested before the rain. A few years ago, the wine had a very sweet flowery nose. It had elegance, breed, and good taste of ripe fruit. Medium body and not much tannin. It should be drunk by now; it was at its peak in the late '70s (1978).
[1979] 16-1/2

1966—Only tasted in half bottles. Powerful nose, very agreeable texture, and flavorful. Medium-to-full body, some tannin, and very well balanced. Harmonious aftertaste. A very delicious wine, perhaps a bit short in the finish (1981).
[1987] 17

1967—Lovely middleweight wine. An attractive bouquet, nicely flavored, but a raw finish (1977).
[1979] 14-1/2

1970—Tasted when the wine was still in its youth. Dark ruby color. Concentrated, closed, and very tannic. It has the attributes of a wine that will become great (1976). Now, finally, it opened up. Rich, ripe red fruit laced with a hint of mushroom that teases both the nostrils and the taste buds. Most enticing! On the palate, the wine is sensuous, rich, and well balanced, with fairly good concentration, depth, and finish (1986).
[2000] 17

1971—Elegant, round, and flavorful. Medium body. At its peak (1980).
[1982] 16-1/2

Cantemerle

1975– Already well advanced and enjoyable. This wine could be ready before the '70 vintage. Lovely nose and taste. Medium body. Long in the mouth. Well balanced. Should evolve very well (1981).
🍷 [1995] 17

1976– Deep purple color. Subdued nose with cassis. Full-bodied on the palate. Concentrated and elegant with sweet, fruit flavors showing through. Good tannin. Long finish. Needs to lose its tannic roughness (1981).
🍷 [1995] 16 +

1978– Dark color. Attractive nose still restrained. Medium-to-full body. Nicely textured and generous. Good balance of tannin and acid. Needs more time. Will make a very good bottle (1983).
[1989/1998] 16-1/2

1979– Medium-dark color. Bouquet of fruit and cedar, not too forward. Light-to-medium body, but a bit lean in texture. Good flavors of fruit. An extra touch of acid unbalances the wine (1983). Middle-of-the-road classified Bordeaux. Medium color, medium body, medium this, medium that. Pleasant little wine, soft and supple, very quaffable. Simple yet seductive fruity flavor. It lacks size and opulence, and still has a hint of astringency in the aftertaste (1986).
🍷 [1991] 15

1980—Light as most wines of this vintage. Has an attractive bouquet and flavor. Nicely balanced. An agreeable wine (1983).

[1990] 14

1981—Medium ruby color. Unyielding and shy nose. Medium body, tannic, and austere. Some ripe fruit flavors enhanced by oak. The wine is well structured and will make a good bottle by 1991 as it opens up and sheds its tannin (1984).

[1991/2001] 15-1/2

1982—Dark color. Deep, smokey, concentrated aroma. Rich and most appealing. Medium body, smooth and round texture. Attractive flavors of fruit and tobacco. Unfortunately, it does not have the depth, concentration, and fineness found in other '82s. However, the wine is very well balanced and relatively long in the mouth. An elegant wine which will mature rather early (1985).

[1988/1998] 16-1/2

1983—A great effort on the part of Cantemerle. Their brand-new facilities have allowed them to bring their winemaking to a point seldom seen in a fifth growth. Bravo! Medium-dark to dark color. Deep cassis aroma not too forward yet, but promising. Full-bodied, great concentration of sweet red berries. Well structured and balanced with rounded tannins. Supple and already enjoyable. This wine has breed and excellent rich cassis/oak finish (1986).

[1991/2005] 18

1984—The new wine-making facilities are paying off. In this difficult vintage, Cantemerle made a very successful wine with relatively deep concentration. Delicious, ripe, plummy/cassis flavors harmoniously balanced in a well-structured wine. A mellow and graceful impression is left on the palate (1987).

[1990/1997] 17

Certan de May

POMEROL

Château Certan

De May de Certan

APPELLATION POMEROL CONTROLÉE

1979

Mme BARREAU-BADAR
PROPRIETAIRE A POMEROL (GIRONDE)
PRODUCE OF FRANCE 75cl

Shipped by : Éts J. PIERRE MOUEIX – LIBOURNE

BORDEAUX RED WINE
CONTENTS 750 ml

PRODUCE OF FRANCE
ALCOHOL 12% BY VOLUME

Imported by CHATEAU & ESTATE WINES COMPANY NEW YORK, N.Y.

1976—Approaching its peak and maturity, but will remain on this plateau quite a few years. This wine is still very concentrated, powerful and intense. It is quite atypical for a '76 to be this opulent. It has a huge, mouth-filling texture laced with rich and generous flavors reminiscent of sweet cassis and tobacco (1986).

[2006] 18

1978—Medium brick purple color. Outstanding, deep, fruity, roasted nose. Most Burgundian in style, a pleasure and a surprise. There is a hint of herbaceousness, but not disturbing in the least. On the palate, the wine is medium-to-full-bodied. Ripe, roasted, fruit and tobacco flavors. The wine is round, supple, and velvety. It has depth, structure, excellent balance. Well-rounded tannin and acid. Luscious aftertaste. A splendid bottle of wine (1984).

[2005] 19

1979—Very dark ruby color. Deep, concentrated nose which is still unyielding, but showing a pleasant hint of sweet fruit. Full-bodied and mouth filling, long and big on the palate. Rich and generous flavors of cedar and ripe red fruit. Concentrated texture, well structured and loaded with tannin. Still very well balanced and long in the mouth. Might surpass the '78, for this wine has much more depth and will need more time (1984).

[1989/2015] 18-1/2+

Appellation Contrôlée: Pomerol

Principal Owner: Madame Odette Barreau-Badar

Average Production: 1,600 cases

Vineyard Area: 4.6 hectares, 11.5 acres

Grape Varieties: 70% M, 30% CF

Average Vine Age: 37 years

Average Yield: 31 hectolitres per hectare

Yves's Classification: Second growth

Food Complement: (10 years or older) veal chop with morels

Certan de May

1981—Very dark purple color. The deep, concentrated nose is still unyielding, but after one hour of breathing in the glass, the soft, gentle, cedar aroma starts to show off. Medium body. Supple cedar and fruit flavors. Very well balanced with good, rounded tannin. Long in the mouth with great depth. A most enjoyable wine (1984).

[1989/2005] 17-1/2

1983—Dark color. Deep, concentrated nose which is quite restrained. On the palate, the wine is mouth filling, powerful and very concentrated. Very hard tannins, through which one can perceive rich flavors of coffee and cassis. It will take a very long time for this wine to round up, mellow down, and acquire a harmonious balance. Hoping for the best . . . yours truly (1986).

[1996/2010] 17

Cheval-Blanc

1945—Very rich and concentrated wine. Mouth filling, generous, deep and complex. Loaded with all kinds of different flavors—blackberry, cedar, tobacco, even chocolate. Long, lingering finish (1986).

[1995] 19 +

1947—Beautiful, flowery, old cedar nose. Big, forward, powerful, fantastic, masculine taste, chewy and concentrated. Exquisite aftertaste, long and lingering. One of the best Bordeaux ever. Tasted in the late '50s in France (it had acquired a big reputation then). Later, I had it several times. It is a wine of deep concentration and of multiple delicious flavors. The wine is enormous,

yet achieves a perfect balance. And what makes this wine superlative is the style, the breed, and the elegance in which all of its components are laced together. Amen! (1984)
[2025] 20 +

1949—Tasted as a *bonne bouche* after a wine tasting. Superb, rich, smooth, delicious flavors. Outstanding balance (1976).
[1995] 20

1952—Gentle, soft bouquet. Velvety and feminine on the palate. A well-made wine. Medium body. The finish could be more romantic (1978).
[1985] 17-1/2

1953—Another magnificent Cheval Blanc! We should all have a case or two. Oui! Oui! Oui! Rich in flavors, round and soft, yet mouth filling. The finish still a bit austere (1976).
[1995] 19 +

1955—I had this wine in several comparative blind tastings. We also had it on the wine list of our restaurant in the early '70s. I never found it very big or powerful. The style is subtle, soft, and gentle laced with a pleasant cedar flavor. Unfortunately, a hint of bitterness in the aftertaste makes the wine unbalanced (1977).
[1985] 16-1/2

1959—It took a longer time than usual for this wine to come around. Cedar and sweet fruit in the bouquet. Full body, rich, velvety, elegant, and delicious. Firm finish (1978).
[2000] 18 +

1961—Should be ready by now. I preferred it to the '59. Dark color. Nice sweet nose, but not too forward. Rich, complex, concentration full of extract, married in a soft, velvety texture (1978).
[2010] 18

1962—Light color. Abundant fragrance of cedar. Attractive cassis and cedar flavors. Soft and elegant. Lacks depth, but is charmingly and exquisitely balanced. A very well-made, medium-bodied wine. Gentle and stylish (1983).
[1990] 17-1/2

1964—I have had this wine more times than I can remember. I also tasted it several times, double-blind, against '64 Figeac and '64 La Croix-de-Gay. Each time the two others in the late '70s scored better. But today Cheval Blanc is superior: Deep, big aroma with a beautiful, attractive bouquet of cedar, yet lacking flower and fruit. Full body. Rich, generous, velvety texture with delicious cedar flavors. The finish is always long, lingering, and romantic (1986).
[1995] 18-1/2

1966—I have enjoyed this wine many times, the last at John Lawless' blind tasting in 1983. Beautiful and enormous cedary nose, blessed with elegance and power. Good texture and flavor. Still a bit restrained and unyielding. Something odd in the aftertaste; almost inky and rough. In my experience, an inky aftertaste in young Right Bank wines has always been an attribute and an advance sign of longevity and intense, concentrated flavors to be enjoyed when those jewels come to maturity (1983).
[2010] 18

1967—This wine was most attractive when young, and scored very well in many tastings. But lately, it is losing its youthful charm and is earthy without flower. It has a nice texture, it is full, but is now lacking fruit and finesse and

Appellation Contrôlée: St-Emilion Grand Cru

Principal Owner: Société Civile du Château Cheval-Blanc

Administrator: Jacques Hebrard

Average Production: 11,500 cases

Vineyard Area: 35 hectares, 86 acres

Grape Varieties: 66% CF, 33% M, 1% Malbec

Average Vine Age: 37 years

Average Yield: 28 hectolitres per hectare

Classified First Great Growth "A"

Yves's Classification: First growth

Food Complements: (5 to 7 years old) rib eye marchand de vin, (10 years or older) lamb sweetbreads

Cheval-Blanc

is a trifle stern and austere. In 1984, served blind against four other '67s—Latour, Lafite, Haut-Brion, and Marquis-de-Terme—Cheval Blanc was the favorite of the evening. I personally preferred Lafite for that day's drinking, but conceded that Cheval Blanc had more depth and concentration. Deep oak and mushroom aroma. Full-bodied, concentrated texture. Flavorful, without much fruit. Long in the mouth. Good aftertaste, well structured (1984).
[1987] 17-1/2

1970—Soft, elegant aroma. Smooth and velvety on the palate. Good amount of well-balanced fruit and tannin. A first-class wine (1981).
[2000] 18

1971—Most attractive aroma of cedar, lilac, and cassis with a hint of mint. Long in the mouth. Flavor of deep cedar and fruit. Perfectly balanced. Great finish. A majestic, silky textured wine (1986).
[1995] 18-1/2

1973—In a 1981 blind tasting against '73 Petrus, '73 Lafite, and '73 Las Cases: Closed aroma with some spice and fruit in the background. Soft and generous on the palate with distinguished flavors. Silky aftertaste (1981).
[1990] 16-1/2

La Conseillante

1978—Dark ruby color. Very fruity nose. Medium-to-full body and fairly good concentration. Flavors of black currant/iron and baked ripe fruit. Good amount of tannin. Should make an elegant bottle in a few years (1982).
🍷 [1998] 16

1979—I preferred this La Conseillante to its '78 older brother. This may be unfair since this wine is more open today and shows more complexity and roundness. Dark color. Medium- fruity aroma with some cedar. It is generous, medium bodied, elegant, and stylish. Long on the palate. Delightful, savory aftertaste (1983).
🍷 [1996] 16-1/2

1980—Medium-light color. Underdeveloped aroma with some fruit and spices. Nice soft texture on the palate, but still has a bit of youthful tannin. Vanilla and clove-like flavors. It has breed and elegance. Will improve (1983).
🍷 [1988] 14-1/2

1981—Medium-to-dark color. Very attractive nose quite forward and full of flowers. Soft and gentle cedar undertones. Medium- to full-bodied, rich, very elegant, and refined. Complex flavors of earth, cedar, spice, and ripe fruit. Delicious aftertaste. Round tannins in a well-balanced wine. Long, lingering finish (1984).
[1990/2006] 17-1/2

1982—I don't think I will join in the general euphoria over this wine. It is very good, but lacks concentration and depth. Medium- to medium-light color. Very attractive cedary aroma. Medium-bodied with a nice, ripe, fruity flavor laced with some herbal undertones which are not overly disturbing. Long in the mouth. A well-structured and enjoyable wine (1986).
[1989/2000] 17

1983—Elegant with a very attractive texture. Good extract, soft, silky, graceful, savory, candy-sweet flavors. One bottle had some disturbing herbaceousness for which I would penalize the wine. I believe that with proper aeration, however, the wine would rid itself of this off odor (1986).
[1990/1998] 17

1984—Tobacco/cedar/gooseberry aroma and flavors enhanced by undertones of spicy oak. Tannin for backbone. Soft and mellow texture and structure. A charmer! (1987)
[1995] 17

Cos-d'Estournel

MIS EN BOUTEILLE AU CHATEAU

CHATEAU COS D'ESTOURNEL

GRAND CRU CLASSÉ EN 1855

SAINT-ESTÈPHE

APPELLATION SAINT-ESTÈPHE CONTROLÉE

PRODUCE OF FRANCE

SOCIÉTÉ FERMIÈRE DES DOMAINES PRATS A SAINT-ESTÈPHE (GIRONDE) FRANCE

RED BORDEAUX WINE — KOBRAND — PRODUCE OF FRANCE

750ml — ALC. BY VOL. 12%

IMPORTED BY KOBRAND CORPORATION NEW YORK N.Y.

1945—Excellent *gout de vin vieux* with depth and style. Not very complex but rich and forward with a cedary flavor. A bit unbalanced. Lacks fruit (1974).
[1976] 16

1947—Lacks fruit and finesse. The proverbial austerity of St-Estèphe is there, but softened. Nevertheless, the wine is attractive and interesting (1976).
[1972] 16+

1953—The nose is a little unyielding (should be more open considering its age). Excellent concentration and depth. Still young and firm with a touch of austerity. Lacks softness, romance, and sweet fruit. Will improve certainly, but without any sense of humor or grace (1976).
[1995] 17-1/2

1955—Old wine-cellar aroma, a hint of cedar. Distinctive, with medium body. Enjoyable texture, but the wine lacks a certain charm and fruit (1975).
[1975] 16

1959—One of my favorite Cos-d'Estournels. When it was 16 years old, it still was not ready. Full-bodied with plenty of tannin and good acid. Very dry and firm, a lot of extract, robust and intense (1975).
[2000] 18

1961—Very similar to the '59. Full, vigorous, rich, extremely concentrated and a lot of tannin. Let us hope that when the tannin is dissolved, some of the fruit will be left. With age, it will achieve a better balance and a touch of elegance (1978). Just starting to unfold and blossom. Very dark and intense in color. Deep mushroom and cassis bouquet. Solid, compact concentration and depth, powerful and sturdy, vigorously structured. Opulent, fruity, woody, mushroomy flavors. Firm, if not austere, aftertaste due to some still undissolved dry tannin (1985).
[2015] 18

1962—Young, austere, and tannic (1976). On the nose, a beautiful, flowery aroma of jasmine, but a bit superficial. Some fruit on the palate, but lacks roundness. Austere, not quite full. Some acid in the aftertaste. Off balance. Overall, pleasant to good (1977).
[1986] 15

Cos-d'Estournel

Appellation Contrôlée: St-Estèphe
Principal Owner: Domaine Prats
Administrator: Bruno Prats
Average Production: 20,000 cases
Vineyard Area: 57 hectares, 141 acres
Grape Varieties: 50% CS, 10% CF, 40% M
Average Vine Age: 35 years
Average Yield: 32 hectolitres per hectare
Classified Second Growth in 1855
Yves's Classification: Second growth
Food Complements: (5 to 8 years old) crown roast of lamb, (12 years or older) roast turkey
Second Label: De Marbuzet

1964—Not a success. When young, it had the color, body, and backbone of a fine wine, but short on fruit. Later, the wine became austere. The body is medium light. No attractive flavors to speak of, and the fruit is gone with the wind (1979).

[1979] 13

1966—Lovely, deep, earthy aroma with good fruit. Medium body. Nicely textured, well-structured enjoyable flavor. Some tannin and extremely long on the palate with a flavorful aftertaste (1983). Young dark color. Deep mushroomy, cedary, fruity aroma. On the palate, the wine is woody with a hint of sweetness, rich and flavorful. It has attractive old tannin and is well balanced. Good backbone. Long and round in the mouth. A very good wine (1986).

[2005] 17-1/2

1967—Showed very well in a horizontal blind tasting against Margaux, La Conseillante, and Pétrus. Light in color. Old cedar aroma laced with a light, distinctive flower. Tired old cabernet flavor. On the light side with some fruit. A wine at its peak. I was pleased with this bottle. I did not find it dried out or typical of a St-Estèphe (1982).

[1982] 15-1/2

1970—Closed and austere (1975). Harsh, closed, and tannic with no fruit showing (1976). Needs another decade. Strange and half-closed nose. The taste is dry and unopened. Good tannin and concentration with subdued fruit. All I can say is wait and wait and wait. Good future but not great (1981). Medium-dark color. Old wine-cellar, mushroomy, woody aroma. Medium body. Earthy, mushroomy flavor. The aftertaste is a bit unbalanced due to some undissolved dry tannin. Long, firm, and dry finish (1986).

[1991/2000] 16

1971—Dark color. Unyielding nose. Medium body. Lacks charm (like most young St-Estèphes), but not as harsh as usual. Supple with mild tannin (1976). Later, more enjoyable but on the light side. Lacks fruit and a certain style. Insufficient depth and concentration for long cellaring (1979).
[1985] 14-1/2

1973—This vintage gave birth to some charming, elegant, quaffable, early drinking wines. What they did not have in concentration was compensated for by subtle and supple feminine characteristics. After many horizontal comparative tastings, I am afraid that Cos-d'Estournel is charmless and does not qualify in that group of light and savory wines (1978).
[1981] 12

1975—The wine was not just austere but was hard as a nail. I found the wine lacking depth (which is strange for a 1975) and did not find much in the background to warrant a great future (1980). Medium-dark color with ruby edges. Unyielding nose. Medium-to-full-bodied. Austere and rough with dried tannins. Woody flavors softened by a hint of sweet berry fruit. Lacks romance and grace. My hopes for this Cos are very limited (1986).
[1990/2000] 15

1976—Attractive fragrance on the nose with good oak overtones. Rich in fruit with appealing flavors on the palate. Medium- to full-bodied. A great amount of tannin. Very good future, much better than the '75. It will also be ready earlier and have a good evolution (1981).
[1995] 17

1978—Another winner for Cos! Dark color. Concentrated nose with an unusual diversity of fragrances. Full-bodied and good ripe fruit. Firm but not austere. Blessed with a certain suppleness. Good depth and loaded with tannin. This wine is not for today's consumption. Will require patience to allow it to reach its peak (1982). Soft nose. Beautiful new style of Cos. Well balanced with harmonious, rounded tannin. Earthy flavor enhanced by sweet, black cherry, not fully opened, but most attractive. Soft, elegant, and stylish (1986).
[1989/2005] 17

1979—Medium-dark color. Aggressive herbaceousness which, fortunately, dissipates after proper aeration, leaving a woody aroma underlined by a hint of cherries. Mouth filling, abundant chewy texture, deep and long. The rounded tannins give this wine an attractive balance, but I am annoyed by a disturbing grassy flavor, and I penalized the wine for this reason. If you disagree, add 2 points to my score (1986).
[2002] 15

1980—Tim Hanni arranged several single-blind tastings of the '80 Bordeaux. The wines were served in flights of five according to their prices. Vinous and closed aroma. Soft and smooth on the palate. Light body. Vanilla flavor with cedary undertone. Lacks concentration (1983).
[1988] 14-1/2

1981—Medium-dark color. Spicy, earthy nose enhanced by subdued ripe berries. Full body. The entrance on the palate is of a powerful and tannic wine, yet the tannins are round, making this wine appear supple and smooth. It shows some excellent ripe fruit, but is presently overwhelmed by the young, spicy, clove-like taste. The wine is well structured and long in the mouth. It is ample and has depth and breed. A harmonious new style for Cos (1986).
[1991/2021] 17+

1982—Dark, opaque, garnet color. Distinctive and distinguished aromas and flavors. Complex, savory components intermingling and complementing one

another. The entrance is loaded with ripe fruit, reminiscent of black currants. It is followed by coffee, clove and cedar flavors. Finishes on a licorice and black cherry overtone. What diversity! At the same time the wine has a rich, opulent texture. It is extremely concentrated and almost chewy. Full of extract, well structured, and backed by a great amount of tannin. A winner! Bravo Monsieur Prats! (1986)
[1995/2020] 19+

1983—I first tasted this vintage in a vertical tasting. The then young '83 fared very well against its older and bigger brothers from '66, '70, '75, '82, and others. Medium-dark purple color. Soft, gentle, vanilla aroma enhanced by a touch of sweetness. Medium body. This Cos has neither the concentration nor the depth of the '82. Yet the wine is supple, round, elegantly balanced, and most of all has a beautiful appetizing flavor. What this bottle does not have in size is greatly compensated for by its graceful finesse. A wine for claret lovers. Burgundians, keep away—you would not understand (1986).
[1993/2005] 17+

1984—Medium-dark, ruby color. Discreet aroma of blackberry and spicy oak. Medium-to-full-bodied, blessed with a chewy concentration unusual for this vintage. Well-structured. Quite expansive, delicious, ripe berry flavors enhanced by some youthful, spicy oak overtone which, of course, will dissolve with time and add extra complexity to this already excellent wine. Firm and robust rounded tannins. Monsieur Prats, the distinguished owner, is producing better and better wines, even in odd years. Bravo Bruno! (1987)
[1989/1999] 17-1/2+

Domaine de Chevalier

GRAND VIN DE BORDEAUX

DOMAINE DE CHEVALIER

GRAND CRU CLASSÉ DE GRAVES

1966

APPELLATION GRAVES CONTROLÉE

JEAN RICARD, PROPRIETAIRE A LÉOGNAN (GIRONDE)

MIS EN BOUTEILLE AU CHATEAU

1959—Rich, concentrated aroma. Most enjoyable flavor. Full-bodied, silky, and fruity. Long on the palate. Has a good backbone. Will be long-lived (1976).
[1999] 18

1961—Very dark color. Young nose with cloves, pepper, and spices. Very rich, concentrated, chewy, with lots of extract. Still a bit unyielding and tannic. Just ready, with a long, great future (1979). Dark color. Deep, cedary nose, not too forward, but great nevertheless. Full-bodied, nicely textured, delightful cedary flavor that lingers in a long, harmonious aftertaste (1985).
[2001] 18

1962—This is a very subtle wine, getting old. It still has complexity, roundness, and breed. The wine is very harmonious on the palate, but lacks concentration. Drink soon with a very light dish (1984).
[1982] 16

1964—An outstanding wine, ready to drink. Beautiful earthy bouquet. Full-bodied on the palate with good extract, fruit and pebbly flavors. Long in the mouth. Well balanced and ready (1979).
[1986] 18-1/2

1966—In 1976, I included a bottle in one of our weekly blind tastings. Of course, the wine was backward and unyielding and I was disappointed with myself for having committed such an infanticide. I did not touch any of the other bottles until 1983. I served it then at two single-blind tastings; one with '66 Haut-Brion and Mouton, '70 La Mission, and a very rare Spanish wine, '66 Vega-Sicilia (which competed very well). '66 Domaine de Chevalier fared well against the competition. It has a medium-dark color and a beautiful big, soft, velvety, earthy bouquet. Medium-to-full body with good texture. Flavorful and well balanced. Complex with a rich and delicate finish. Will continue to improve a few years (1986).
[1996] 18

Appellation Contrôlée: Graves

Principal Owner: Société Civile du Domaine de Chevalier

Administrators: Claude Ricard and Olivier Bernard

Average Production: 5,000 cases

Vineyard Area: 15 hectares, 37 acres

Grape Varieties: 65% CS, 5% CF, 30% M

Average Vine Age: 16 years

Average Yield: 30 hectolitres per hectare

Classified Graves Cru Classé

Yves's Classification: Second growth

Food Complements: (5 to 8 years old) côte de boeuf, (12 years or older) sautéed duck liver with truffles

1967— Aromatic and ample. Medium body. Has a touch of acidity. Drink soon (1977).

[1978] 14

1970— A very successful wine and much more advanced than one would expect for the vintage. Not quite as great as '70 La Mission, but close to it. It has a very forward and intense nose with the typical earthiness of a Graves. Laced with ripe fruit, cassis, and cloves. Big and mature on the palate, yet elegant with good complexity. Well structured, rounded tannin, and delightfully flavored. Long, luscious, lingering finish (1985).

[1995] 17-1/2

1971— The nose is thin and reminiscent of cacao and dried flowers. Light body, yet supple. Enjoyable but without great concentration. A bit short on the finish. It has the breed and finesse of a grand cru, but does not have enough stuffing to succeed. Probably better a few years ago (1984).

[1981] 14-1/2

1973— Probably the most powerful and concentrated '73 wine I have had in years. It almost equals in quality the '66 and '70 of the same château. The nose is very rich and aromatic with caramel, vanilla, and oak. On the palate, the wine is full-bodied and very elegant with a good backbone of tannin and delicious extract. A surprisingly marvelous wine which will last for many years to come (1984).

[1993] 17-1/2

1975— Closed and unyielding. Some fruit behind all the tannin. Will need a long time to open up. Reminds me of the '66 when young. Should make an excellent bottle (1979). I was wrong. An overdose of tannin in this somewhat light and mildly concentrated wine renders it unbalanced, impenetrable, severe, even acrid. There is no way for this wine ever to become homogeneous. I expected better (1986).

[2000] 13-1/2

1976— The color is rich but already quite advanced. Deep nose, delicate and complex. Refined bouquet of ripe red fruit and prunes. Medium body and well structured. Its mouth-filling texture gives the wine a warm, homogeneous character. Long, harmonious finish. A great wine (1984).

[1996] 17-1/2

1978— Earthy, deep, concentrated nose with cassis complexity. Full body with great concentration but still a bit restrained compared to the '78 Ducru, Latour, La Mission, and Mouton tasted at the same time. Very fruity and nicely flavored. Reminiscent of black currants and ripe, baked cabernet. Medium tannin. Finishes well but austere compared to the other wines. When young, Domaine de Chevalier is always the least forward of the many classified growths. (1983).

[1988/2000] 17-1/2+

1979— Similar to the '78. Dark color. The nose is earthy with nice intensity of fruit and cedar. Mouth-filling, the flavors are now reaching their full potential. It does show a certain complexity of fruit, black currants, cedar and pebbly *terroir*. It has style and breed. All of the components are blended into a splendid balance. I predict that by 1988 this wine will be round, rich, generous, and complete (1983). Medium garnet color. Deep, concentrated, black currant aroma. The nose has style and breed. Full body. Rich, luscious and most appealing on the palate. Delicious and generous cassis flavors embodied in a silky and chewy texture. The well rounded tannin gives the wine elegant balance and a long, exquisite finish (1987).

[1988/2005] 17-1/2

Domaine de Chevalier

1980—Tasted in two single-blind tastings against '80 La Conseillante, Latour, l'Evangile and La Mission. Medium ruby color. Attractive, elegant nose with a soft flowery aroma and a hint of vanilla. Light-to-medium body, velvety, round and supple. It has elegance, style, and a slightly inky aftertaste. A light wine which is well made and ready to drink. But like all of the '80 vintage Bordeaux, it lacks concentration, intensity, and amplitude (1983).
[1988] 15

1981—Medium-to-dark color. The nose is unyielding but deep. Medium-to-full-bodied and well structured. Ripe red fruit flavors piercing through the tannin. Elegant balance, long, and deep in the mouth. A wine that should become quite attractive and complex (1984).
[1991/2011] 17

1982—Medium purple color. The aroma is soft and gentle. Spicy and predominantly clove-like with a touch of vanillin oak. On the palate, the wine is tannic and rough, but it will mellow down. Don't we all? It has good fruit, spice, and oak flavors, but today it is a bit ungenerous and quite unyielding. The finish is lovely and tells me a lot about the future of this wine (1986).
[1995/2015] 16-1/2

1983—Medium-to-dark color. Deep, attractive aroma of coffee laced with sweet red fruit—a very seductive combination. It is medium- to full-bodied. It has breed, concentration, and good depth. It is a bit restrained today, yet it is harmonious. Long in the mouth. All of these qualities are beautifully escorted by an outstanding flavor of coffee, hot pebbles and ripe cassis. A great wine. I can already hear the sarcasm of some smart aleck asking me if I go through the vineyards sucking hot pebbles since I seem to know how they taste (1986).
[1990/2003] 17

1984—Medium ruby color. Discreet bouquet. Medium body. The entrance is of spicy oak flavors, followed by abundant cassis and an agreeable roastiness. Some sturdy tannins to shed. Long with a relatively good depth. The finish is a bit austere, but the wine needs more time to mellow and open a bit (1987).
[1990/2000] 16-1/2

Ducru-Beaucaillou

1981
CHATEAU DUCRU-BEAUCAILLOU
APPELLATION SAINT-JULIEN CONTROLEE
SAINT-JULIEN

Appellation Contrôlée: St-Julien

Principal Owner: Jean-Eugene Borie family

Average Production: 15,000 cases

Vineyard Area: 45 hectares, 111 acres

Grape Varieties: 65% CS, 5% CF, 25% M, 5% PV

Average Vine Age: 30 years

Average Yield: 33 hectolitres per hectare

Classified Second Growth in 1855

Yves's Classification: Second growth

Food Complements: (4 to 6 years old) leg of lamb, (10 years or older) roast quail

Second Label: La Croix

1947—Outstanding. Full-bodied, velvety, and elegant. A long flavor of cedar on the palate. Exquisite balance. Top wine at its peak, but will last a few more years for it still has good concentration of fruit and tannin (1981).
[1990] 19

1949—Tasted with the '47, the '49 was not quite as deep and lacked breed. Nevertheless, the wine is rich and medium-bodied. It has fruit and cedar undertones with a delicate balance and finish (1981).
[1981] 16

1952—Austere, unyielding and slightly tannic with some acid which makes it a bit unbalanced. It is nice, dry, cool, a little distant, and lacks warmth and generosity. The taste is a bit burnt and disappointing (1979).
[1976] 12

1953—A great wine that I have enjoyed many times. Deep, concentrated aroma with cedar and ripe fruit. Soft, elegant, and long on the palate. Cedar flavor. Well balanced. Will not improve, but will last (1979).
[1990] 18

1955—A very well-made wine for this vintage. Beautifully subtle with old cedar aroma. On the palate, medium-to-full body. Elegant flavors, well structured and balanced. Good finish. A very enjoyable wine ready to drink (1982).
[1988] 17

1959—Deep, rich, complex aroma. Full, mouth-filling, and concentrated with a good amount of extract. Fruit and cedar flavors are well balanced. Still a little tannic, but not the least bothersome. A wine of *longue garde* which may still improve (1979).
[2000] 18

1961—The last time I had this wine was in a horizontal single-blind tasting held by Lee Kramer. The surprise was that we all preferred the Ducru to the well-publicized and renowned '61 Lynch-Bages. The nose is outstanding, deep, and concentrated, with that old savory cedar aroma laced with a flowery fragrance. On the palate, great texture, with fruity and flowery flavors. Exquisite balance. A delicious, long and lingering finish. A great wine. Beware, I found many bottle variations in the late '70s (1983).
[2005] 19

1962—I have had this vintage in many double-blind tastings. My notes are much more consistent than for the '61 vintage. Flowery and attractive aroma but not too forward, a bit shy. On the palate, good texture. Fruity, deep, and balanced with a smooth, lingering finish. (1979). Great, fragrant, cigar-box and tobacco aroma. Smooth, velvety, medium-light body. Elegant balance. Nicely flavored. A delicate and graceful wine (1985).
[1989] 17-1/2

1964—Medium-to-light color (almost fading). Old wine-cellar and mushroom aroma. On the palate, the wine is unmistakably claret in style, meaning it is very subtle, delicate, dainty, and sensual. Its exquisite, refined, cedary flavor can be appreciated only by the most keenly discriminating or fastidious claret lover (1986).
[1984] 17

1966—When tasted young in a vertical double-blind tasting, I faulted the '66 vintage for its unyielding nose. I found it big on the palate. Great texture. Gentle, as well as elegant and mouth-filling, with subtle fruit. Nice tannin. By 1980 the wine opened up and its aroma showed cedar and flower. The wine also became fuller and rounder. It still has a lot of tannin to shed and will certainly become a near classic by 1986 (1980). Full-bodied, excellent flavor and texture. Powerful, concentrated, rounded wine (1985).

[2006] 18

1967—Not bad when the wine was six to eight years old. It has lost the attributes and charms of its youth. It has gained neither wisdom nor softness with age (1980).

[1977] 14

1970—In the late '70s, I found this vintage quite unyielding but of delightful quality and great concentration. It needed a lot of time to mature. Today, this vintage is rich, full, velvety, round, supple, and concentrated. It has a good amount of tannin, cedary flavor, and, of course, the proverbial celestial Ducru balance (1983).

[2005] 18

1971—This wine is ready and will not become any better. It was already drinkable "with reserve" in 1976. It is now at its peak and very attractive. Medium body with a soft, gentle cedar flavor. Delicately balanced (1983).

[1985] 16

Ducru-Beaucaillou

1973—Medium-dark color. Stern aroma with no fruit. Fairly concentrated with good texture but lacks fruit, suppleness and roundness. It still might soften. A bit unbalanced by a hot finish. This wine seems to be young and atypical for a '73 vintage. There is a chance that this wine may improve (1982).
[1990] 14-1/2

1975—The nose is unyielding with some cedar undertones. Full body, austere, and a lot of tannin. Difficult to evaluate; Mademoiselle Ducru is not showing very much. This is a wine that we will have to taste and retaste. My prediction is that by 1990 it will have developed into a deep, concentrated, flavorful wine (1982). When retasted in 1986, Mademoiselle Ducru was not a demoiselle anymore, but rather an old maid. After 14 years, the wine is still annoyingly rough and tannic, which partially hides, for the time being, the rich, concentrated flavors of ripe cassis and cedar (1986).
[1990/2010] 17-1/2

1976—Time and time again, when two good vintages follow one another we invariably have the tendency to compare them. In many cases the second year appears lighter, more forward, and more enjoyable when young than the first. A dozen years later we say, "How could I compare them? They are in a different class." Applying this rule, '76 Ducru is lighter than '75, more advanced, much more enjoyable today. The ideal wine for a restaurant but not for my personal cellar. I find good fruit with a lot of charm on the nose. It has good flavors of vanilla and cedar. Medium-to-full body, velvety, elegant, and excellent balance. Still some tannin. Long in the mouth, but the finish is still a bit austere. Needs more time to get out of its shell (1981). As predicted, it is now soft, velvety, and elegant. It has the breed of the great aristocrat that Ducru is. Medium-bodied, blessed by a graceful and harmonious balance, enhanced all the way by a savory, creamy cedar flavor (1986).
[1995] 16-1/2

1978—Deep, earthy, perfumed, and fruity on the nose. Big and full on the palate. Flavorful with breed, depth, and excellent balance. Lingering with good tannins for cellaring. A great wine (1983).
[1988/2005] 18

1979—A well-made Ducru but of a smaller stature than usual. Nice bouquet with cedary overtones. Medium-to-full body on the palate. Well structured, appealing flavors of fruit and cedar. Good balance. A good bottle (1983).
[1994] 16-1/2

1980—Light, subdued aroma enhanced by some vanillin oak. Light body. Spicy flavor reminiscent of cloves. Attractive luncheon wine (1983).
[1987] 13-1/2

1981—Medium-dark ruby color. Deep, concentrated nose of cassis, cloves, and oak laced with the exciting, soft, characteristic St-Julien cedary overtone. Medium-to-full-bodied. Powerful entrance followed by a luscious flavorful ripe red fruit laced with oak and cedar. Deep, rounded tannins. Very long in the mouth (1984).
[1989/2006] 17

1982—Very dark color. Soft, cedary, concentrated nose enhanced by ripe berry laced with roasted coffee. Full-bodied, mouth filling, and loaded with rounded tannin. Powerful, deep, and concentrated. Rich and flavorful with a long and elegant, lingering finish (1984).
[1993/2015] 18-1/2

1983—The nose is restrained. In the mouth, the wine is medium-bodied with a certain breed but lacks style and amplitude. Medium purple color. Good tannin—not too much, not too little—in balance with the good-to-average concentration of the wine. Lovely texture. Long finish. These notes were

written in a blind tasting. Once the identity of the wine was revealed, I wrote, "Disappointing wine for such a renowned property." A good wine but not in the class I would have expected. Backward and severe. Time should help (1986).
[1995/2005] 16

1984—Medium-light Ducru, gentle, mellow, and slender. Its redeeming qualities are to be found in its delicate and elegant balance and its more-than-charming cedary flavors. It reminds me of the '73 Ducru at the same age (1987).
[1992] 15-1/2

Duhart-Milon-Rothschild

MIS EN BOUTEILLE AU CHÂTEAU
CHATEAU
DUHART-MILON-ROTHSCHILD
1982
PAUILLAC
PRODUCE OF FRANCE
APPELLATION PAUILLAC CONTRÔLÉE
75cl
GRAND CRU CLASSÉ

Appellation Contrôlée: Pauillac

Principal Owners: Domaines Barons de Rothschild

Administrator: Eric de Rothschild

Average Production: 12,500 cases

Vineyard Area: 40 hectares, 99 acres

Grape Varieties: 70% CS, 5% CF, 20% M, 5% PV

Average Vine Age: 20 years

Average Yield: 28 hectolitres per hectare

Classified Fourth Growth in 1855

Yves's Classification: Third growth

Food Complements: (4 to 6 years old) lamprey à la Bordelaise, (10 years or older) salmis of pigeon

Second Label: Moulin de Duhart

1961—Dark brick color with amber edge. Concentrated tobacco-like nose. Dense on the palate with good depth. Ripe fruity flavors, very tannic, and getting old. When the tannin dissolves, the fruit could be all gone. Watch out! (1979)
[1981] 15

1966—Deep ruby color. Powerful nose full of cassis. Straightforward on the palate, one-dimensional. Nice depth. Earthy and dusty flavors enhanced by a hint of black currant. Lacks elegance and charm (1980).
[1992] 15

1970—A corpulent wine with plenty of oak. Still very hard and austere. Lacks finesse and generosity. Good fruit in the back-ground, but we will have to wait a long time for it to mature and show more of itself (1982). Disappointing!—the least one can say after waiting 16 years. The wine is harsh and astringent, obtrusive, lacking fruity flavors. Instead, one gets an overpowering, dried, woody mouthful (1986).
[1995] 12

1973—Below-average quality for this château. Hard, austere, light body. Short finish. The redeeming qualities are the color and some fruitiness (1978).
[1978] 11

1975—Dark brick red with amber edges. Sweet candy-like, fruity bouquet. Full-bodied, mouth-filling texture, concentrated flavors of rich, ripe cassis. Full of extract, sensual, generous, savory. A warm and opulent wine (1985).
[1995] 18

1976—Medium ruby color. Nice fruity aroma with a hint of sweetness. Medium body. A lovely, light-structured wine that is ready to drink (1980).
[1990] 14-1/2

1978—Deep blackberry aroma and flavor. Medium body. Lacks the style and elegance of its brother, Lafite, although it bears some resemblance in the taste. Nicely balanced, but firm. As the vines (replanted in the '60s) are getting older, the quality of this property improves each year. Watch this château for future vintages (1982).
[1998] 16

1979—Even better than the '78, it has achieved charm, roundness, and suppleness. It has elegance and breed. The nose and taste also have a wonderfully complex cedar component along with its cassis-like fruit. The wine is well structured. Good amount of tannin. Long in the mouth (1982).
[1999] 17

Duhart-Milon Rothschild

1981—Dark color. Deep, soft, round, with cedar bouquet. Most attractive. Medium-to-full body, round, supple, and elegant. Excellent cedar flavor. Long in the mouth, and good depth. A very good future for this Duhart-Milon. Bravo! (1984)

[1989/2001] 16-1/2

1982—Dark color. Deep but muted nose of tobacco, clove and ripe fruit. Mouth filling, smooth, and attractive flavors of cedar and rich, baked ripe fruit. The wine is still backward with a good backbone of tannin. It is deeply structured, has depth and length, and is quite powerful (1985).

[1992/2012] 17+

1983—Dark purple color. The nose is extremely concentrated, yet it is a bit restrained. It is showing some oak, some stemminess (which is not overly offensive), and some good ripe fruit in the background. Rich and very concentrated on the palate, full of extract, loaded with tannin. A huge wine which will require a long time to mature. It is deep, long and almost rough. It will make a good bottle (1986).

[1995/2013] 17+

1984—Medium color. Soft cassis/earthy/oaky aroma which has breed and complexity. Medium weight on the palate. The entrance is a bit tannic but it is followed by a generous, distinguished flavor of cassis and oak. Warm, gentle, and long aftertaste (1987).

[1988/1994] 16

Durfort-Vivens

1959—Medium-dark brick color with amber edge. Attractive, soft, and elegant nose with cedar overtones. Medium body, round, and supple wine. Delicate flavor and structure. Well balanced. To be enjoyed with white meat (1979).

🍷 [1989] 15-1/2

1964—Harvested before the rains. Fully developed nose with an excellent bouquet. Lovely flavor on the palate, but a bit unbalanced by an overdose of tannin. The wine is aging rapidly. Drink it quickly for I am afraid its lovely attributes will have vanished when the tannin softens (1978).

[1978] 16-1/2

1966—Like the '64, this is a very tannic wine. Lovely and somewhat elegant bouquet. Light, flavorful ripe fruit. Long in the mouth. The tannic backbone damages the wine's breed and finesse (1982).

[1990] 14

1967—Lean, feeble wine with a good, elegant Margaux bouquet (1978).

[1975] 13

1970—The wine was firm and austere when young. Lately it is becoming more supple, but it is still restrained. It has a fair concentration (1981). Vigorous, hard, and coarse. Biting tannic aftertaste. Lacks finesse. Inharmonious wine (1985).

[1995] 14

1971—More attractive than its '70 older brother, more mature and more forward. Its texture and structure resemble a '70. Dark color. Deep tobacco nose with a hint of sweetness. Long in the mouth with good balance. Some tannin (1981).

[1991] 16

1973—Hard, austere, lean, and tannic. Not at all the gentle Margaux style (1978).

[1981] 12

1975—Medium-dark brick red. Unyielding nose. Medium-light to light body. Dry texture and finish, some nice earthy flavor. Balance is satisfactory. Drink up (1985).

[1985] 13-1/2

1976—Medium ruby color. Attractive bouquet and quite perfumy. Rich and elegant on the palate. The wine is round, soft, and has good flavors of cabernet. Tannic finish like most of the Durfort-Vivens, but should soften up and achieve a relatively good development (1980).

[1990] 15

1978—Hard to assess. Undeveloped aroma and taste. Medium dark color. Very tannic on the palate and long in the mouth. Will mature slowly (1982). Interesting nose, intermingling berries, cherries, and wood, not overwhelmingly expansive but present. Some astringent tannin unbalances the wine. Medium body and straightforward. The simple berry and oak flavors are subdued and palatable. Finishes all right if not a bit sharp. A food wine (1985).

[1988/1998] 14

1979—Medium color. Nice fragrance of cherries and vanillin oak. Medium body. It has breed and style with some elegant flavors. Tannic finish, but this vintage is much more harmonious than its older brother of the '78 vintage (1982).

[1988/1999] 15-1/2

1980—Light ruby color. Fresh, fruity nose. On the palate, the wine is supple, round, light, with a cassis-like berry flavor. A small and lean wine (1986).

[1986] 13-1/2

1981—Medium color. Flowery fragrance mixed with cassis. The attack on the

Appellation Contrôlée: Margaux

Principal Owner: Lucien Lurton

Average Production: 7,000 cases

Vineyard Area: 19 hectares, 47 acres

Grape Varieties: 82% CS, 10% CF, 8% M

Average Vine Age: 22 years

Average Yield: 33 hectolitres per hectare

Classified Second Growth in 1855

Yves's Classification: Third growth

Food Complements: (4 to 6 years old) beef stroganoff, (12 years or older) Peking duck

Second Label: Domaine de Cure-Bourse

Durfort-Vivens

palate is elegant and round. The fruit is quite apparent and develops well in the mouth. It is followed by a trace of vanillin oakiness. The wine is complex and long in the mouth. The finish is a bit unbalanced by too much acid and tannin, but this is a minor flaw due to its youth that I am sure aging will correct (1984).

[1991/2006] 16+

1982—Medium color. Nice aroma of sweet fruit reminiscent of cassis laced with oak. On the palate, the wine is medium-to-medium light, but in good balance with each component. It is supple with enough tannin for aging. The fruit flavors are elegant and are enhanced by vanillin undertones. A good wine, easy to drink in a few years (1985).

[1989/1998] 16

1983—A good effort from this property, which made a wine more in keeping with its real second-growth classification. Medium- dark color. The nose shows some subdued but attractive ripe berries laced with cedar. On the palate, it is fairly well concentrated. Rough tannin counter-balanced by a rich fruitiness. When the tannin rounds up, which will take a long time, this wine will be a very good bottle, for it has a certain length and depth and shows good breeding (1986).

[1995/2005] 17

1984—Gentle, medium-light second growth. Smooth and mellow with attractive berry/spicy flavors. Elegantly balanced. Quaffable, easy-drinking wine. Should make a good restaurant wine for the next five years (1987).
[1992] 15-1/2

L'Evangile

1982
CHATEAU
L'EVANGILE
POMEROL
MIS EN BOUTEILLES AU CHATEAU
Appellation Pomerol contrôlée
75cl
PRODUCE OF FRANCE
SOCIÉTÉ CIVILE DU CHATEAU L'ÉVANGILE
Héritiers P. DUCASSE
PROPRIETAIRES A POMEROL (GIRONDE)

Appellation Contrôlée: Pomerol

Principal Owner: Héritiers P. Ducasse

Administrator: Louis Ducasse

Average Production: 4,300 cases

Vineyard Area: 13 hectares, 32 acres

Grape Varieties: 67% M, 33% CF

Average Vine Age: 34 years

Average Yield: 32 hectolitres per hectare

Yves's Classification: Second growth

Food Complements: (3 to 6 years old) civet of duck au Pomerol, (10 years or older) stuffed medallions of hare in strawberry Bordelaise vinegar

1961—Very dark color. Outstanding nose of perfumy fruit, raspberries and cedar. Full-bodied, rich, and luscious. Magnificent flavors of cedar and ripe merlot. Velvety and remarkable elegance in the finish. Still young and could improve (1980).
[1995] 18-1/2

1964—Beautiful and powerful nose of luscious cassis laced with cedary fragrance. Mouth filling, chewy, the same opulent flavors already found on the nose. Velvety texture. A sensual bottle (1986).
[1990] 17+

1966—Very well made. Round and soft full-bodied wine. Very fruity, easy to drink, and very well balanced. A wine that has finesse and elegance (1979).
[1990] 17-1/2+

1967—Attractive when young, but getting old and should be drunk up by now. Delicate wine, perhaps a bit overchaptalized. Not too flavorful, and a disturbing, awkward finish (1978).
[1977] 14-1/2

1970—When six years old, it was unyielding, mouth filling, loaded with tannin, and long in the mouth. But nothing exciting about it. Today the wine has opened up and shows some rich qualities. Earthy, iron, violet, and cedar aroma and flavor. Well-knit, velvety texture, and a seductive elegance and class (1986).
[1995] 17-1/2

1971—Old and feeble. Herbaceous flavor reminiscent of wet straw. Quite unpleasant (1986).
12

1973—This was one of my everyday table wines from 1979 to 1982. Soft, round, with delicious cedar flavor. Medium body and well balanced. Silky finish. A very charming and delicious wine that went perfectly with roast chicken served with *pommes de terre rissolees* and *haricots verts au beurre* (1983).
[1985] 16-1/2+

1975—One of the 15 best wines of the vintage. Dark ruby/purple color. Raspberry fragrance on the nose laced with vanilla, cedar, and spice. Full-bodied, rich, powerful wine. Very concentrated and fleshy. It has breed, depth, and finesse. Will make a great bottle of wine when the tannin dissolves (1983).
[1988/2005] 18-1/2

1978—Much like the '73 vintage in flavor and style but with more concentration and depth. The nose is loaded with sweet fruit, black currants, and cedar. Medium body. Delicious and rich flavors. Much finesse and well balanced. Drink now (1985).
[1993] 16-1/2

1979—Again, one of the best of the vintage. In general, '79 was better in Pomerol and St-Emilion than in the Médoc and Graves. It also seems that they

L'Evangile

achieved better quality than their '78. Medium-dark ruby color. A delightfully big, mature nose full of ripe merlot, cedar and vanillin oak. Medium-to-full body, luscious, and supple. Outstanding rich and generous flavors. Good tannin and long finish. This wine is very enjoyable and savory (1986).
[1996] 17-1/2+

1980—A very spicy wine, bigger in weight than other '80s. However, it lacks fruit and has an inky aftertaste. Needs more time (1983).
[1987/1992] 14

1981—Medium ruby color. Intensely fragrant bouquet of soft flowers laced with cedary overtones. Light-to-medium body. Round texture with attractive cedar and fruit flavors. Lacks depth and concentration. Otherwise, the wine is very charming with its rather light components in perfect balance (1984).
[1988/1995] 15-1/2

1982—Dark purple color. Deep, rich, floral bouquet enhanced by cassis and cedar. The aroma is beautiful and forward. Mouth-filling, chewy texture, deep, and very concentrated. Marvelous flavors of ripe fruit, cedar, and oak. Loaded with round tannin. Supple, balanced, long and generous in the mouth (1985).
[1992/2012] 18-1/2

1983—Dark color. Deep, concentrated nose but still underdeveloped. Very concentrated texture, full of extract. Loaded with fruit, oak, and marvelous flavors of coffee and tobacco. The taste is reminiscent of Trotanoy or Latour-a-Pomerol. This L'Evangile has a great backbone of rounded tannin and wonderful depth. Lingering, sweet berry flavor (1986).
[1993/2007] 18

1984—Light, lean, and mellow wine. Delicate, fruity flavors overshadowed by some unpleasant herbaceousness (hay). Elusive finish. Drink soon (1987).
[1990] 13-1/2

Figeac

CHATEAU - FIGEAC
SAINT-EMILION PREMIER GRAND CRÛ CLASSÉ
ST ÉMILION
Appellation St-Emilion 1er Grand Crû Classé Contrôlée
1982
MIS EN BOUTEILLES AU CHÂTEAU
MANONCOURT PROPRIÉTAIRE A SAINT-ÉMILION (FRANCE)
Bouteille Nº 192528
PRODUCE OF FRANCE
750 ml

Appellation Contrôlée: St-Emilion Grand Cru

Principal Owner: Thierry de Manoncourt

Average Production: 12,500 cases

Vineyard Area: 38 hectares, 94 acres

Grape Varieties: 35% CS, 35% CF, 30% M

Average Vine Age: 38 years

Average Yield: 29 hectolitres per hectare

Classified First Great Growth "B"

Yves's Classification: Second growth

Food Complements: (3 to 6 years old) breast of mallard with chestnuts, (8 years or older) noisette of veal

Second Label: Château du Grangeneuve

1959—Medium color with amber edge. The nose is soft and gentle with a lilac, earthy, mushroom fragrance. Delicious ripe grape flavor. The wine is full-bodied, deep, and has enormous flavors. No subtle complexity here, but, instead, a powerful, opulent nectar. I love it (1984).
[1989] 18+

1961—Dark color, slight brownish edge. Beautiful nose with plenty of fruit followed by a cedar aroma for which this château is well known. Full-bodied, rich, big, plummy, and excellent flavor. The finish is a bit odd. It lacks weight and sweetness (1981).
[1991] 18

1962—Medium dark. Charming, soft bouquet. Medium body, well structured, and balanced. Good taste of fruit and cedar. Round and velvety. A very good wine at its peak. Should not be kept too long (1978).
[1982] 17-1/2

1964—I have always loved this wine. We had it at many tastings from 1975 until 1986. At a single-blind tasting at Mr. Kramer's in 1983, it was served with '64 Haut-Brion, Cheval-Blanc, Pétrus, and La Croix-de-Gay. Big, full, excellent concentrated aroma. On the palate, the wine was outstanding. Luscious and cedary, well balanced, rich and generous. Long, velvety, lingering finish. A marvelous, opulent St-Emilion! (1983)
[1985] 19

1966—Tasted at the St. James restaurant in Bordeaux with Messieurs Gabriel and Eric Dulong (father and son wine negociants). The wine was rather mature. Dark color. Deep, fragrant bouquet, with an almost Burgundy-like aroma. Huge and mouth-filling with a great texture and concentration. It has a fruity and delightful cedar flavor. Long on the palate. Great balance with some useful tannin. A great wine (1981).
[1996] 18

1970—Dark ruby color. Deep bouquet with enjoyable and concentrated scents. Full body. Outstanding flavor. The wine is big, soft, ample, velvety, and extremely well balanced. Distinguished aftertaste. I take my hat off to Mr. Manoncourt. His wine is complete and ready to drink, unlike many '70s which are still not mature (1983).
[1994] 18

1971—Elegant, soft bouquet with cedary overtones. Light-to-medium body. Harmonious wine, almost-sweet taste. Lacks tannin and backbone for long keeping. Drink it now while it is still young and charming (1979).
[1983] 16

1973—Attractive, deep, cedar and tobacco aroma. Medium body. Appealing concentrated flavors. Nice texture. Cedar aftertaste. A little tannin gives the

Figeac

wine good backbone. Very enjoyable wine that went perfectly with my very rare lamb chop served, of course, without the abominable mint jelly (1986).
[1988] 16

1975—Dark color. Nice, open bouquet. Full-bodied and well structured. Extremely flavorful with a hint of sweetness in the background. Good tannin that needs to dissolve. Will be a great bottle in the very near future (1981). Beautiful, dark ruby color with amber edge. Deep, rich, intense, aromatic bouquet of cassis and tobacco. On the palate, the wine is warm, generous, huge, powerful, fleshy, velvety, and harmoniously well balanced. It has gorgeous cedar and cassis flavors which linger unctuously in the aftertaste. A chewy texture which has depth and length. A remarkable wine! (1986).
[2005] 18+

1976—Dark color. Concentrated nose with fruit, cedar, wood, and tobacco aroma. Quite seductive. Full-bodied. Deep flavors but not as forward as the nose yet. Fruity, velvety, and generous. Long, smooth, cedar finish. A great success in this vintage (1984).
[1996] 17-1/2+

1978—Dark color. Charming fruit and cedar on the nose. On the palate the wine is closed, unyielding, austere, and tannic. Very hard to assess its future (1981). Starting to unfold and blossom. The nose shows in a bashful way a refined, redeeming cedar, cassis, and tobacco aroma. Deep and concentrated on the palate, the wine is supple and round, heavily structured, and loaded with tannin. Even though it is already palatable, it will continue to improve for many, many years. For the time being, the flavor is attractive but one-

dimensional. Having known and followed Figeac for thirty years, I know this one will acquire complexity, nuances and grace (1986).
[1988/2008] 17

1979—Disappointing considering the price and reputation of this fine property. The wine is unbalanced, with unattractive flavors. A touch of bitterness in the aftertaste. Although there are some good components, it is not too pleasant a drinking wine (1983). Medium-light, innocuous flavors, lacks depth and length (1986).
[1994] 13-1/2

1980—Cloves and spiciness show through the unyielding nose. It is round and supple on the palate with a good backbone. It has character and style for the vintage. A well-made wine. The grapes were picked very late, on October 20th (1983).
[1986] 14-1/2

1981—Pleasant, round, and soft wine with some redeeming flavors of cedar and red ripe berries. An easy wine to drink, but it lacks depth, concentration, and generosity to qualify in the big leagues (1984).
[1993] 15

1982—Medium-dark ruby color. Forward and attractive nose of young spicy clovelike bouquet enhanced by cedar and ripe red fruit. Full-bodied, powerful, and virile, yet supple. Well- developed and precocious flavors of spice, berry, oak, and cedar. Loaded with youthful tannin. Deep and well balanced. Finishes elegantly and with style (1985).
[1992/2010] 18+

1983—Probably the best St-Emilion of the vintage. Medium dark. Voluptuous cedary aroma. In one bottle, I found a hint of stemminess which dissipated after aeration. Great concentration of ripe fruit. Delicious, creamy aftertaste of cedar. Deep, long, intense, distinguished. A splendid wine (1986).
[1992/2010] 18+

1984—In the years when the merlot grape fails to flower properly, Cheval-Blanc and Figeac always come out ahead of their neighbors, since only one-third of their properties is planted in merlot. Most attractive, abundant aroma and flavors of cedar, rich cassis, and tobacco with a certain aromatic toastiness. The hefty tannin gives this otherwise smooth and velvety wine a gutsy finish which will also provide an adequate longevity (1987).
[1989/1999] 17+

La Gaffelière

1947—Fragrant bouquet. Outstanding taste with good backbone. Long, round, velvety aftertaste. A great bottle that will hold a few more years (1978).
[1986] 18+

1953—Soft and gentle, very mature. Rich, round, and very flowery. Should be drunk by now (1976).
[1976] 18

1959—Brick color with amber edge. Very rich nose but a strange fragrance. Medium body. Elegant with soft and round texture. Nice wine (1981).
[1981] 15-1/2

1961—Concentrated deep color. The nose has cedary overtones. Full-bodied and mouth-filling. Great depth, complexity, rich, and powerful. Abundant

Appellation Contrôlée: St-Emilion Grand Cru

Principal Owner: Count de Mallet-Roquefort

Average Production: 8,000 cases

Vineyard Area: 20 hectares, 50 acres

Grape Varieties: 10% CS, 25% CF, 65% M

Average Vine Age: 44 years

Average Yield: 36 hectolitres per hectare

Classified First Great Growth "B"

Yves's Classification: Third growth

Food Complements: (3 to 6 years old) New York strip steak grilled over wood, (8 years or older) civet of goose

Second Label: Château de Roquefort

flavor of cedar, ripe red fruit, and a touch of earthiness. Unfortunately, some woody, dry tannin unbalances the aftertaste and finish. Drink up (1985).
[1985] 17

1962—Like most '62s, which were very pleasant and attractive in the mid '70s, they should be consumed by now. Extremely palatable and balanced with a taste of mellow ripe fruit and a hint of cedar (1979).
[1979] 16-1/2

1964—Sweet, flowery aroma with many beautiful different scents. Some bottles are a bit restrained. Big in the mouth, vigorous, with some still untamed tannin, it does not seem to grow old. The taste of old wood and mushrooms is pleasant. The wine is balanced and has a good finish (1983).
[1994] 17

1966—Round and supple with good harmony. Gentle, elegant, and charming, yet straightforward with no complexity (1978).
[1990] 16-1/2

1967—Was disappointing when young, but by 1983 the nose showed some fruit with a cedary overtone. Unfortunately, it was laced with a bothersome wet-grass smell. Medium body, fair texture, and concentration. A little fruit and cedar flavor. Nice aftertaste (1983).
[1987] 15

1970—A powerful wine. Quite forward with a big and deep bouquet. Concentrated full body. Sweet fruity flavors. Plenty of tannin. Harsh finish. Will improve but it is already delicious. Quite precocious for a '70 and for La Gaffelière (1980).
[1999] 16-1/2

1971—This vintage of La Gaffelière is certainly not as open, round, flavorful, and lingering as Magdelaine or La Fleur-Pétrus. Nevertheless, the wine is pleasant. Good fruit but somewhat restrained. It needs more time. Many vintages of La Gaffelière require a longer period to supple up (1977). Fully opened and at its peak now. Soft, round, aromatic bouquet and flavor. Medium- to-medium-light concentration. Getting old. Drink without delay while it is still charming (1986).
[1986] 15+

1973—Light and soft body. Should be drunk by now (1980).
[1980] 14

1975—Young nose with a deep and concentrated aroma. Very elegant on the palate. Supple and harmonious, medium-to-full body. Still hard as many La Gaffelière are when young. I predict that this wine will have a very good future (1979). This wine has aged harmoniously. It is, therefore, well balanced and drinks very well. Medium-bodied, attractive fruit, oak, and mushroom flavor. Round and supple in structure. Good finish (1986).
[1995] 17

1978—This is a good wine, but there is a predominant herbaceous flavor I dislike. It has a certain depth but lacks complexity. I do not see this wine as memorable even when fully mature (1982).
[1990] 13

1979—Tasted side by side with the '78 vintage, the '79 was more to my liking. Fruity perfume with vanilla and cedar. Medium body. Agreeable flavors. Good tannin. Long on the palate. Needs to be at least ten years old (1982).
[1989/2000] 15-1/2

La Gaffelière

1981—Feeble and lean on the palate, not very long in the mouth. A light luncheon wine. Not up to its potential (1984).
[1991] 13

1982—I have enjoyed it at every tasting. Medium ruby color. Unyielding nose with some spice. Medium-to-full body. Rich, opulent, warm, round, cedar and fruit flavors. Good backbone of rounded tannin. Long in the mouth and well balanced (1986).
[1992/2002] 17

1983—Medium color. Medium-to-medium-light body. Not too much concentration here, nor depth either, yet it is elegant and well balanced. A redeeming quality of fresh gooseberries laced with a hint of cedar and oak. It has charm and a certain sex appeal. It is a true and distinctive St-Emilion (1986).
[1990/1998] 15-1/2+

1984—Light, pinkish color. Gentle, mellow, and lean. Agreeable, simple, and delicate, fruity flavors. A wine to drink right now and for the next two or three years while it still possesses some of its youthful attributes (1987).
[1990] 14

Gazin

Appellation Contrôlée: Pomerol

Principal Owner: Etienne de Bailliencourt

Average Production: 8,250 cases

Vineyard Area: 24 hectares, 59 acres

Grape Varieties: 80% M, 15% CF, 5% CS

Average Vine Age: 32 years

Average Yield: 31 hectolitres per hectare

Yves's Classification: Third growth

Food Complements: (3 to 6 years old) roast beef, (10 years or older) calves' sweetbread with fresh herbs and truffles

1961—Bright, medium-dark color. The nose is not too forward, but has a discreet, attractive bouquet of fruit, cassis, and cedar. The wine is well structured but it is still austere and unyielding. It has a good backbone and plenty of tannin. Needs more time (1979).
[2001] 16-1/2

1964—Nice dark color. Rich and fragrant cedary/fruity bouquet. Quite powerful. Full-bodied, rich flavors, mouth-filling texture. Very well balanced. Good aftertaste. Long in the mouth (1977). Medium-dark color. Deep minty and fruity aroma. On the palate, the wine is still young in flavor. The tannins are not totally dissolved. Well-structured, long aftertaste, a bit austere (1985).
[1996] 16

1966—Resembles the '61 vintage. Full-bodied, but firm, austere, and unyielding. Plenty of tannin. Good prospect (1979).
[2000] 16-1/2

1970—Medium-dark ruby color with amber edges. Deep, subdued cedar nose. Full-bodied, with a soft, round, silky texture. Concentrated, savory cedar flavor. Loaded with rounded tannin. Long and powerful finish. A great, generous, merlot wine which took 16 years to blossom, and which will continue to mature and develop for many years (1986).
[2010] 17-1/2

1976—Dark color. Like many Gazins, the nose is bashfully subdued. On the palate, the wine shows some redeeming qualities. It is medium full, supple, and balanced with a cedary undertone. It has good, rounded tannin. Finishes long. A fine Pomerol in this vintage (1985).
[1993] 16

1978—Very much like the '76 in style and structure, but more developed and advanced. This makes it more attractive for today's drinking. Charming cedary bouquet. Medium body, rich, good depth and balance. Flavorful and good tannin. Finishes well (1981).
[1995] 16

1979—Medium-dark color. Clove and ripe merlot aroma, not too forward. Medium body. Lovely fruity/cedary flavors laced with a good backbone of tannin. Well-built and long aftertaste (1983).
[1996] 16

1981—Medium dark. Attractive, soft, and deep cedary cassis aroma. Medium body. Very supple, even velvety. Extremely enjoyable cedar and black currant flavors. Appears to have a hole in the middle and a short finish (1986).
[1993] 15-1/2

1982—Dark color. Unyielding and restrained nose. Medium body. Austere from a lack of fruit. Tannic, lacks romance, elegance and softness. Other than that, the wine has good concentration and is firmly structured. It is like drinking espresso coffee without sugar. *A chacun son goût!* (1985)
[1992/2006] 15

Gazin

1983—Medium color. Deep nose but rather restrained, showing spiciness enhanced by a sweet fruitiness. Medium- to medium-light body, nicely rounded and slightly concentrated, yet appealing with soft, rounded flavors. Well balanced. A nice Pomerol (1986).
[1990/2000] 15-1/2

1984—Picnic wine. *Vin de qualité ordinaire.* Château Gazin should not have bottled this wine under its label (1987).
🍷 [1989] 12-1/2

Giscours

1959—Harmonious wine with breed and concentration. Well structured and long in the mouth (1979).
🍷 [1990] 17

1961—Very dark color with amber edge. Fragrant bouquet full of fruit. Rich and powerful, yet elegant. Chewy on the palate with great depth and lovely flavors of baked ripe black currant (1984).
🍷 [1991] 17

Appellation Contrôlée: Margaux
Principal Owner: G.F.A. du Château Giscours
Administrator: Pierre Tari
Average Production: 25,000 cases
Vineyard Area: 68 hectares, 168 acres
Grape Varieties: 67% CS, 33% M
Average Vine Age: 25 years
Average Yield: 33 hectolitres per hectare
Classified Third Growth in 1855
Yves's Classification: Third growth
Food Complements: (5 to 8 years old) rack of lamb, (12 years or older) roast veal loin

1962—Light-bodied wine with attractive flavor and bouquet. Easy to drink. It does lack the backbone and depth to make it great (1978).
[1978] 14

1964—Similar to the '62 in body, flavor, and texture. Should be drunk by now (1978).
[1978] 14

1966—This vintage of Giscours is very firm and dry. It has lost its fruit and flesh. It lacks finesse. Drink it up (1978).
[1978] 14

1967—A *vin de qualité ordinaire*. Drink it up (1978).
[1974] 12

1970—Dark color. Subdued aroma starting to open, showing an attractive ripe fruit. Rich and concentrated on the palate. It has depth, good tannin, and a chewy texture. The elegant flavors are long and lingering in the mouth. A great wine that will continue to improve for a few more years (1983).
[2005] 17-1/2

1971—Some bottles are very open and delicious while others are backward and tannic in the style of the '70 vintage. Very deep color with amber edge. Most attractive nose of oak and ripe cabernet. Very concentrated texture, full body, deep, and powerful. Flavorful, good tannin, and long in the mouth. A big success for this vintage (1982).
[1991] 17

1973—Now past its prime, but even today you can see how charming and well balanced the wine was. It still has its seductive berry flavor. Some of these '73s were really attractive in the late '70s (1986).
[1979] 15-1/2

1975—Dark color. Spicy aroma with ginger undertones now showing a deep, sweet berry bouquet. On the palate the wine is very concentrated and chewy. It has good texture and lovely ripe cabernet flavors. It is full-bodied and long in the mouth with plenty of tannin. This wine, rather ample and fat, has an unctuous, rich, cassis/chocolate aftertaste (1985).
[1988/2005] 17-1/2

1976—Firm and austere when young. It is now open and very supple. It has reached the beginning of its maturity. Extremely pleasant flavors with good backbone and depth (1983).
[1993] 16-1/2

1978—Very dark color. Deep aroma, unopened but showing some ripe cabernet in the background. Extremely concentrated and full-bodied on the palate. Atypical style for a Margaux, but who cares since the wine is well made. Long in the mouth and very tannic. Will make a great bottle but we will have to wait a long time (1983). Very dark ruby color. Deep, rich, concentrated bouquet of berries and plums jumps right out of the glass! Full-bodied, abundant concentration of fleshy, juicy, ripe black currants. Mouth-filling extract, generous texture. A powerful and opulent wine which will continue to mature and develop for many years. Served during the dinner-gala at the Waldorf when I won the U.S. Sommelier's contest. Quite a memorable wine for me! (1985)
[2005] 18

1979—Exceptionally well made for the vintage. When young, it was even better than the '78. Dark purple color. Plenty of fruit on the nose. Full body.

Giscours

Very rich, delicious texture, and flavors reminiscent of ripe red fruit and cassis. Great structure and balance. Generous finish with good tannin. A winner! (1983)

🍷 [2000] 18

1980—The perfect restaurant wine. Medium-light concentration, forward, displays seductive flavors of ripe sweet fruit. Round and soft texture, exquisite balance. The wine is lightweight but every component is in proportion. A harmonious wine. Ready to drink (1986).

🍷 [1992] 16

1981—Medium ruby color. Attractive, deep flowery fragrance. Soft and generous. Some deep flavors on the palate. Rounded tannin. Deep cassis and oaky aftertaste. Long in the mouth and quite well balanced. A very good Margaux (1984).

[1989/2006] 16-1/2

1982—Medium-dark color already showing some amber in the edge. The nose is closed, but a fragrance of deep cassis and vanilla escapes. Full-bodied, velvety texture, and supple. Rich cassis flavor and good concentration. The lack of acidity makes this wine a bit flabby. Should be drunk and enjoyed relatively young. It does not have the depth of a long-lived Giscours (1985).

[1989/1999] 16-1/2

1983—Medium-dark color. The nose is uncomplicatedly forward and quite fruity. Medium-bodied, soft and velvety texture. Rich and full of ripe berry flavor. Unctuous and long-lasting on the palate. Most charming wine for early consumption. Drink young (1986).

[1989/1996] 16-1/2

1984—Medium-dark color. Deep cassis/oaky aroma followed by the same delicious flavors. Well textured, round, relatively deep and concentrated, rich, fleshy, and expansive. Long and lingering finish (1987).

🍷 [1995] 16-1/2

Grand-Puy-Lacoste

Château Grand-Puy-Lacoste
Mis en bouteilles au château
Saint Guirons
Pauillac
(Médoc)

Société du Château Grand-Puy-Lacoste, Propriétaire

Appellation Contrôlée: Pauillac

Principal Owner: Borie family

Administrators: Jean-Eugene and Xavier Borie

Average Production: 14,000 cases

Vineyard Area: 35 hectares, 86 acres

Grape Varieties: 70% CS, 25% M, 5% CF

Average Vine Age: 32 years

Average Yield: 36 hectolitres per hectare

Classified Fifth Growth in 1855

Yves's Classification: Third growth

Food Complements: (4 to 6 years old) mousse of duck livers, (10 years or older) veal cordon bleu

1959–Harsh when young, still a bit tannic but quite pleasant now. Delightful flavor of cedar. Medium body. Good spicy aftertaste (1981).

[1989] 16

1961–Medium-dark color. Deep earthy aroma with mushroomy fragrances enhanced by sweet ripe fruit. Mouth-filling, attractive flavors, rich and concentrated. Still young. Good tannin and long in the mouth. Lovely finish, but a bit tannic. A well-made wine (1984).

[2001] 17-1/2

1962–Nice ruby color. Soft and elegant bouquet. Same characteristics on the palate with good flavors of fruit. Round texture, medium body, easy to drink, and very enjoyable (1979).

[1987] 16-1/2

1964–Past its prime now, yet it still shows some surprising, redeeming attributes in its somewhat rustic style. The pronounced, rich cassis aroma and flavor are, of course, the main factors that make this wine so enjoyable. The chewy yet rough texture along with good depth and an oaky component give the wine a rustic structure. Drink now (1987).

[1981] 16-1/2

1966–Even when this wine was 10 years old, its nose was uncompromisingly closed. Yet on the palate, it showed good fruit, concentration and depth. Now it has opened up showing a very fragrant aroma full of ripe fruit. It is full-bodied on the palate with excellent flavors of cabernet. It is long and well balanced (1980).

[2000] 17

1967–Getting old now. Losing its fruit and attractiveness. Should be drunk (1981).

[1977] 14

1970–Oaky, mushroom aroma. On the palate, the wine did not mature as well as predicted. Some dry, aging, acidic tannins unbalance the wine and are quite bothersome. The wine shows some one-dimensional fruit with an austere, woody flavor. Overall, the wine lacks generosity, warmth, and romance (1986).

[1990] 13-1/2

1971–Tawny red. Spicy and oaky nose. Elegant and round on the palate. A bit unbalanced by acid but not overly offensive. A charming wine easy to drink (1981). Medium ruby color with amber edges. Oaky mushroom aroma followed by a hint of bell pepper and spice. Medium-light body, fluid texture, attractive woody, oaky flavors. Good balance but the tannin is becoming dry and angular. Therefore, drink the wine without delay, before it becomes austere and sharp (1985).

[1983] 15-1/2

1973–Very much like the '71 vintage but with less depth and concentration. Appetizing flavors. Drink now (1981).

[1981] 15

1975–A very well-made wine. Plenty of fruit and cassis in the aroma. Medium-to-full body. Good concentration of cabernet. Nicely textured. Good tannin. Will make a good bottle in a few years (1981).

[1995] 17

1976–Harsh and austere with some fruit in the background. It will need more time to round up and mature, but will there be enough fruit to sustain that wait? (1981)

[1990] 14

1978—We shall have to wait a long time for this wine. The color is very dark and the wine is very tannic. It has a deep and concentrated nose with cabernet and oak. It is loaded with tannin, which currently makes the wine severe. It has a mouth-filling texture with concealed flavors of fruit and cedar. It is long-lasting in the mouth. Very good future (1981).

[1990/2005] 17-1/2

1979—Dark color. Deep nose with fruity and tobacco aroma. Medium body, round, and rich, delicious flavors. Good tannin. An extremely precocious, attractive wine that came to the market at a very low price (1983).

🍷 [1995] 17

1980—Light and attractive, with breed. Needs time to open. Good-to-fair concentration and depth. It has fruit in the taste and aftertaste. Some tannin. Light and enjoyable wine (1983).

🍷 [1989] 14-1/2

1981—Medium-dark-to-dark color. Spicy, deep, concentrated, and unyielding nose. Full body. The flavors are quite withdrawn. The texture is severe. It lacks softness, roundness, and elegance. However, the wine is well structured and has good depth. I predict a relatively good future for this wine (1984).

[1993/2006] 15-1/2

1982—The first thing that struck me was its extremely dark purple color. Good sign I said. The nose, although unyielding and more in the traditional Bordeaux style (versus the 1982 Bordeaux-California forwardness), showed some attractive spiciness laced with deep ripe berries. Concentrated, full-bodied, yet tight with a tannic structure. Excellent berrylike flavor escorted with oak. Powerful, deep, and very well balanced. Great rich rounded tannin gives this wine a long and lingering finish (1985).

[1992/2010] 18

Grand-Puy-Lacoste

1983—Medium color. Deep, peppery aroma. Medium body. Good concentration, well-textured, elegant structure, appealing black currant flavors. It is well balanced but lacks complexity and a certain romance and style (1986).
[1990/1998] 15

1984—Medium color. Discreet nose shows after the wine breathes awhile. Some oak with a hint of berry, but lacks finesse. Concentrated, tannic, needs more time. Some redeeming qualities, such as its structure and a surprising depth for a 1984. A cabernet wine that is a bit austere but has a foreseeable future (1987).
[1990/1995] 15

Gruaud-Larose

Appellation Contrôlée: St-Julien

Principal Owner: Cordier family

Average Production: 32,000 cases

Vineyard Area: 78 hectares, 193 acres

Grape Varieties: 63% CS, 9% CF, 24% M, 3% PV

Average Vine Age: 35 years

Average Yield: 40 hectolitres per hectare

Classified Second Growth in 1855

Yves's Classification: Second growth

Food Complements: (4 to 6 years old) wild duck in wine sauce (10 years or older) beef Wellington

Second Label: Sarget de Gruaud-Larose

1947—Tasted at a dinner party. Round, supple, and fruity. Good concentration, generous, and elegant. Still young for its age (1976).
[1990] 18

1949—Beautiful bouquet enhanced by cassis. Good depth on the palate. Luscious, rich, and gentle. Great balance and long lingering finish (1978).
[1990] 18-1/2

1953—Deep aroma, ripe cabernet nose, and perfumy bouquet. Rich, warm, and elegant on the palate. Still some tannin indicates a good longevity (1975).
[1993] 17-1/2

1955—Lighter than its older brothers. It has charm and breed, but lacks depth and length. Nevertheless, it is a good, elegant wine. Drink now, for it will not improve (1979).
[1983] 16

1959—Tasted once at my restaurant, brought by one of our regular guests. I could not get much out of the nose. On the palate, the wine was chewy, concentrated, and rich. Not well balanced, too much acidity. But it did have a good flavorful aftertaste (1977).
[1989] 14

1961—I was flabbergasted the first time I tasted this wine which was already 20 years old when I tried it. Very dark color with a brick edge. Deep, fragrant bouquet like an explosion of flowers. Enormous on the palate. Full of extract, supple, round and velvety. Delicious flavors of black currants with a touch of cedar. Extremely concentrated with plenty of rounded tannin still present. This is a powerful, fleshy wine made to live a long time (1982).
[2020] 19+

1962—Wonderful aroma of cassis and cigar box. Deep and concentrated on the palate. Full of extract. Long in the mouth. A great and complete wine that is still young (1985).
[1990] 17

1964—This château made a great wine in this controversial year. It is a big wine loaded with fruit that is round, fleshy and supple. Good depth and balance (1985).
[1985] 17

1966—Tannic, hard, and backward (1976). A little window opened through that thick, firm concentration and tannin. I forecast an excellent future. This wine has great depth and a powerful personality (1983). Dark purple color with no amber edge. Deep but unyielding nose with some cedar. Full body and excellent flavors of blackberry and oak. Nicely textured, long in the mouth,

Gruaud-Larose

rich, velvety, and extremely well balanced. This wine is still not fully ready and will continue to mature. A huge and well made wine (1984).
[1988/2010] 18+

1967—Severe, acidic, stern, therefore unbalanced. Lacks fruit and style. I do not see much future (1982).
[1977] 14

1970—Another powerful wine from this château. The wine has a very good concentration of fruit. It is well structured, with depth and complex flavors. All of these components are harmoniously blended with one another. It is a rich, mouth-filling, and plummy wine (1985).
[2005] 18

1971—Attractive, fruity aroma enhanced by a touch of mint. On the palate, a bit coarse and austere. Medium body. Lacks elegance and generosity but could improve (1980).
[1995] 16

1973—Medium-dark color. Nice, concentrated aroma with some cedar and flowery overtones. Medium to big on the palate. Smooth, elegant, good fruit, and flavorful. Velvety aftertaste. A charming wine. I preferred it over the '71 (1981).
[1983] 16-1/2

1975—Extremely hard to assess. This wine is very tannic, closed in, concentrated, and intense. All of the attributes of a wine for long aging. It reminds me of the '66 when young. There is no question in my mind that this will be a great wine when ready (1980). Dark, dark color. The bouquet starts to blossom and to unfold its petals, showing in a bashful way a refined, plummy, black currant, cedary aroma. Deep and concentrated on the palate, supple and round, yet the wine is firmly structured and loaded with tannin. Even though it is starting to become palatable, it will continue to improve for many, many years. A humongous wine (1986).

[1992/2010] 18-1/2

1976—Light nose showing some fruit and wood. Medium-light body, pleasant flavors, soft and delicate. Unbalanced by some bitter tannin. Drink up (1985).

🍷 [1986] 14

1978—I should call Château Gruaud-Larose the Château Latour of St-Julien, because when the wine is young and from a great vintage it is closed and unyielding. One has to wait a very long time before the wine comes around. Dark in color. Cassis and cedar on the nose. Medium-to-full body. Well structured with a good backbone. Lots of tannin. Again the potential is there and patience will be rewarded (1982). Opaque in color. Deep, deep blackberry aroma. Mouth-filling, meaty, generous, fleshy, delicious, ripe red fruit flavors firmly backed up by oak and cedar. Loaded with undissolved, rounded tannin. A huge, forthcoming and powerful bottle (1986).

[1989/2008] 17+

1979—Dark color. Unyielding nose showing some fruit in the background. On the palate, the wine is more advanced than the'78. It is full-bodied, well built, and has depth and complexity. Cedary flavors and ripe fruit. Good, firm aftertaste and tannin. A long-lived wine (1982). Dark color. Rich and very attractive blackberry aroma. Full-bodied, rounded tannins, long and deep. Good concentration, full of extract. Chewy texture, warm and generous. Luscious and savory black currant, plum, and cherry taste and aftertaste (1986).

🍷 [2005] 17

1980—For $10.00 or less a bottle when first released, one could not go wrong. We might have had to wait a little longer for this 1980 than for others. When young, it was more restrained and tannic, but today it has lovely fruit and cedar flavors. It has fairly good depth and texture (1985).

🍷 [1990] 14-1/2

1981—It is not often that Gruaud-Larose is head and shoulders above Ducru and Léoville-Las-Cases, but this time I believe it is. Another eight years of age will determine the validity of my assertion. The wine is rich and deep. It has a black currant flavor followed by oaky components. It is mouth-filling and thick with great texture. Sweet red fruit lingering in the finish. This wine is one of the best of the vintage (1984).

[1993/2025] 18-1/2+

1982—The '81 Gruaud-Larose was one of the best of its vintage, and certainly the best value. But the 1982 is even superior! It has a very dark purple color. Deep, rich, concentrated aroma of black currants. It is powerful and mouth-filling on the palate. It has great concentration, depth, balance, breed, and style. Delicious cherry/cassis/oaky flavor. Rounded tannin and long- lasting in the mouth. Superb! (1985)

[1992/2012] 19

1983—The first time I had this wine was in New York, participating in one of the rigorous wine judgings held by the International Wine Review. In this particular flight, wines were served blind at random. I had Margaux, Pichon-Lalande, and Gruaud-Larose side by side in that order. You wine lovers know how difficult it is for any wine to follow Margaux and Pichon- Lalande, but this Gruaud-Larose was outstanding and came out of this challenge undefeated. Opaque color. Fantastic aroma of roses, violets, and cassis. Mouth-filling, soft, round, supple, yet full of extract, savory cedar and ripe sweet cabernet fruit. Generous with exquisite balance. Loaded with gentle tannin. Aristocratic in style. Rich, deep, and long in the mouth (1986).

[1993/2010] 18+

1984—Like a Cordier wine in style—luscious and voluptuous. Very, very dark purple color. Deep, intense, concentrated, plummy aroma that needs more time to blossom fully. Less precocious than its stablemate, Talbot, but even more concentrated. Full of extracts, abundant black currant flavor. Rich, generous, opulent, and powerful. Expansive cassis aftertaste. A huge wine blessed with oodles of fruit and rounded tannin (1987).
[1991/2004] 18+

Haut-Bailly

CRU EXCEPTIONNEL

CHATEAU HAUT-BAILLY
GRAND CRU CLASSÉ
APPELLATION GRAVES CONTRÔLÉE
1970
Daniel SANDERS · PROPRIÉTAIRE à LÉOGNAN (Gironde)
MIS EN BOUTEILLES AU CHATEAU
DÉPOSÉ ROUSSEAU FRÈRES IMP

1961—Dark color. Deep, earthy, black currant nose. Full-bodied with powerful, intense concentration and depth. Earthy, baked ripe grape flavors abundantly forward and long in the mouth. Rich and forceful wine created to last a long time (1985).
[2010] 18

1962—Nice medium-dark color with amber edge. Earthy nose and very pleasant light bouquet. Round and supple on the palate. Quite advanced. Attractive flavors. Unfortunately, the wine is a bit unbalanced by distracting acidity (1978).
[1979] 15

1964—Better than the '62 vintage. The wine should be at its peak. It is deep and powerful, yet supple. Round and very well balanced. The nose and flavors are of hot pebbly earthiness found in great Graves. Good tannin and finishes well (1980).
[1994] 17

1966—A very successful vintage. I personally preferred it to the '61. It has more style, elegance, and breed. It achieves an outstanding balance. Delight-

Haut-Bailly

Appellation Contrôlée: Graves

Principal Owner: Société Civile Sanders

Administrator: Jean Sanders

Average Production: 8,500 cases

Vineyard Area: 23 hectares, 57 acres

Grape Varieties: 34% CS, 18% CF, 27% M, 17% PV, 2% Malbec, 2% Carmenere

Average Vine Age: 35 years

Average Yield: 38 hectolitres per hectare

Classified Graves Cru Classé

Yves's Classification: Third growth

Food Complements: (5 to 8 years old) veal loin steak with chanterelles, (12 years or older) quail galantine with duck liver foie gras

Second Label: La Parde de Haut-Bailly

ful earthy nose with ripe fruit and a delicious flavor of tobacco and coffee. Good extract and cedary component. A rich and mouth-filling wine (1985).
[1996] 18

1967—Delicate, gentle, round, and soft. Light-to-medium body with some good flavors (1978).
[1980] 15

1970—I bought many a case of this vintage in 1976. It was not as backward as many other '70s. Medium color. Attractive, full cedary nose followed by a beautiful bouquet. Medium body, extremely supple, and round. Very well balanced and very good fruit, cedary flavors. Velvety aftertaste with no disturbing acidity. Delightful, easy to drink. At its peak. Drink soon (1987).
[1985] 17

1971—Smooth and elegant nose with cedar aroma. Light body. It has a bite of acidity. Lacks the depth and concentration of the '70 but is pleasant with its soft, cedary flavors. Drink now without delay (1983).
[1983] 15

1973—Light, austere, and firm. It lacks the charming flavors of other 1973s or other Haut-Bailly vintages (1979).
[1979] 12

1975—I find it a bit lean for the vintage. It lacks flesh. Medium color. Quite open nose. Medium-bodied and forward, lacking complexity and depth (1979). Old, feeble and diluted. Light color, no extract or depth on the palate. Disappointing for this good property and great vintage (1987).
[1983] 13

1976—Medium color. Cassis/cherry aroma, but not too deep. Attractive fruity flavors on the palate. Already quite developed, supple, and lean. A wine to enjoy in the mid '80s, but not of *longue garde* (1982).
[1988] 14-1/2

1978—Medium ruby color with amber edges. Light and graceful cedary bouquet. Medium-bodied, expansive flavors of cedar and black cherry. Not too complex, but well balanced, and, therefore, round and harmonious. It lacks the depth, fleshy richness and opulence that would make this wine great. However, on the positive side, it has absolutely no flaw and has an extremely seductive, gentle flavor. A very amiable and likable wine (1987).
[1993] 16

1979—If the '78 lacked fruit, this one is loaded with it. Dark color. Deep, earthy nose of black currants and vanilla oakiness. Full body. Sweet, ripe, fruity flavors. Quite forward. Rich and round, backed by a good amount of tannin. It achieves an impeccable balance with depth, fruit, acidity, texture, and style. A graceful, savory, charismatic wine (1985).
[2005] 17-1/2

1981—Medium color. Soft and very attractive cedary bouquet. Medium-light body with a gentle balance of fruit and vanilla. Softly textured with light depth. Traces of rounded tannins. The wine is savory, very supple, and easy to drink (1984).
[1994] 16

1982—A true charmer! It conquers you the moment you sniff the wine—a beautifully smooth cedar fragrance jumps out of the glass. The wine is extremely flavorful with hints of cedar and black currants. It is precociously forward. It has a velvety texture and is elegantly structured. Subtle, stylish, and extremely well balanced. It lacks the depth and concentration of other '82s, but compensates with its voluptuous and savory elegance (1985).
[1987/1995] 18

1983—Wine buffs or neophytes will tell you that when the flavors are delicious and the wine is well balanced, they are already greatly satisfied. This Haut-Bailly might have neither the concentration, nor the depth, nor the amplitude of a first growth, but it has beautiful, creamy, savory cedary flavors enhanced by some delicious ripe cassis. It is divinely balanced with rounded tannin, not too much, not too little. It has breed and is extremely appealing. A delicious wine and a precocious one at that (1986).
[1988/1995] 17+

1984—Medium-light body. Underdeveloped aroma. Mellow, gentle, lean structure and depth. Restrained vanillin/cedar/fruit flavors. A delicate but well-balanced Graves that has breed and charm (1987).
[1992] 15-1/2

Haut-Brion

Appellation Contrôlée: Graves

Principal Owner: Domaine Clarence Dillon

Average Production: 12,000 cases

Vineyard Area: 44 hectares, 109 acres

Grape Varieties: 55% CS, 20% CF, 25% M

Average Vine Age: 30 years

Average Yield: 26 hectolitres per hectare

Classified First Growth in 1855; Graves Cru Classé in 1953 and 1959

Yves's Classification: First growth

Food Complements: (7 to 8 years old) venison steak, (12 years or older) roast breast of squab with foie gras sauce

Second Label: Château Bahans-Haut-Brion

1949—Tasted only once as a *bonne bouche* at a dinner. Deep and concentrated velvety nose. Earthy and supple on the palate. Full-bodied. Lacks some roundness in the finish. A powerful wine (1977).
[2000] 18

1952—In a blind tasting held by Lee Kramer, we had this wine against a few second growths of the '53 vintage. Full of flowers, round, roasted, and deep, beautiful earthy aroma. Superb on the palate, big, rich, velvety, long, and well balanced. I loved it (1978).
[2000] 18-1/2

1953—Earthy and concentrated. Rich and flavorful. Has depth and character. Long and round. A great wine (1978).
[2000] 19

1955—A very successful wine of this vintage. Perhaps a bit more elegant than the '52 and '53, although it does not seem to have the amplitude of its older brothers. Nevertheless, it has an excellent *gout de terroir*. Full-bodied, round and rich (1979).
[1995] 18

1959—Very dark color. Deep, earthy, and very ripe cabernet nose. Full-bodied, concentrated texture on the palate. Round with a touch of tannin. The wine has just reached its peak (1984).
[2020] 18

1961—The first time I had this wine it was 15 years old. We were assembled at Dr. Herb Stone's where he provided four '61s. Deep, forward, earthy aroma with no complexity. Some austerity could still be noted (1976). On the palate, the wine is big, rich, velvety, earthy, and generous. Long, lingering finish. Great depth and balance. A monumental wine (1980).
[2025] 19

1962—This wine showed very well in a few horizontal double-blind tastings. It has a big, deep, forward aroma—just great. The aroma has a character of its own, similar to a Burgundy. Enormous on the palate, flavorful, earthy, round, and supple with a good amount of smooth tannin. A great wine (1978).
[2000] 19

1964—I have never experienced a wine with so many bottle variations—you never know how it is going to turn out. Is it possible that they harvested before and after the rains, kept the good grapes and the watery ones in separate vats, then bottled each separately? The best bottles have an attractive flowery aroma, are big, complex, and aristocratic. Mouth-filling and great texture,

Haut-Brion

loaded with ripe fruit. Velvety and supple. Well balanced and long finish. Rather advanced (1979). Fantastic, big, elegant wine with outstanding creamy cedary flavors (1985).

[1990] 18-1/2

1966—Tasted blind against other '66s. Beautiful, soft aroma and straightforward. Cedary flavor, rich velvety texture. Extremely elegant but lacks backbone (1983).

[1995] 18

1967—Medium-dark color. The nose is unyielding. Good concentration on the palate, which is more open than the nose. Sweet, deep, cherrylike flavor with a cedary overtone. A bit unbalanced in the aftertaste, nevertheless quite good. It seems more like a Right Bank wine than a Graves (1979).

[1995] 16

1970—Like most of the '70s from good families, it still does not show enough. "Mademoiselle Haut-Brion, would you please not be so prudish, disrobe and

show yourself!" Underdeveloped aroma. Quite rich, good body and texture, yet not fully opened and still a bit dormant. Finishes shorter than other premier crus of that vintage. Needs a few more years. La Mission is better and more generous in this vintage (1983).
[1990/2005] 17

1971—I tasted this vintage when the wine was still very, very young. It had a very dark color. Big concentration on the palate. Rich, well made (1975). I had a hard time locating this bottle and had to barter all kinds of other wines for it. I was handsomely rewarded, however, for this wine is voluptuous, opulent, and generous. Medium-to-full body blessed with an exquisite balance. Delicious flavors of rich, sweet black currant, tobacco, cedar, truffles and *tutti-quanti*. Concentrated, velvety texture. A warm and sensual wine (1987).
🍷 [2000] 18

1973—Attractive bouquet, medium body. A bit austere for the vintage. I wish it were a bit fruitier and softer (1981).
🍷 [1990] 15-1/2

1975—Outstanding! In a blind tasting of all of the '75 vintage first growths, I rated this wine second best after Lafite. On the nose, I find jasmine, cedar, spices, and cloves. A young wine on its way to greatness (1981). Full-bodied, cedary, velvety texture. Exquisitely well balanced. I did not get the earthiness normally attributed to Haut-Brion, and I thought that it was Pétrus or Cheval-Blanc. A warm and generous wine (1985).
🍷 [2010] 19

1976—Very attractive wine. Perfumy and earthy. Good flavors on the palate with lovely fruity nuances enhanced by a *gout de terroir*. Medium-to-full body. The wine has breed, style, and is quite graceful (1981).
🍷 [1996] 17

1978—Complex, deep, earthy aroma with good fruit. Mouth-filling, almost chewy, laced with rich fruit and earthy flavors. Round on the palate with a long, lingering finish. Plenty of tannin and acid for longevity. A great Haut-Brion! (1983)
[1988/2010] 18

1979—This was served as a mystery wine at a dinner party where we had already shared a '59 Pichon-Baron and a '66 Cheval-Blanc, and just before we were to pour an excellent '59 Eitelsbacher Karthauser Hofberger Trockenbeerenauslese. Technical tasting of a wine under these conditions is unfair to the wine, but it is fun, if not crazy. California cabernet-type on the nose, very rich and concentrated, young. Full-bodied on the palate with good tannin, inky taste. Almost a *vin de presse*, but because of that I see a good potential for its future. I would buy it (1983). Opaque color. Deep, earthy, cigar box, cassis aroma. Huge, mouth-filling, full-bodied wine. Extremely concentrated, powerful yet harmonious, and blessed with a graceful balance. Loaded with attractive, rounded tannins which still need a few more years to dissolve. Be patient until the wine blossoms to its fullest around 1991. A magnificent Bordeaux! (1987)
[1991/2009] 18-1/2

1980—Not at all bad for this difficult vintage. Black currants, earthy, with a touch of vanilla on the nose. Medium-to-light body. Complex flavor of cedar and cassis. Some tannin and a nice counterbalance of acid. Good show, old boy! (1983)
🍷 [1992] 15

1981—A wine made in the attractive style of Professor Peynaud—which is to say, precociously harmonious, round, and supple. Already enjoyable to taste and even to drink. Ruby color. Ripe, baked cabernet nose laced with oak and

cassis. Very forward. Deep, full body, almost velvety texture. The tannins are rounded. Long in the mouth with a delicious taste and aftertaste of hot pebbly, sweet fruity, vanillin and oak flavors (1984).
[1989/2005] 18+

1982—Medium-dark purple color. Unyielding aroma with some red fruit and tobacco scents piercing through. Medium-to-full body. Round and supple. Delicious cabernet flavors. Nicely concentrated texture. Rounded tannin. Velvety finish (1985).
[1991/2012] 18

1983—Medium color. Soft, understated aroma of spice and cedary cassis components. Medium-to-full body with good concentration. Most appealing flavors, reminiscent of cigar box, cassis, and tobacco. Very well balanced, distinguished. This wine has breed followed by good intensity of flavors. A very successful wine, supple and mouth-filling, only lacking a little depth, yet it is generous (1986).
[1992/2005] 17-1/2

1984—A delicious, warm, harmonious, creamy wine. Abundant flavors of tobacco laced with rich, sweet berries. Medium in size and quite precocious. A seductive and graceful little wine (1987).
[1989/1995] 17-1/2

D'Issan

1961—Tasted several times from half bottles. Each time the wine was excellent with good fragrance on the nose. Full body, soft, and round on the palate. Deep with exquisite flavors of fruit and cedar. Long in the mouth (1978).
🍷 [1995] 18

1964—One of the Médocs harvested before the devastating rains. Soft, elegant, well balanced. Good backbone and depth (1976).
🍷 [1984] 16-1/2

1967— Disappointing and closed (1977). Soft, elegant, and cedary bouquet. Light, subtle, and very elegant on the palate. Archetypal Margaux. Long, lingering aftertaste. A great wine for a '67. It lacks only amplitude and depth as do most wines of this vintage (1983).
🍷 [1987] 16

1970—Very severe and closed. When will it open? (1983)

1971—Dark ruby color. Stalky nose with some oaky overtones. Attractive on the palate. Light-to-medium body. Lacks backbone, concentration, and depth (1978).
🍷 [1981] 14-1/2

1973—Small but pleasant wine with good one-dimensional fruity flavor. Well balanced and easy to drink. Not for long cellaring (1979).
🍷 [1980] 14

1975—Medium-dark ruby color. Medium body. Well-structured, chewy texture. Fruity, clovelike flavors a bit simple. The tannins are now rounded and less offensive (1986).
🍷 [1995] 15-1/2

1976—Light to very light color—its amber edges demonstrate an advanced maturity. Lean and feeble on the palate. Some diluted fruit helplessly tries to

redeem the quality of the wine, but to no avail. It lacks depth, density, concentration, and many other attributes (1986).

[1986] 13

1978—Medium color. Very forward blackberry aroma, quite attractive but lacking complexity for my taste. Medium body, mouth-filling, round, generous, and also harmonious. Delicious ripe berry flavors. It has the rare silky texture only known to great and successful Margaux. Long, graceful, and distinguished wine (1986).

[1992] 17+

1979—Dark, ruby color. Unyielding aroma with some fruit and wood in the background. Full-bodied and mouth-filling. Outstanding rich cassis flavor. Well structured, chewy texture, and long on the palate. Good depth. Overall, a yummy wine (1983).

[2000] 17

1981—Medium ruby color. The aroma is quite forward, made of subtle ripe fruit. Already quite delicious on the palate with softness and elegance. Very like Margaux in style. Good tannic finish. A good example of a well-made d'Issan (1984).

[1988/1999] 15

1982—Medium ruby color. Very spicy nose reminiscent of cloves. Full-bodied and well structured. Clovelike, woody, fruity flavor. A wine made in a more traditional style, and made to last. The tannins are therefore firm and uncompromising (1986).

[1993/2007] 17

1983—Medium-dark color. Deep cherry, spicy aroma. Full-bodied, concentrated, luscious, rich, mouth-filling, and long in the mouth. Extremely appealing wine. Easy to taste and quite precocious for a wine with so much depth and intensity. Keep it up d'Issan—I have not tasted anything this good since your '61 (1986).

[1989/2000] 17+

D'Issan

Appellation Contrôlée: Margaux

Principal Owner: Madame Emmanuel Cruse

Average Production: 11,000 cases

Vineyard Area: 32 hectares, 79 acres

Grape Varieties: 80% CS, 20% M

Average Vine Age: 18 years

Average Yield: 33 hectolitres per hectare

Classified Third Growth in 1855

Yves's Classification: Third growth

Food Complements: (5 to 8 years old) sautéed quail with grapes, (12 years or older) pâté en croute

Lafite-Rothschild

Appellation Contrôlée: Pauillac

Principal Owner: Domaines Barons de Rothschild

Administrator: Gilbert Rokvam

Average Production: 25,000 cases

Vineyard Area: 90 hectares, 225 acres

Grape Varieties: 70% CS, 5% CF, 20% M, 5% PV

Average Vine Age: 40 years

Average Yield: 25 hectolitres per hectare

Classified First Growth in 1855

Yves's Classification: First growth

Food Complements: (7 to 8 years old) filet mignon with cèpes, (12 years or older) roast chicken with gratin dauphinois

Second Label: Moulin des Carruades

1945—Full, rich, and elegant with good concentration. One of the best Lafites (1978).
[2000] 19-1/2

1947—Soft and rich, delicate and flavorful (1976).
[1985] 19

1949—Outstanding, complex aroma—deep with a flowery jasmine overtone. The nose is aristocratic but not too forward. On the palate, great elegance, round, flowery, and complex. Long, lingering finish. Tasted against seven other Lafites (1977).
[1985] 18

1950—Attractive nose and flavor. A bit on the light side (1978).
[1975] 16

1953—I was surprised that this wine scored higher than the '49 (which I have loved). But tasted side by side, the bouquet and the flavors of the '53 were better, a bit more forward yet delicate, complex, and elegant. A wine with extreme finesse and breed (1977).
[2000] 19

1955—A fine and elegant wine. It has all of the Lafite's complexity, its savory flavor, richness, and breed (1977).
[1990] 18-1/2

1959—It took a long time for this vintage to mature. But at last by 1980 it started to open up and lose the excess tannin of its youth. It is now big and forward. It does not resemble Lafite in style, and compensates for this lack of delicate finesse by resembling its powerful first-growth neighbors, Mouton and Latour (1980).
[2020] 18-1/2

1961—The aroma of this wine starts with a smooth bouquet of violets which intensifies and blossoms into an outstanding and near perfect aroma. The wine is full on the palate, concentrated yet gentle, with a savory hint of old cedar wood. It has breed, great balance, finesse, and tannin. Outstanding extract of fruit. Perfect lingering finish. At its best, a superlative wine. However, Lafite '61 suffers from bottle variation and a few bottles were disappointing (1980).
[2020] 20

1962—I had this vintage in many blind tastings and my scores were always high. Most people mistakenly shunned '62, which was underrated and overshadowed by the great '59 and '61. The precious nectar is soft, with an almost velvety aroma of jasmine flower overtones—a great fragrance. Medium-to-light body with an elegant gentleness, smoothness, and breed. The wine is also well balanced and long in the mouth. An old princess of a wine (1985).
[1990] 17-1/2

1964—In the mid '70s, I did not find this wine of much interest—it was light, thin, and unbalanced. Not a good Lafite but alright for lunch. Retasted blind in 1982—once against '64 Haut-Brion and '64 Latour, the second time against '62 and '66 Lafite—I did not find the mediocre wine I described earlier. Medium-light, soft, and round. Flavors reminiscent of mushrooms and wet forest soil. The proverbially subtle and elegant Lafite balance is right there to conquer you, and the wine remains the great queen that Lafite is (1985).
[1986] 17

1966—Medium-red brick color. Soft, round, velvety fragrance that is quite forward. Medium-to-full body. Very elegant, round, supple, velvety, and

Lafite-Rothschild

complex. It has breed, excellent texture, good depth. Long, lingering finish. It lacks, perhaps, the concentration expected in a '66, but it makes up for it by displaying a graceful, complex femininity full of elegance and finesse (1984).

[1996] 18-1/2

1967—Medium, brick color. Soft and round. Gentle nose with a cedary, jasmine aroma. Medium body, smooth and delicate, yet aristocratic in style. Extremely flavorful and very well balanced. Neither concentrated nor has much depth, but a very well-made '67. Finishes with a long, silky aftertaste (1984).

[1986] 17

1970—In a horizontal tasting at Atlanta's Rue de Paris wine room, the contenders were La Mission, Latour, Mouton, Haut-Brion, and Cheval-Blanc. Lafite finished dead last (La Mission was my favorite). The nose was restrained. Medium body, subdued, and somewhat unyielding flavor. It lacked flesh and amplitude, and had too much tannin to shed for the overall fruit concentration (1983).

[2000] 17-1/2

1971—Now that most of the '71 Bordeaux are at their peak, Lafite is certainly not one at the top. It is light, lean, and flat. Has good flavor of cedar, but the wine seems to be fading and cracking up (1983).

[1983] 13

1973—I had this vintage several times when it was young and also recently, and I always liked it. It is full of charm, with a fine bouquet. It has a complex cedary flavor that lingers on the palate. Medium-bodied, the finish is smooth and elegant. It is not a long-lived Lafite, but it is extremely pleasant with a delightful flavor (1983).

[1986] 16-1/2

1975—The first time I had this wine was in a first-growth blind tasting held by Frank Stone in 1981. I preferred Lafite over all the other wines, but I could not identify it, for it was rich and fleshy and atypical for Lafite. Soft, warm, opulent coffee aroma enhanced by violets and cedar. Big, full-bodied, and loaded with fruit. Good concentration and breed. Velvety texture. Great balance. Long, lingering finish. Rather forward for such a young Lafite (1983).

[2015] 19

1976—A splendid and celestial Lafite, atypical of the vintage. Very dark color. Distinguished and graceful bouquet of cedar and cassis. Full-bodied, lusciously concentrated, intense, rich cedary, tobacco flavors followed by an explosion of deep, scented, ripe berry fruit. Complex, great depth and length. Long, lingering finish. Plenty of tannin and extract to carry this wine to a venerable age (1986).

[1988/2010] 19

1978—Another winner! I am not really a Lafite lover, but the '75, '76 and '78 vintages could easily convert me. These vintages are unusually forward for their age. This one is immediately attractive on the nose with vanilla and fruit. On the palate, it has depth and concentration which forecast a fairly good longevity. It is luscious, elegant, full, and fleshy. It has a good amount of tannin and achieves a beautiful balance (1983). Ruby color with amber edges. Beautiful, classy, and elegant cedary nose. Medium-to-full body, soft, luscious, velvety, and very feminine. "A real and perfect claret in the true sense of the word," said George Gore of the Abbey Restaurant, who was savoring the nectar across the table from me. Lingering, graceful, cedary finish. This exquisite, refined Lafite is only for the most keenly discriminating claret lovers (1986).

[1988/2003] 18-1/2

1979—I am being converted to Lafite. This '79 impressed me as its siblings of '75, '76 and '78 did. Perhaps, though, without the intensity of these greater vintages. Round with good structure. Vanilla with a hint of cedar, laced together in marvelous complexity. Some tannin and fruit concentration tells me to lay down this wine and await the reward (1983). Beautiful ruby color. Deep aroma still not too accessible in 1986. Medium-full-bodied, quite concentrated with good depth. It does not have the elegance found in other Lafites such as the '78 and '80. However, in its different, more powerful style, the wine is round, supple, long in the mouth, aristocratic, and harmonious. Some tannin to shed. The black currant aftertaste is extremely appealing (1986).

[1990/2005] 17-1/2

1980—On the light side but with breed. Has fruit with nuances of cedar on the palate. Some depth. To be drunk in a couple of years when the tannin dissipates (1983). Very elegant, charming, light and flavorful (1986).

[1990] 16-1/2

1981—Dark color. Soft, elegant, flowery, vanillin nose. Mouth-filling in the attack, concentrated, rich ripe sweet fruit. In the style of the proverbial Lafite— that is to say with the subtle, refined, elegant flavors expected of this property. Powerful tannins suggest a long and slow maturity. Very deep and long in the mouth. An excellent bottle! (1984). Outstanding cedary, velvety nose, most elegant and most Lafitelike. Medium-bodied, long and velvety as a true, feminine Lafite should be—elegance personified. Already enjoyable, but it would be a pity to drink it so soon (1986).

[1991/2011] 18-1/2

1982—Dark purple color. Deep, concentrated nose with very attractive oak and ripe berry bouquet. On the palate, the entrance is immediately mouth-filling and powerful, yet round. It is followed by excellent extracts and overwhelming flavors of ripe fruit. A majestic balance of acidity, rounded tannin, and depth. The well-structured and exciting texture give this Lafite a rich, powerful, and mellow finish (1985).

[1992/2012] 18-1/2+

1983—An outstanding wine, but completely different in style. Both Jim Gaby and I thought this was the '83 Latour. This wine has the attributes and the characteristics of a Latour. It is dark in color. It has a beautiful, deep concentration with sweet ripe cassis enhanced by attractive woodiness—absolutely marvelous! Here is a wine that has amplitude, style, generosity. It is very concentrated, full of extracts and magnificent ripe cassis flavors. The wine is huge, yet harmonious and even graceful at such a young age. Deep, complex, loaded with rounded tannin. Long and lingering finish. A splendid wine (1986).

[1995/2013] 19

1984—Medium-dark, ruby color. Tobacco/cedar aroma. Medium-to-full body, round, very elegant texture and structure. Extremely well balanced with each component in the right proportion. This is a wine that has distinction, breed, and complexity. Not a big Lafite but a very good one (1987).

[1991/2000] 17-1/2

Lafleur

1959—Dark color with amber edges. Big cedar/truffle nose. Full-bodied. Exquisite flavors of cedar, cherries, and truffles. Nice amount of tannin for longevity. Dry finish (1978).

[1999] 17-1/2

1962—Dark color. Deep, huge nose full of ripe fruit. Mouth-filling and very big on the palate. Rich flavors—intense and concentrated. Good tannin and a long, lingering finish. An excellent wine that will improve and age very well (1979). Dark color with amber edge. Mushroom and old-wine-cellar bouquets—what the French call *sous-bois*. Deep, full-bodied, concentrated, still young. Quite atypical for a '62. Rich, long, round, followed by the most attractive flavors of wood, ripe berries, and mushrooms. Long and generous on the palate. Outstanding wine (1986).

[1992] 18

1964—Another huge wine from this property. I had the pleasure of savoring it in two horizontal tastings against Latour, Figeac, Cheval-Blanc, and La Mission. Both times it was equal in quality to its august company. Very dark in color, considering its age. Big, forward, earthy, and black cherry aroma. Full-bodied, concentrated, deep, intense, and fat. Mouth-filling with excellent plummy/fruity flavors. Good tannic backbone. Long in the mouth (1979).

[1999] 18+

1967—Quite concentrated for a '67. The wine is austere and hard (1976).

[1987] 15

1970—Heavily structured, unyielding, deep, and unopened. Tannic (1978). Just barely opening up. The wine is still restrained, but fortunately a few of its attributes are piercing through. The bouquet is intensely concentrated. On the palate, the wine is not any less intense or concentrated. As expected, it is enormous in size and, unfortunately for today's drinking, it is still astringently tannic. But a load of rich and luxurious sweet merlot flavors are waiting in the

Lafleur

Appellation Contrôlée: Pomerol
Principal Owner: Marie Robin
Administrator: Jean-Pierre Moueix
Average Production: 1,250 cases
Vineyard Area: 4 hectares, 10 acres
Grape Varieties: 50% M, 50% CF
Average Vine Age: 42 years
Average Yield: 29 hectolitres per hectare
Yves's Classification: Second growth
Food Complements: (3 to 6 years old) noisette of lamb Edward VII, (10 years or older) filet of beef Lucullus

background for the tannin to dissolve. Therefore, there will still be plenty of fruit left when that happens, which is good news (1986).
[1989/2009] 18

1971—Nice color. Attractive fruity aroma with cedary/spicy overtones. Medium body. Delicious velvety texture and taste. Long in the mouth. A great charmer! (1978)
[1991] 17-1/2

1975—This is a huge wine. Comparable to the '64 in structure and in style, perhaps even bigger. Very dark color. Outstanding nose full of sweet ripe merlot. Enormous full body, majestically Burgundian in style. Concentrated nectar. It is luxurious, opulent, and delicious. It finishes in a long aftertaste that lingers forever. Still has a load of tannin to shed. We shall have to wait patiently for this magnificent bottle. When I was in Pomerol in 1978, it was rumored by several property owners that the Robin sisters had made an elixir in 1975, and so they did (1981).
[1990/2025] 19-1/2+

1976—It was very difficult to locate even one bottle of this vintage. A light-textured wine, lacking acidity and tannin. Nevertheless, the ripe berry flavors are quite attractive and leave a good impression on the palate. It is a delicate but graceful wine that should be drunk rather soon (1986).
[1988] 15

1978—If '76 Lafleur was light and delicate, the '78 is quite the opposite. The wine is huge, even gutsy, due to a certain lack of finesse and complexity. It is John Wayne pushing the swinging doors of the saloon, walking decisively straightforward and with an imposing, rough, tannic look in his eyes. Did you get or see the picture? (1986)
[1990/2005] 17-1/2

1979—Very dark color. If it were not for the color, this huge wine could pass for a big Burgundy with its marvelous explosion of ripe fruit on the palate. The wine has depth and concentration. It is loaded with tannin, long in the mouth. Like the '75 vintage, we shall have to wait a long while (1982).
[1990/2005] 18-1/2

1981—When tasted blind against the '81 Gazin and the '81 Vieux-Château-Certan, Lafleur was the least interesting of the three. I find the aroma of this wine odd and unattractive: wet straw and herbaceous. It has a supple, soft, and medium body. Round tannin. A nice peppery/vanilla taste. Unfortunately, that wet straw and herbal nose is unpleasant and distracting. It is an easy-drinking wine. It lacks complexity and does not seem to have all of its components laced together (1984).
[1987/1995] 15

1982—Great breed and character. Deep, round, voluptuous with excellent balance. The flavors are creamy, gentle, and generous, showing an outstanding ripe sweet fruit. Extremely elegant wine, very stylish but also very precocious. I have to agree with a friend of mine, Jim Gaby, who found some good underlying rounded tannin with a medium, acid backbone, surrounded by ripe candy/plummy merlot (1986).
[1992/2003] 18

1983—Even though the wine has some great qualities, on one occasion I found it so stemmy and so herbaceous that I downgraded it drastically. When I tasted it side by side against its '82 older brother, I did not perceive any of that disturbing herbaceousness. Good depth with medium concentration. The wine is rich and powerful, yet round, supple, with a silky texture. It has a very ripe sweet raspberry flavor, which lingers in a long aftertaste (1986).
[1992/2003] 17

1984—Intensely fruity and rich in oak and tannin, giving the wine a certain style and appeal. Medium-to-full-bodied, relatively deep and complex for this vintage. Long and flavorful aftertaste (1987).
[1990/2000] 16

La Fleur-Pétrus

1961—Dark color with amber edges. Huge nose with a beautiful, soft cedar and fruity aroma. Very elegant. Full-bodied, velvety, and mouth-filling. Delicious flavors and aftertaste. My kind of wine! (1978)
🍷 [1991] 17-1/2+

1964—Beautiful, mouth-filling wine. Jammy and full of extract, deep, forward, and rich. Exciting, appetizing flavors reminiscent of ripe sweet merlot and cedar. A good backbone of dry tannin gives this wine an interesting balance in a more rustic style (1986).
🍷 [1990) 17

1970—For years this wine would not show anything except its concentration, depth, and tannin. It was firm, austere and well structured. Today, it is finally beginning to open up and show a good deep cedary nose. On the palate, the wine is concentrated and full-bodied. Good texture with a delightful cedary flavor. Still some tannin to shed. It is not quite ready for me (1983). The wine is opening up. Start drinking (1986).
🍷 [1999] 17-1/2+

1971—This wine is at its peak right now and should be drunk within the next few years. Aromatic cedary bouquet with good fruity overtones. Medium body. Very elegant, soft, and round. Delicious cedary flavor. Good creamy texture and perfect balance for this medium-weight wine. Excellent lingering finish. A very delightful, feminine wine! (1982)
🍷 [1982] 17

1973—Medium color. Attractive cedary bouquet. Light to medium-light body. Soft and gentle. Flavorful and well balanced. A charmer which is also elegant (1978).
🍷 [1981] 16

La Fleur-Pétrus

Appellation Contrôlée: Pomerol
Principal Owner: Jean-Pierre Moueix
Average Production: 3,500 cases
Vineyard Area: 9 hectares, 22 acres
Grape Varieties: 75% M, 25% CF
Average Vine Age: 30 years
Average Yield: 35 hectolitres per hectare
Yves's Classification: Third growth
Food Complements: (3 to 6 years old) rack of lamb en croute with truffle sauce, (10 years or older) creamed chicken casserole

1975—A rich, intense and concentrated wine. The nose is still a bit restrained, yet through this bashfulness appears an ample sweet-berry bouquet laced with coffee and chocolate. It is opulent and powerful in the mouth with great depth and length. It has delicious flavors of rich black currants and sweet plums. It is loaded with rounded tannin. A "macho" wine with class (1986).
[2005] 18+

1976—Medium-light concentration. Gentle cedary flavor. Suave, debonnaire, quaffable and easy-drinking wine. Lacks concentration and depth, but it is seductive nevertheless (1986).
[1986] 15

1978—This wine lacks concentration and depth. It has good, flavorful components, such as cedar and fruit, but a bothersome herbaceousness spoils the fun (1982).
[1990] 13

1979—Same as the '78—perhaps a bit more forward with more character and style. It lacks the elegance and soft, round texture to which I am accustomed. The wine is also unbalanced and has a sharp finish. The body is medium-light and lacks flesh (1982).
[1992] 14

1981—When tasted side by side with its '76 brother, it was very much in the same style. Medium-to-medium-light body. Charming cedary flavors laced with jammy, plummy fruit. It is most delicious and the taste lingers in the mouth. Well balanced, but perhaps lacks a bit of acidity. Not for long aging (1986).
[1993] 16

1984—Medium-dark color. Deep oak/cedar/spicy bouquet. Medium-bodied with bashful, cedary flavor enhanced by subdued black currant. Sturdily structured. Tannic. Long, deep aftertaste (1987).
[1990/1995] 16

Lascombes

Appellation Contrôlée: Margaux

Principal Owner: Société Anonyme Lichine (a subsidiary of Bass Charrington)

Administrator: Alain Maurel

Average Production: 38,000 cases

Vineyard Area: 91 hectares, 225 acres

Grape Varieties: 65% CS, 3% CF, 30% M, 2% PV

Average Vine Age: 20 years

Average Yield: 38 hectolitres per hectare

Classified Second Growth in 1855

Yves's Classification: Third growth

Food Complements: (5 to 8 years old) hamburger, (12 years or older) aiguillettes of duck breast

Second Label: Château la Gombaude

1959—Typical Margaux. Soft and complex bouquet. Gentle and smooth on the palate. Good depth, feminine, and aristocratic. Plenty of fruit and nicely flavored, but unfortunately some bothersome acidity (1976).
[1989] 17

1961—Great depth and concentration. Rich and fruity but a bit coarse due to dried tannin. Full body and long finish. A very good wine (1977).
[1999] 17

1962—Attractively complex, full, with a nuance of spicy cloves. A well-made wine with good fruit, graceful velvety texture and balance. A delicate and elegant Margaux (1984).
[1982] 16-1/2

1966—Dark ruby color with some advanced aging and amber edge. Fully matured with seductive, unctuous, and elegant Margaux flavors and bouquet. Suave, complex, and elegant wine. Long and gracefully balanced (1986).
[1996] 17

1967—Honest nose, not big but attractive and smooth. Round on the palate with good fruit. Some excess tannin disturbs the balance. It finishes long. I regard this wine as a typical Margaux style—smooth and feminine with breed (1978).
[1979] 17

1970—Showed good potential when young, even through the tannin. Concentrated, undeveloped scents with some cedar. Spicy and cedary flavors just opening. Young on the palate. Needs more time. Will be good (1983). Medium ruby color with amber edge. Soft oak and cedar aroma. Medium-to-full body with a round and luscious texture. Oak, cedar and fruit flavors all in harmony and balance with one another. Well structured, distinguished and enticing wine with beautiful, rounded tannin. Long, long, cedary aftertaste (1987).
[2003] 17-1/2

1971—Bordeaux Nouveau. Dark pink, light, round, fruity, and lively. Not in its class. Finishes a bit off balance (1976).
[1979] 13

1973—Light ruby color. Small on the palate. Unattractive flavors and texture. Even the '74 vintage is better (1977).
[1979] 10

1975—For years I avoided trying this wine. "Life is too short," I was thinking, "one can only enjoy so many wines in a day and they might as well be great ones." When I did taste it—not expecting anything—I was pleasantly surprised. The wine was full-bodied and rich in flavors. Good depth, especially well balanced for a Lascombes—meaning no astringency of any kind (1986).
[2000] 16-1/2

1976—Made in a lighter style than other '76s. This wine is very enjoyable now and should not be laid down beyond 1986. It has a soft, forward bouquet with good fruit and vanilla undertones. Very soft and feminine on the palate.

Lascombes

Medium-to-light body. Not much tannin. Flavorful and velvety. Ready to drink and enjoy today (1981).

[1986] 15

1978—Spicy and fruity aroma along with a green and unpleasant stemmy flavor. Some fruit, plenty of tannin, and unbalanced (1981).

[1990/2005] 13

1979—Dark color. Attractive bouquet. Light-to-medium body. Not much depth. Round and supple. Oaky flavors and light texture. Fairly well balanced. A good, innocuous wine (1984). Much better than I expected. Medium dark ruby color. Deep aroma of spice and oak. Medium body and concentrated texture. Spice and oak flavors. The fruit has not quite blossomed yet, and is still overshadowed by rounded tannin. Round, with good extract. Stylish yet powerful. Exciting long and concentrated black currant aftertaste (1987).

[1989/2001] 16-1/2

1981—Light color. Medium-light body with not much character. Little fruit without much complexity and rather ordinary style. A bit green and stemmy with a little unpleasant, sharp tannin (1986).

[1990/2001] 13

1982—Medium-dark color. The nose is tight and restrained. However, some attractive berry and vanillin oak pierces through. Intense and concentrated on the palate. Rich and powerful with breed and style. The flavors are full of ripe red fruit such as cassis, plums, and cherries. Good balance and long aftertaste (1986).

[1992/2002] 17

1983—When I learned the name of this wine after tasting it blind, I could not believe it. Yet I was happy that this second-growth property is making a comeback to its true rank and level. I will not say bravo yet, but "It's about time." Medium concentration, opulent, rich, deep, with a delicious cassislike aroma and flavor. It is harmonious and even graceful, followed by a little

tannic backbone. Rather quaffable and therefore quite precocious (1986).
[1988/1995] 17

1984—Medium-light color. Spicy oak laced with mulberry aroma and flavors. Light and quaffable with a graceful balance, each component in perfect proportion. Feminine, silky finish. A real claret (1987).
[1992] 16

Latour

MIS EN BOUTEILLE AU CHATEAU
GRAND VIN
DE
CHATEAU LATOUR
PREMIER GRAND CRU CLASSE
1967
APPELLATION PAUILLAC CONTROLEE

Appellation Contrôlée: Pauillac

Principal Owner: Société Civile de Château Latour (Pearson group)

Administrator: Jean-Louis Mandrau

Average Production: 18,000 cases

Vineyard Area: 50 hectares, 124 acres

Grape Varieties: 75% CS, 10% CF, 10% M, 5% PV

Average Vine Age: 33 years

Average Yield: 40 hectolitres per hectare

Classified First Growth in 1855

Yves's Classification: First growth

Food Complements: (8 to 10 years old) venison, (15 years or older) rabbit chasseur

Second Label: Les Forts de Latour

1945—Outstanding aroma of ripe fruit, old oak, and cedar. Marvelous velvety texture. Magnificent taste with depth, magnitude, and grandeur. Wonderful lingering finish. The best Latour I have ever tasted. It finished first in a vertical-blind tasting of vintages from 1934 to 1964 (1978).
[2015] 20+

1949—Tasted twice in the late '70s. Not typical for a Latour. Although I scored it the same as the '49 Lafite, I preferred the Latour. Like all Latours, it has depth and concentration, yet it is silky and smooth. It has a zest of sweetness in the aroma that is most enticing. Exquisitely balanced with a delicious aftertaste of cedar (1979).
[2000] 18

1952—*Arome de vin vieux.* This is a layman's expression in the southwest of France for a wine of modest origin that has lost its fruit but has retained a certain attractive quality in the nose. This wine is deep and concentrated, but the lack of fruit and the excess of tannin render this vintage quite severe. Hot finish (1978).
[2000] 16-1/2

1953—Mushroom and damp earth aroma. Good flavors but with a hole in the middle. Lacks backbone and fruit. The texture and aftertaste are good, but the wine is relatively disappointing for a Latour of such a great vintage. Most growers harvested two weeks later than Latour, which suggests that an early picking was a mistake for this property (1978).
[1980] 16-1/2

1955—In vertical Latour tastings, I have always found this wine better than the '52 and '53 vintages. Deep, concentrated, fair amount of fruit. Powerful (like all the great Latours), well balanced, and lingering finish. Ready now but can last until 2010 (1981).
[2010] 19

1959—I did not realize that I had tasted this vintage so many times until I went through my notes. Both in vertical and horizontal tastings the wine scored well and always ended up at the top or near the top. It finished right behind the '45 and '61 superstars in a vertical tasting of vintages from 1934 to 1964. Very dark, almost inky in color. The nose is big, forward, yet has a very stylish bouquet reminiscent of cedar and violets. Powerful and even enormous on the palate. Full of fruit, outstanding texture, robust, and rich. Excellent aftertaste. High in alcohol and tannin. A long-lived Latour, BRAVO! (1982)
[2030] 19-1/2+

1961—Huge, beautiful, deep, and velvety aroma. On the palate, it is concentrated, powerful, and mouth-filling. Full of fruit, yet silky, round and aristocratic. Marvelous aftertaste. A mixture of majestic power, breed, and elegance that lingers in a perfect finish. This wine commands respect. The Charles de Gaulle (or Winston Churchill) of clarets (1985).
[1988/2050] 20

Latour

1962—Brilliant dark color. Concentrated, deep, chocolatey, cassis aroma showing grandeur and style. Big, mouth-filling wine. Great depth and concentration of cassis and tannin. Unfortunately, the tannin is stern which unbalances the wine and renders the finish a bit astringent (1985).
[2002] 17

1964—As in the '53 vintage, Latour picked early but this time it paid off. By the time they were finished on October 8th, heavy rains came for two weeks. This diluted the wines of other growers (such as Lafite and company). Deep, earthy cabernet nose a bit closed. I would like more fruit in it. Full body and good depth. Not soft but smooth. Lacks fruit which makes the wine a bit austere (1981). A powerful, intense Latour that has mellowed down, tamed its tannin and finally is showing an opulent, generous and succulent flavor. The texture is soft as velvet, yet chewy. The balance is perhaps one of the most important attributes of this wine and all components are in perfect harmony with one another. The load of rounded tannin and rich, concentrated extracts suggest great longevity (1986).
[1988/2025] 18

1966—The color is very dark, similar to a California cabernet. The nose is closed, showing only a great but subdued berrylike concentration. Full body with plenty of tannin hiding in the fruit. Will be a classic if you can wait until 1990 or later (1978). Dark ruby color with no amber edge. The nose is deep with some fruit in the background but still unyielding and not quite developed. Mouth-filling texture, well structured, and loaded with tannin that gives it a strong backbone. Long, long powerful finish. Needs more time (1984).
[1990/2030] 19

1967—I was never impressed by this vintage. The wine is full but monastically austere. It lacks flower and fruit. It is a powerful cabernet without finesse and softness. It is "le Grand Charles de Gaulle as Mother Superior" (1984).
[2000] 16+

1970—Most '70s from good families were more backward than we thought. The '70 Latour was no exception, being very austere for many years. It had rich, concentrated, full-bodied flavors, and was loaded with tannin; the prospect of a great wine (1982). Dark color with no amber edge. Deep nose but unyielding. Ripe berry aroma. Full body, not opened yet. Some exciting flavors now of cassis/oak/cedar. Concentrated, powerful, great depth and structure. Loaded with tannin. Excellent balance and aftertaste. Long-lasting on the palate. A huge wine (1984). Very dark color with amber edge. Deep berry, mushroom, earthy nose. Big, mouth-filling wine, attractively textured and very concentrated. Great backbone of rounded tannin. Powerful finish. Needs another 12 years to blossom completely (1986).
[1998/2035] 19

1971—Since 1977, the wines of this vintage have been gentle and soft. We were able to enjoy them sooner than their brothers of the '70 vintage. But now the '70s are waking up and the '71s are getting tired. The '71 Latour is the exception. Though it is of a lighter style than the '70, it still has enough concentration and tannin for many more years of aging in the bottle. It has charm, length, and character with a savory cassis/oak flavor. "General de Gaulle on a holiday" (1986).
[2005] 17-1/2

1973—More advanced and forward than the '71. This wine has relatively good depth and a charming concentration of fruit. Medium- to full-bodied style, atypical of a Latour. It is gentle, even gay. "Mon General as a female impersonator? *Pourquoi pas*?" Deep cedar/cassis aroma. Medium body, soft, round, and very well balanced like many good '73s. Long, soft, and lingering finish. It had more depth and length than the mystery wine served at this tasting, which I found to be the '73 Les Forts de Latour (1984). Deep, concentrated, cigar-box nose laced with rich, ripe black currants. Soft, round, silky texture and flavor. Long and lingering on the palate. A wine with a fantastic balance which makes it extremely loveable (1985).
[1995] 17+

1975—Deep, earthy, cabernet fragrance. Concentrated texture, beefy with great elegance, rich, and tannic. The cassislike fruit is showing well, which is rare for a six-year-old Latour. Therefore, I did not find the wine austere, even though it is certainly a *vin de longue garde* (1981). Deep cassis aroma followed by oak and damp earth. The nose is still young and subdued. Very concentrated and tannic on the palate with plenty of black currant/berry flavors begging to blossom. Dense, powerful, even overpowering, yet it is still backward. I would wait another 10 years (1986).
[1996/2035] 18-1/2

1976—When I had this wine for the first time, I did not like it much. The price had doubled within a few years, which did not help. It showed to be austere and backward. Tannic with very little fruit, but a healthy, concentrated

texture (1980). Medium color. Unyielding nose with a hint of sweet cassis in the aroma. Medium- to full-bodied sweet black currant flavors. A disturbing inky aftertaste which should be dissolved in a few years. Good balance, some tannin, and finishes well. Not a great Latour but passable (1984).
[1990/2005] 16-1/2

1978—In a horizontal tasting against Mouton, La Mission, Domaine de Chevalier, and Ducru-Beaucaillou: All wines were very forward, except Domaine de Chevalier. Latour finished second behind La Mission. Big with floral dimensions, has depth and concentration. Mouth-filling, round, some velvet mixed with good, earthy, ripe cabernet. Not austere yet has a fair amount of tannin (1983). Medium-dark color. Beautiful, soft, round, and deep ripe cassis aroma with a hint of sweetness. Medium-to-full body, excellent cassis/oak flavor. Nice texture. Still young but round and powerful. The well-rounded tannin makes this Latour more approachable and precocious, making this wine more attractive when young (1984).
[1988/2020] 18-1/2

1979—Medium-dark color, a shade darker than the '78. The nose is still clovey and has the spicy character of a young, promising wine. Medium-to-full body, good depth, and quite rich. Well-balanced, great soft tannin, and excellent texture. Long-lasting on the palate. A very enjoyable wine (1984).
[1990/2010] 17-1/2

1980—Surprise! Not bad for this vintage. It is more open than any Latour at age three. It has depth and is medium-bodied. It is quite forward. The nose and taste display cedar and violets with a long finish. Extremely well balanced. Even the tannin is not too bothersome and tells us, "Don't worry, put me away until 1987-88 and I will show you who I am." That's a deal and I'll wait! (1983)
[1988/1995] 16-1/2

1981—Very dark color but the edge already shows some amber. Outstanding spicy bouquet enhanced by black currants and oak. Quite forward, elegant and complex. Full-bodied on the palate with fairly dense concentration. It shows good, complex, fruity/woody flavors. The wine has already rounded up a bit and is very delicious (1984).
[1991/2011] 18-1/2

1982—Extremely dark opaque color. The darkest of the group we tasted blind. On color alone, you could tell it was the Latour. Deep, concentrated, and earthy nose with some undertones of cassis and bell pepper. Not too forward yet. Rich, full-bodied, mouth-filling texture. Very concentrated and powerful, yet round, supple, and aristocratic. Outstanding flavor of ripe cabernet fruit that needs to open up. Dense. Tannic aftertaste followed by a long, lingering, fruity finish (1985).
[1997/2025] 19+

1983—Although the wine is very good, I cannot help being disappointed. In a blind tasting, I thought it was '83 Lynch- Bages. This Latour lacks amplitude and greatness. Medium purple color. Deep and subdued nose, which is normal at this age. Medium-to-full-bodied, good concentration. Excellent, mouth-filling, round texture. Supple balance yet well structured. Plenty of rounded tannin that is not assertive. Nicely flavored with cassis and oak, young but distinguished. Long-lasting on the palate. A very good wine, but not a real Latour (1986).
[1992/2005] 17

1984—Medium-dark color. Spicy, clovelike, woody nose enhanced by rich, opulent, mulberry acents. Full-bodied, concentrated (especially for this light vintage), with forceful tannins forecasting a better-than-average longevity. Dominant flavors of berries overshadowed today by spice and oak. Long and vigorous aftertaste (1987).
[1991/2005] 17-1/2+

Latour-à-Pomerol

Appellation Contrôlée: Pomerol

Principal Owner: Madame Lily Lacoste-Loubat

Administrator: J.P. Moueix

Average Production: 3,850 cases

Vineyard Area: 9 hectares, 22 acres

Grape Varieties: 80% M, 20% CS

Average Vine Age: 35 years

Average Yield: 38 hectolitres per hectare

Yves's Classification: Third growth

Food Complements: (3 to 6 years old) veal kidneys, (10 years or older) sautéed duck liver on leaf spinach

1961—One of the best '61s I have ever had. Very dark color. Outstanding nose, deep and forward with opulent bouquet of ripe fruit, oak, and spice followed by an overtone of cedar. On the palate, the wine is full-bodied, mouth-filling, warm, and round with great depth. Marvelous concentrated texture and flavors of cedar and ripe fruit backed by good tannin for longevity. The finish is long and lingers forever. A superb, concentrated, rich, portlike wine (1982).

[2015] 20

1966—A very rich and opulent wine. Dark brick color. Deep aroma of sweet cassis, truffles and tobacco. Full-bodied, mouth-filling, and powerful with excellent extract. Outstanding flavors already described on the nose. Chewy texture, deep, long, and lingering. A great wine (1986).

[2000] 18

1970—Dark color. Deep, concentrated nose with a beautiful bouquet of cedar, oriental spice, and ripe merlot grapes with a hint of violets, truffles, and iron/earthiness. Rich fruitiness with a complex, earthy taste with raspberries and truffles. Full-bodied, deep, and concentrated. Velvety and generous with some good tannin still to shed. Very long finish. Bravo! (1983)

[2010] 18

1971—Dark red with amber edge. Unyielding nose. A very velvety wine with great depth but finishes short. Strange wine (1976). Mellow, round, soft, but on the decline. Drink up (1986).

[1986] 14

1973—A very slow-maturing wine. Very good garnet color, darker than most '73s. Concentrated, unyielding, and disturbing inky flavor in the aftertaste. Seems like a *vin de presse* which can be a sign of greatness to come (1980). Nevertheless, I bought a case and am glad that I did. The wine displays a deep cedar/cherry/truffle bouquet. On the palate, it is concentrated and mouth-filling. Earthy/iron/cedar flavors. It has depth and a rich velvety texture. Some tannin is long-lasting in the mouth. This wine is atypical for this vintage and will age well (1984).

[1995] 16-1/2

1975—Medium brick color. Butterscotch, creamy, cedar nose. Not typical. Soft entrance, then astringently unbalanced in the middle. Rounds up in the aftertaste and becomes very velvety with a long, cedar finish. This is a good, simple, attractive wine. Lacks depth, concentration, and complexity (1984).

[2000] 16+

1976—In a vertical tasting, I found the wine most drinkable with a velvety, medium body. The soft, mellow richness gives this wine great elegance. The savory flavors composed of oak, fruit, and spice are most enticing (1986).

[1993] 17

1978—Very intense and full of ripe fruit on the nose and on the palate. The flavors are of prunes and overripe plums. Already very supple and round. Slightly flabby finish due perhaps to a lack of acidity (1986).

[1993] 16-1/2

1979—Tasted blind beside the '81, '78, '76, and the great '66. This wine is also very forward, chewy yet creamy. An expansive wine (and expensive, too), which goes down the throat easily, harmoniously, and seductively. Ah, my friends, merlot can do wonders. Beginners should start with this varietal; it is the easiest to enjoy of all the red grapes (1986).

[1988/2000] 17+

1981—Much darker than the other vintages of this property, this wine is also much more restrained. However, it shows great promise. The nose has a rich and powerful, scented bouquet. It is very concentrated on the palate with a silky texture. The flavors are of mushrooms, truffles and cedar, enhanced by

Latour-à-Pomerol

ripe berries. It is firmly structured with tannin. Needs much more time to open up (1986).

[1993/2010] 18

1982—Dark to very dark ruby color. Deep, spicy, clovelike, plummy, cedary aroma with a hint of disturbing herbaceousness which will disappear in time. Full-bodied, luscious, round texture. Great concentration of ripe fruit, oak, and cedar which is delicious and generous. Rich, opulent, and viscous. Well balanced. Long, lingering finish (1986).

[1990/2012] 18-1/2+

1983—Medium-dark color. The nose is uncompromising and quite restrained. Most appealing fruit and cedar flavors. Full-bodied, rich and powerful. Deep and very long-lasting on the palate, loaded with rounded tannin. A great Pomerol (1986).

[1992/2003] 17

1984—Unyielding, austere, and tannic. Let us hope the fruit survives when the tannin has dissipated (1987).

[1992/2002] 14

1945—Outstanding wine from a great vintage. Excellent nose, deep and aromatic. Rich, full, and concentrated on the palate. Velvety, round, and long with great depth and texture. A classic (1975).
[2000] 19-1/2

1953—Soft, round, cedar aroma. Very typical St-Julien on the palate—smooth, round, and elegant flavors with graceful cedar overtones. Well balanced. A most enjoyable wine (1977).
[1990] 18

1959—Very successful in this vintage. Better than the '61. Soft, velvety, and savory cedar flavor. Round and full-bodied. Well structured. A great wine (1979).
[1989] 18

1961—Medium dark. Deep velvety aroma with cassis. Expansive elegant bouquet. Mouth-filling, deep, and concentrated with great extract. Good round tannin and beautiful balance. Long- lasting on the palate. A great wine, perhaps lacking intensity of flavor (1984).
[2001] 18

1962—Good fruit and style on the nose. Pleasant flavors which are disturbed by a dry and austere aftertaste. Medium body. It has breed and character but is embodied in a stern texture. Drink up soon (1984).
[1985] 16

1964—Harvested before the rain. Deep ruby color. The nose is restrained but has some elegance. Well-textured, ripe, fleshy cabernet flavor (1986).
[1985] 16

1966—Probably their best vintage of the '60s. Ripe cabernet nose just opening up. Full on the palate with lots of vitality. Still a bit firm. Nevertheless, an excellent wine that has plenty of tannin for a long life (1981).
[1988/1999] 18

1967—A bit tired, showing a disturbing, dry, tannic astringency in the finish. Also losing some of its fruit and flavor. A pleasant wine to which we must bid farewell (1982).
[1979] 14-1/2

1970—Finally opening up after 15 years. Still not ready but becoming enjoyable. Rich with breed and style. Full body with cedar flavor. Long in the mouth but still a bit tannic and restrained for today's drinking (1985).
[2000] 17-1/2

1971—Relatively round and supple. Perfumed and flavorful but lacking breed and intensity (1981).
[1986] 14-1/2

1973—A light wine but with some charm. Good flavors of fruit and cedar. Well proportioned and balanced. I prefer it to the '71 (1981).
[1986] 15-1/2

1975—Deep but closed aroma. Big and powerful on the palate. Rich, velvety, and round. Good tannin but needs more time. Enjoyable now but will improve (1981). Opaque color. Mouth-filling, full-bodied wine. Robust tannins begging to dissolve. Intense and deep concentration. Subdued yet most attractive cedar flavors followed by an oaky, rich, ripe, fruity aftertaste. At this point, the wine is predominantly restrained and as deeply concentrated as its stablemate '75 Langoa Barton. Today, both wines are very similar and need more aging to differentiate their respective qualitative attributes (1986).
[1993/2015] 17

Léoville-Barton

Appellation Contrôlée: St-Julien

Principal Owner: Barton family

Average Production: 16,000 cases

Vineyard Area: 40 hectares, 99 acres

Grape Varieties: 70% CS, 7% CF, 15% M, 8% PV

Average Vine Age: 25 years

Average Yield: 36 hectolitres per hectare

Classified Second Growth in 1855

Yves's Classification: Second growth

Food Complements: (4 to 6 years old) hare Périgourdine, (10 years or older) roast wild duck with chanterelles

Léoville-Barton

1976—I guess one could call this '76 Léoville-Barton "the great charmer." Whatever this wine is lacking in depth and concentration is marvelously compensated by a delicious, expansive, cedar/sweet, ripe berry aroma and flavor embodied in a velvety texture all of which is laced in a remarkable, soft, graceful balance (1986).

[1990] 17

1978—Concentrated aroma with fruit, oak, and even a *gout de terroir*, not typical for a St-Julien. On the palate, it has excellent flavors of cassis mixed with a hint of herbaceousness and ripe cabernet. Medium body and well balanced with good acidity. A wine with moderate tannins for a Barton but should have an appealing future (1982).

[1990/2008] 16-1/2

1979—Very similar to the '78 but slightly lighter and a bit more ready to drink. Attractive nose composed of fruit and cedar fragrances with the same flavors on the palate. Medium-light body. Nice balance and finish. A lovely wine (1982).

[1988/1995] 15

1980—This vintage is not at all restrained as many young vintages of this property can be. Some very attractive cedar and fruit flavors, embodied in a harmonious texture and structure, followed by a hint of tannin. Not a big wine but an enjoyable one (1986).

[1991] 15

1981—Medium color. Deep nose with fairly good concentration. The aroma is still subdued but shows young overtones of spices, cedar, and fruit. These flavors are subdued, and presently overwhelmed by the young clove spiciness. Quite elegant and round. Medium-to-full body. Good concentration with an attractive aftertaste of cedar and cassis. The wine has good depth, is well textured and balanced. Long, round finish (1985).

[1990/1999] 16-1/2+

1982—Very dark color (a good sign). The nose is more traditional and less forward than is found in the wines of other properties. Not much aroma but some fruit, cedar, oak, and spice are apparent. Full-bodied, deep concentration with cedar/oak overtones. Unyielding, backward, tannic, and long in the mouth. To be aged for many years, but should be very rewarding, especially for the price at which it was sold (1986).

[1997/2025] 17-1/2

1983—Ronald Barton, now deceased, was not ignorant of modern viticulture nor of modern progressive techniques of vinification, but he did not believe that aging, so necessary to the perfection of a wine, could be passed over rapidly. The more slowly the wine matures, the more promising the result. Therefore, he grew very little merlot (only 15 percent) on his estate. His wines are more often than not, tannic, backward, and unyielding for many years. They are the old guard, typical of the way Médoc wines were generally produced until the early '70s. The '83 is no exception to this philosophy. The wine is hard and very tannic, to the point of being astringent. It is very dark in color, which is a good sign. It has a muted but great concentration of fruit to await the development of its rough tannins. Right now, it is very spicy, quite closed and not too indulgent. The Barton family is one of just two families in the Médoc who have maintained their properties from the time of the 1855 classification to the present day (1986).

[1998/2020] 16-1/2

1984—Medium-dark color. Deep yet restrained spicy oak enhanced by an abundance of black currant. Medium body, hefty and forceful in character due to its firm and almost austere tannins. Wait a few years for the wine to round up a bit (1987).

[1991/2000] 16-1/2

Léoville-Las-Cases

1945—Very soft and elegant wine. Medium body, smooth, and velvety. Good cedar overtones. Not typical of a '45 in style (1974).

🍷 [1990] 17-1/2

1947—Las Cases at its best. Gently soft, silky, with magnificent flavors enhanced by cedar. The wine has great balance. It goes down one's throat like "little Jesus Christ in velvet pants," to borrow a favorite Burgundian expression. Long-lasting finish on the palate (1980).

🍷 [1990] 19+

1955—Excellent bouquet. Soft with a cedar overtone. Rich on the palate. Velvety, round, and full. Extremely flavorful. A great wine! (1980)

🍷 [1995] 18

1959—A big wine from a great vintage. Perhaps even more intense than the '55. Very rich and mouth-filling with exquisite flavors of fruit and cedar. Fleshy and generous, yet complex and long-lasting on the palate. Another great wine (1981).

🍷 [2000] 18-1/2

Appellation Contrôlée: St-Julien

Principal Owner: Société Civile du Château Léoville-Las-Cases

Administrator: Michel Delon

Average Production: 30,000 cases

Vineyard Area: 80 hectares, 197 acres

Grape Varieties: 65% CS, 13% CF, 17% M, 5% PV

Average Vine Age: 28 years

Average Yield: 33 hectolitres per hectare

Classified Second Growth in 1855

Yves's Classification: Second growth

Food Complements: (4 to 6 years old) baron of lamb, (10 years or older) pork chop glazed with cheese

Second Label: Clos du Marquis

1973

Grand Vin de Léoville

du Marquis de Las Cases

SAINT-JULIEN-MÉDOC

APPELLATION SAINT-JULIEN CONTROLÉE

PROPre SOCIÉTÉ DU CHATEAU LÉOVILLE LAS CASES A SAINT-JULIEN (Gde)

MIS EN BOUTEILLES AU CHATEAU 73cl

IMPRIMÉ EN FRANCE PRODUCE OF FRANCE BERTHON · LIBOURNE

1961—Dark color. Deep bouquet predominantly of oak with a hint of cedar. Full-bodied, coarse, woody flavor. A bit of dried-out tannin is bothersome. Disappointing for this vintage and property, this wine lacks flesh and generosity. Austere finish (1986).
[2000] 15

1962—Almost sweet cedar in the bouquet. Round, medium body, and well balanced. Long in the mouth. Still a fine wine (1983).
[1990] 17-1/2

1964—Nice complex aroma but not very deep. Some fruit and cedar flavors. Medium body. Awkward balance. An attractive, mellow wine growing old. At its peak now. Drink up (1983).
[1982] 16-1/2

1966—Shows more maturity than other '66s of its class. A classic St-Julien. Wonderful bouquet of cassis and cedar. Deep, intense concentration on the palate. Delicious flavors, full, velvety, and harmonious. Elegant balance with an unctuous cedar aftertaste. A winner (1982).
[1995] 18-1/2

1967—Some acidity makes this light wine unbalanced. It also gives the impression of being diluted. Getting tired now. Drink it up (1980).
[1978] 13-1/2

1970—Rich wine. Long in the mouth. Gutsy, deep, concentrated, and stylish. A successful wine with some rustic tannin in the aftertaste (1986).
[1995] 17

1971—An unharmonious balance is spoiling the broth! Too much woody tannin overpowering delicate and light fruit has prevented this wine from blossoming with grace. Now that some of the vigorous tannin has been shed, the fruit has faded and lost its intensity, leaving a dry, coarse, and austere wine (1986).
[1999] 13-1/2

1973—In a double-blind wine tasting, we all preferred it to the '73s of Pétrus, Lafite, and Cheval-Blanc. Perhaps the best wine of the vintage, although by no means a big wine nor of *longue garde.* Delicate, supple, and harmonious, with good texture. Delicious flavor, velvety aftertaste, and a long, lingering finish. Extremely attractive wine due to a perfect balance and delicious cedar taste (1986).
[1988] 17+

1975—A very powerful and complete wine, among the best of the vintage. Great concentration on the nose. Deep and full-bodied on the palate. Rich and full of tannin. Needs more time for it is still closed and hard to access. Wait until 1990 before opening a bottle (1982). Opaque garnet color. Deep, concentrated, unyielding nose from which escapes a subdued and attractive plum/ripe berry/oak aroma. Huge body, powerfully structured with a great load of firm tannin begging to dissolve. At this point the wine is predominantly restrained and deeply concentrated, showing a rich but muted black currant/oak/cedar flavor. Be patient, for this wine is a work of art for your children to enjoy (1987).
[1993/2025] 19

1976—Not as concentrated or tannic as the preceding vintage. Extremely elegant with style and character. Ripe cabernet flavors enhanced by a hint of cedar. Impressions of sweetness. Velvety, smooth, round, and supple. Medium body, well balanced. This château definitely makes great wine year after year (1982).
[1988] 17

Léoville-Las-Cases

1978—Very dark color. Very fruity with cedar and cherry nose. Big, full, intense flavors on the palate. Great depth and loaded with generous ripe cabernet fruit. Plenty of tannin. You will be well rewarded if you let it rest until 1990 (1981). Opaque garnet color. Very deep and concentrated black currant and oak bouquet laced with a hint of youthful spicy cloves which will shed away with time. Full-bodied, chewy, mouth-filling texture with oodles of ripe berry flavors still restrained and contained by rounded tannin. Great depth and saturated concentration, harmonious and stylish. A splendid wine which will last for a few decades, and which we will commence drinking in a few years (1987).

[1993/2020] 18-1/2

1979—Big, forward, smooth aroma with a hint of vanilla and cedar. On the palate, stylish, aristocratic, velvety, supple, and round. Plenty of fruit with good cedar overtones. Fine finish but still a bit tannic. A great wine. Presently more enjoyable than the '78 (1983).

🍷 [2000] 17-1/2

1980—Medium-light color. Soft, elegant, and fruity cedar aroma. Medium-to-light body. Round, nicely textured, velvety, buttery, with excellent balance (1983).

🍷 [1986] 16

1981—Dark color. Spicy cloves with a gentle creamy, cedar nose laced with ripe cabernet fruit. Most delightfully deep bouquet. Medium-to-full body with concentration and depth. Velvety texture followed by a luscious cedar flavor.

Rich and long lasting on the palate. Extremely well balanced. A first-class wine (1984).
[1988/2011] 17-1/2+

1982—Very dark purple, almost inky color. Deep gooseberry nose followed by a cedar/oak fragrance timidly showing through. Full-bodied, deep, and concentrated. Sappy texture with an excellent cedar/black currant flavor. Still young and full of virile tannins, yet it has breed, elegance, and power. The attractive aftertaste, composed of cassis, cedar, coffee, and plums, lingers in a long, velvety finish. Watch for this wine around 1995 (1986).
[1993/2015] 18-1/2+

1983—Medium-dark color. Beautiful aroma of cedar and ripe fruit. On the palate, the wine is round, silky, elegant, yet it is full-bodied with great concentration. The appetizing flavors of ripe fruit and cedar are long-lasting and lingering. A wine that has class, style, and charisma, meaning that you like it at first swallow (1986).
[1990/2005] 18

1984—Medium-dark color. Deep clove/spicy aroma followed by a mellow, creamy, cedary bouquet laced with rich berry fruit. Medium-bodied, fairly concentrated for this vintage. Delicious cedar flavor embodied in a velvety texture, gracefully balanced, and a smooth lingering finish. A sensuous and seductive wine (1987).
[1989/2000] 17+

Léoville-Poyferré

1945—Damp forest-soil mushroom aroma. On the palate, the wine still performs well. The tannin has rounded up and the fruit, laced with oak and mushroom, gives this wine a very appealing *gout de vin vieux*. This is how wines were made in the olden days (1986).
[1990] 17

1959—Not the best '59 by any means. Good *gout de vin vieux*, predominantly mushroom and damp earth. There is enough concentration and backbone to make this wine quite enjoyable for a few years (1979).
[1990] 15

1961—Big, full, fruity, mushroom aroma with a hint of cedar complexity. On the palate, not as concentrated as many '61s. Smooth, elegant, refined, with exquisite flavors. A trifle unbalanced. Long, lingering finish (1983).
[1990] 17-1/2+

1964—Nice fruity aroma. Coarse flavor and a bit light. Nothing to write home about (1981).
[1980] 14

1966—Charming bouquet. Powerful. Some acidity (1976). Elegance and breed. It is mouth-filling and almost complete (1982). Medium-red brick color with amber edge. Deep, cedar aroma laced with mushroom and cassis. Medium-to-full body, round, well structured, good depth. A little astringency in the aftertaste due to a hint of dry tannin but not unpleasant in the least. Long in the mouth with an old cedar flavor (1986).
[1996] 17

1967—Not typical of a '67. It was slow to evolve and has become a nice supple wine with good texture and flavors (1979). Medium-light color. Sweet cedar and vanilla bouquet. Medium- light body, round and smooth. Charming cedar

Léoville-Poyferré

flavor. This is a very tasty wine, not big but with every component in the right proportion (1985).

[1985] 16

1970—Like most of the other '70s, it is maturing slowly. Good concentration, light-to-medium body, and a nice flavor of cabernet. Needs a few more years (1979).

[1995] 16

1971—Brick-red color. Common and lively nose with a violet bouquet. On the palate, medium body, round, lean, and gentle. Lacks depth. Straightforward with ordinary vinous flavors (1987).

[1986] 15-1/2

1973—Medium-dark color. Old cedar bouquet. Well balanced with a lingering, warm, soft finish. Undertone of cherries. Medium body, light texture, supple, and velvety. A charming wine that drinks easily, typical of a well-made '73 (1980).

[1985] 16

Appellation Contrôlée: St-Julien
Principal Owner: Cuvelier family
Administrator: Didier Cuvelier
Average Production: 23,000 cases
Vineyard Area: 54 hectares, 133 acres
Grape Varieties: 65% CS, 35% M
Average Vine Age: 35 years
Average Yield: 36 hectolitres per hectare
Classified Second Growth in 1855
Yves's Classification: Second growth
Food Complements: (4 to 6 years old) sautéed skirt steak with shallots, (10 years or older) veal steak in mushroom cream sauce
Second Label: Château Moulin-Riche

1975—Medium-dark color. Closed and awkward aroma. Tastes better and is cleaner than it smells. Medium body. Needs more time (1978).
[1995] no score

1976—Medium-dark color. Deep aroma of fruit, cloves, and cedar. On the palate, the wine is soft and complex. Full of fruity flavors with overtones of vanilla and cedar. Its tannins are now soft and supple, which makes the wine well balanced. Bravo! (1987)
[1990] 16+

1978—Medium-dark color. Intense, rich, ripe cabernet aroma with cedar overtone. Medium-to-full body on the palate. Rich texture and flavor, long and well balanced. Good tannin. Round and supple. Aromatic. A successful wine (1987).
[1988/2000] 17-1/2

1979—Well developed and already quite forward. Very attractive aroma. Concentrated with an overtone of cedar and cherries. On the palate, similar to the '78. Round, supple, and full with a rich, fruity texture. Enjoyable now (1987).
[1995] 17

1980—Nice varietal nose, small but pleasant. Attractive on the palate. Fruity, cedar flavors. Medium-to-light body (1983).
[1986] 14-1/2

1981—Medium color. Deep, aromatic nose with ripe fruit laced with a winsome St-Julien cedar bouquet. Good concentration but the flavor is currently unyielding and very spicy. Soft and round, most enjoyable. Medium-to-full body. Fairly good finish. Should make a very good, round, luscious wine after shedding some of its tannin (1986).
[1989/1998] 16+

1982—Very dark purple color. Outstanding, deep, aromatic black currant aroma with a hint of sweetness and earthy undertone. The nose is marvelous and precociously forward. Mouth-filling, concentrated, and extremely flavorful. Full-bodied, round, and velvety. Great balance of acid and rounded tannin. Long, lingering, silky finish (1985).
[1989/2005] 18

1983—Medium-dark color. Deep, exquisite fruity aroma. Most attractive, ripe, silky berry flavors typically found in a great Margaux. Medium-to-full body. Round and supple. Fairly concentrated. Long and well balanced. Luscious finish (1986).
[1990/2003] 16-1/2

1984—Hard, tannic, and austere. Very little fruit piercing through yet. The question is, will there be enough of it when the harsh tannin recedes? (1987)
[1992/2000] 15

Lynch-Bages

1945—Oaky/mushroom aroma. Dry tannic entrance, woody flavors enhanced by mushrooms. Lacks softness and charm. Dry finish (1986).
[1975] 14

1949—Damp earth and mushroom aroma. Delightfully savory and mouth-filling entrance, followed by a stern and firm aftertaste of cabernet and oak (1980).
[1989] 17-1/2

1952—A full-bodied wine loaded with fruit. Intensely concentrated when young. High in alcohol (1975).

[1980] 17

1953—Full-bodied and loaded with fruit. Very fleshy, rich, powerful, and delicious (1978).

[1978] 18

1955—Red brick color with amber edge. The aroma is rich and extremely complex. A beautiful wine, deep, with a touch of mint and a lot of flavor. The wine has reached its optimum age (1983).

[1980] 16-1/2

1959 —Very dark brick color with amber edge. Aroma of spice, cinnamon, mint and eucalyptus. High in alcohol, still young. Full-bodied, mouth-filling. Flavorful, nicely balanced. The finish is a bit stern due to some dried-out tannins (1986).

[2009] 17

1961—I have had the pleasure of trying this wine several times in recent years in horizontal double-blind tastings. Although the wine press often rates it as one of the best '61s, I find it very good, but certainly not at the top. Beautiful, deep, concentrated aroma of mushrooms. On the palate, it is not overwhelmingly fantastic. Rich with good texture. Mouth-filling with austere oaky flavor.

Lynch-Bages

Appellation Contrôlée: Pauillac

Principal Owner: Cazes family

Administrator: Jean-Michel Cazes

Average Production: 25,000 cases

Vineyard Area: 70 hectares, 173 acres

Grape Varieties: 70% CS, 10% CF, 15% M

Average Vine Age: 30 years

Average Yield: 33 hectolitres per hectare

Classified Fifth Growth in 1855

Yves's Classification: Second growth

Food Complements: (4 to 6 years old) chateaubriand, (10 years or older) partridge with truffles

Second Label: Château Haut-Bages-Averous

Still plenty of tannin, some of which has become dried-out and astringent (1984).

[1991] 17

1962—Cassislike aroma. A bit coarse on the palate at first, followed by a nice flavorful texture with good fruit and a long, lingering finish. A full-flavored and robust wine with oak and black currant flavors. A very delightful wine with a little metallic touch characteristic of the great cabernet sauvignons of Pauillac (1981).

[1985] 17

1964—Not showing well. Harvested too late during the rain (1975).

8

1966—Not fully developed, still a bit hard. Medium-to-full body, good texture. Flavorful but lacks the style, breed, and complexity usually found in a Lynch-Bages (1980). In a horizontal-blind tasting, deep and concentrated. Cassis with a touch of eucalyptus. Still rough and unpleasant on the palate and a bit unbalanced. Lacks complexity and breed, but a good rustic type of wine (1983).

[1996] 16

1967—Light structure and body. Still has some attractive fruit. Palatable but should be consumed now (1978).

[1978] 14

1970—A very powerful, concentrated wine with all the components of a great claret. Very dark color. Beautiful bouquet with cassis, cedar, and oak. Deep, ripe cabernet flavors. Full body. Plenty of tannin guarantees longevity. Hold off from drinking now. Will become a fantastic wine (1982). Big nose of oaky and damp earth character. Full-bodied, deep, concentrated, mouth-filling texture full of extract and rounded tannin. Powerful, almost pungent, oak flavor lacking only the rich, sweet cabernet fruit that would give this wine elegance and finesse. Long-lasting, chewy aftertaste. A huge wine with a great longevity ahead (1987).

[1988/2018] 18

1971—Nice cabernet nose. Gentle fruit and attractive flavors. Well balanced. Medium body. No faults, a well made wine (1981).

[1986] 16

1973—When I first tasted this wine, I found it unattractive, closed, a bit vinous, and high in alcohol. It had good flavor but was unbalanced by too much acidity—rough on one side, breed on the other. I called it the "marriage of the princess with the peasant." A year and a half later, I found a small aroma of different scents. Some fruit, good texture, and relatively good depth. Leaves a fine impression of merlot and cabernet on the palate. I like this wine. It developed well for a '73 (1980).

[1986] 15-1/2

1975—I expected this Lynch-Bages to be comparable to the '70. I am disappointed. On the nose, it is unopened. On the palate, it does not have depth or concentration. It does have some redeeming good flavors but does not qualify as a big leaguer (1981).

[1995] 14-1/2

1976—Stern, concentrated nose. Some fruit and an attractive oak flavor. Medium body, fairly good texture. Finishes well. Has all the indications of becoming good but not great (1982).

[1990] 14 1/2

1978—The best vintage from this château since 1970. Dark color. Black currant and cedar nose. Sinewy texture with fruity flavors. Loaded with tannin. Soft, round, supple with medium body. Attractive yet simple cabernet flavors. Well-balanced oak/mushroom aftertaste (1982).

🍷 [1995] 16-1/2

1979—Similar to the '78 with perhaps less tannin and depth. Nevertheless, a very good Lynch-Bages with a fruity, cedar nose. Medium to full on the palate with a ripe cabernet flavor and a hint of cedar. Suppler than the '78. Good tannin and acid (1982).

[1988/1995] 16

1980—Some fruit and spice on the nose. Vanilla and cedary flavor. Well-structured, light-to-medium body. Very little tannin, but in proportion for this light and lean wine. Delightful, elegant aftertaste. A well-vinified wine from this weak and controversial year (1983).

[1985/1987] 15

1981—Medium-dark color. Attractive, young red fruit aroma with spice and oak. Medium body, dry and not too generous. Very tannic and austere. Good concentration and length. Should make a very good wine but we shall have to wait (1984).

[1993/2011] 16-1/2

1982—Medium-dark purple color. Deep but underdeveloped aroma of ripe fruit. Excellent berry/oak flavors. Full body, very concentrated, rich texture. Very well structured. Long in the mouth with a strong backbone of tannin. Will make a great bottle of wine (1985).

[1995/2020] 18

1983—A fabulous wine and a fantastic value! Medium-dark color. Deep coffee aroma laced with concentrated black currants. Opulent coffee and sweet ripe cassis flavor. Full body, loaded with extracts. Rich, intense, chewy concentration. It has great depth and plenty of rounded tannin. A huge, aristocratic wine. Splendid! (1986)

[1991/2013] 19

1984—Outstanding wine in this mediocre-to-average vintage. A very good value . . . not to be missed! Rich, opulent, cabernet aroma and flavors. Delicious coffee/tobacco/cassis concentration embodied in a fleshy, mellow texture backed up by excellent, rounded tannins (1987).

[1988/1994] 18

Magdelaine

1959—Brick color with amber edge. Soft, perfumed nose, not too forward. Round, creamy, and flavorful. Medium-to-light body. Good backbone in the finish (1979).

🍷 [1986] 15-1/2

1961—Fading rapidly and should be consumed. Medium-dark brick color with amber edge. Weak but attractive nose of cedar and earth. Lacks fruit on the palate and suppleness, which makes the wine austere. Earthy flavor. Overall, the wine lacks backbone and is past its prime (1981).

🍷 [1976] 14+

1962—Deep, earthy aroma with rich cedar overtone. Mouth-filling with a

Appellation Contrôlée: St-Emilion Grand Cru

Principal Owner: Jean-Pierre Moueix family

Average Production: 5,000 cases

Vineyard Area: 11 hectares, 27 acres

Grape Varieties: 20% CS, 80% M

Average Vine Age: 33 years

Average Yield: 42 hectolitres per hectare

Classified First Great Growth "B"

Yves's Classification: Second growth

Food Complements: (3 to 6 years old) mallard breast salmis, (8 years or older) confit of goose with cèpes

vigorous balance. Delightful flavors of fruit and cedar. Long-lasting on the palate. Probably at its peak by now (1977).

[1984] 17-1/2

1964—Deep, full-bodied wine but not in the same class as '64 Figeac or La Gaffelière. Unbalanced (1979).

[1984] 15-1/2

1966—Hefty wine with good extract. It has depth and roundness but lacks elegance. Fine tannin warrants longevity. Start drinking now (1980).

[1996] 16-1/2

1967—Very pleasant cedar fragrance and flavor. Light body. Subtle, gentle, and palatable but should be finished by now (1978).

[1978] 14

1970—A very slow-maturing wine just starting to open up. The nose is concentrated with some cedar. Big and mouth-filling. Cedar and red fruit flavors on the palate. Graceful, concentrated, creamy texture. Great aftertaste. Well balanced with a nice lingering finish (1983).

[2003] 17+

1971—One of my favorite wines during the late '70s. In a 1981 blind tasting against '71 Cheval-Blanc and '71 Pétrus, this wine was at its peak and extremely charming. Smaller than the other two, it displayed a creamy elegance with its soft, mellow, merlot characteristics. Smooth cedar flavor with a beautiful balance. What a wine! Drink now (1983).

[1985] 17

1973—Typical creamy, floral, merlot nose of Magdelaine. Velvety texture. Fruity, cedar flavor. Great balance, still with a light backbone of tannin. The finish is good and sound. Exceptionally well made for this vintage. A surprisingly good bottle of wine (1979).

[1986] 15

1975—Like the '70, this wine is backward, although it already displays some very attractive fruity/vanilla/earthy flavors. Good concentration and powerful tannin (1979). Just starting to open up, showing great depth and concentration. Harmonious cedar/oak/berry flavor. Long-lasting and powerful (1987).

[1995] 17

1978—Disappointing from such a fine property. Medium-dark ruby color with some brownish edge. Attractive fruity nose and flavor but a bit simple. Medium-light body and thin in texture, due, perhaps, to a lack of acidity (1986).

[1988] 14

1979—Very much like the '71. Beautiful, charming aroma of soft cedar fragrances. On the palate, it has elegance, and reasonable depth with good fruit and cedar flavors. Will be a very enjoyable and charming wine in a few years (1983).

[1992] 16

1981—Medium color. Very concentrated, unyielding, spicy nose reminiscent of cabernet franc. Medium body and texture. Good concentration. The wine has breed and character. Finishes well (1985).

[1992/2001] 16

1982—Medium ruby/garnet color. Spicy, oaky nose with a hint of cedar that

Magdelaine

will become more apparent as the wine ages. Some bottles show an attractive fruity aroma, others don't. On the palate, the wine from these bottles is rich and powerful; others are rounded and medium-bodied with soft, dormant flavors. Some bottles seem as if they will be ready soon; while others that are more concentrated and tannic suggest long cellaring (1986).

[1992/2002] 17+

1983—As with the '82, Magdelaine suffers from bottle variations. One is hard and tannic; the other is round and supple with the generous and delicious, creamy, cedar flavors typical of Magdelaine. One has style, breed, and gentleness, the other is full-bodied and uncompromising. Start enjoying the former by 1992 and wait until 1997 for the latter. If you do not know which style of '83 you have, send me a bottle and I'll taste it for you! (1986)

[1992/2005] [1997/2013] 16-1/2

1984—There is no 1984 Magdelaine.

Margaux

Appellation Contrôlée: Margaux

Principal Owner: Mentzelopoulos family

Average Production: 20,000 cases

Vineyard Area: 75 hectares, 185 acres

Grape Varieties: 75% CS, 20% M, 5% PV

Average Vine Age: 32 years

Average Yield: 25 hectolitres per hectare

Classified First Growth in 1855

Yves's Classification: First growth

Food Complements: (7 to 8 years old) sautéed lamb chops, (12 years or older) sweetbreads in red wine sauce

Second Label: Pavillon Rouge de Château Margaux

1945—Atypical style for Château Margaux. Nevertheless, rich and forward, ripe varietal fruit, and smooth texture. Lacks a certain finesse. Extremely big and intense (1977).

[2000] 19

1947—Beautiful, forward, and velvety bouquet. Rich and full on the palate. It appears younger than its age would indicate (1978).

[1995] 18

1952—Like the '45 vintage, I found it different than its usual feminine style. It is big and austere, smooth but not completely open (1975).

[1990] 16

1953—An outstanding Margaux. Almost perfect. I would be content just to smell this wine. It has a majestic bouquet with magnitude and elegance. On the palate, the wine is concentrated, velvety, rich, and achieves great elegance. Long, lingering, perfumed finish. A magnificent wine (1977).

[1995] 20

1955—Small, underdeveloped nose. Elegant, velvety texture and flavor with some fruit in the background. Attractive but light. Tasted with several other vintages, none of which showed very well on this occasion (1977).

[1990] 17

1959—In a vertical tasting, this wine showed some flower, was mouth-filling, but lacked fruit. It was still tannic and rough (1977). In another vertical tasting, a bottle from the same case showed much better. Old-cedar aroma. Big and rich on the palate. Soft, delicate flowers. Smooth and elegant (1982).

[2010] 18-1/2

1961—Magnificent bouquet, reminiscent of the '53 vintage. Medium-to-full body with loads of fruit. The tannin is not completely dissolved yet, the wine is still showing its adolescence. Great aftertaste. Flavorful, rich wine (1979). Elegant, graceful, and divine. Start drinking (1984).

[2011] 19

1962—Austere, tannic, and not too well balanced. Needs more time (1975). Château Margaux is notable for its distinguished bouquet and this vintage is no exception. Exquisite fruit and cedar flavors. Velvety texture and now very well balanced. Medium-light body. Beautiful aftertaste of roses and cedar that lingers forever (1983).

[1990] 17-1/2

1964—I last tried this wine in a horizontal double-blind tasting against Léoville-Las Cases and La Mission. The Graves and the St-Julien scored better. Small, unopened nose. Medium- light body. Good texture and balance but lacks fruit and elegance. Whatever makes Château Margaux so special is definitely not here (1983).

[1990] 16

1966—At Dr. Herb Stone's double-blind tasting, elegant, soft aroma of violets. Typical, subtle, aristocratic Margaux on the nose. On the palate, big, rich, and smooth. Almost sweet with great flavor of ripe cabernet. Well structured. Long, lingering finish (1981). Old wine-cellar aroma of mushrooms, forest soil, with a touch of fruit. On the palate, it is rich, full, complex, silky, and aristocratic. It is blessed with an excellent, graceful, mouth-filling texture (1982).

[1999] 18+

1967—In a horizontal double-blind tasting, the challengers were Pétrus, La Conseillante, and Cos-d'Estournel. Flowery and attractive bouquet. Good old

Margaux

cabernet flavor. Medium-to-light body. A well-made wine with a fair support of fruit and a good balance. The acidity found in its youth is now gone. At its peak (1982).

[1984] 16+

1970—When this vintage was still available, I did not buy any. I found the '70 Palmer, at half the price, far better in quality. Margaux was not as big and concentrated as the other '70s. Some complexity and fruit, but nothing overwhelming. Some tannin and acidity (1977).

[1990] 15

1971—In comparative tastings of '70s versus '71s, we preferred the '71, which was more forward than its older sister. I was not overwhelmed by the quality of either. Not much to tell (1976).

[1990] 15+

1973—Very pleasant like many well-made '73s. Flavorful with a light body. A charmer for this vintage (1979).

[1983] 16

1975—Disappointing for such a great vintage. Not in the class of the first growths. Small, unopened spicy nose. Nice jasmine but bad acid in the aftertaste. Light body. Quite disappointing (1981).

[1990] 14-1/2

1976—What is going on at Margaux? Dull, one-dimensional flavor. No concentration of fruit. No style, no breed, no charm. Another disappointment (1981).

[1985] 13-1/2

1978—A miracle! Past vintages of Margaux were the least attractive of all the premier crus. Today, it is the best '78 claret. What a change! The new owners have done well. Bravo! The fragrance of this wine is overwhelming, with black currants, violets, berries, and cedar overtones. It has concentrated, beautiful flavors. Smooth yet rich and full. Long on the palate with great balance. A classic that will live long (1982).

[1990/2020] 19

1979—Another masterpiece. The new owners have again created a heavenly nectar. I even like '79 better than the '78, but this is a wine for earlier drinking. Deep, great floral dimension with cassis, violets, and oak. On the palate, full-bodied, round, rich, and fruity. Silky texture, long and generous. The best wine of the vintage (1983).

[1989/2005] 19

1980—Never two without three, as the saying goes. They did it again at Margaux! Even in this light and difficult year, Margaux is more than attractive. It has intense perfume, depth, and elegance. Cassis laced with cedar and good soft tannin for an adequate longevity. The best wine of 1980 (1983).

[1995] 17

1981—A magnificent wine! What can I say? Very dark color. Deep, complex, powerful aroma with black currants/violets/vanilla oak laced with sweet red fruit. Rich, mouth-filling wine with great rounded tannins (in contrast to the harsh tannins found in the '81 Latour). Exquisite, complex flavors that were already found in the nose. Great depth and length, full of extract, chewy texture, elegant, and creamy. Wonderful finish. An outstanding wine which needs a few more years to show its full potential (1984).

[1991/2011] 19+

1982—Dark color with a purple tinge. Soft, velvety, concentrated nose (typical of a great Margaux) with an aroma of ripe cassis laced with bell pepper and a hint of herbaceousness. Full-bodied, rich, round, and silky. Mouth-filling with enjoyable extract and velvety texture. Ripe, concentrated berry flavor, with breed and elegance, yet powerful and long in the mouth. Excellent Margaux but not the best wine of the vintage as their '78, '79, '80, and '81 were (1985).

[1997/2025] 18-1/2+

1983—Without doubt, the best wine made in 1983. It has a very dark purple color. Outstandingly beautiful, deep aroma loaded with sweet berries. A huge, rich, luscious, mouth-filling wine, full of extract and rounded tannins.

Opulent with a delicious cassis flavor. More Pauillac in style than Margaux. A magnificent, aristocratic wine which explodes in your mouth (1986).
[1995/2015] 19-1/2

1984—Medium-dark purple color. Subdued, ripe black currant aroma. Medium-to-full-bodied, rich, complex extract of cassis. Penetrating and, at this young age, vivacious with some tannin to be shed. A very good Margaux successfully made in a difficult year, but not quite the leader of this vintage (1987).
[1992/2004] 17

La Mission-Haut-Brion

CHÂTEAU
LA MISSION HAUT BRION
APPELLATION GRAVES CONTRÔLÉE
Grand Cru classé
1970

SOCIÉTÉ CIVILE DES DOMAINES WOLTNER
PROPRIÉTAIRE
BORDEAUX
FRANCE
MIS EN BOUTEILLES AU CHÂTEAU

1945—Dark color, showing some age at the edge. Velvety nose with a deep Graves earthiness. Intense flavors of fruit and mushrooms. Nicely balanced. Medium body, rich and powerful. Finishes long on the palate. A great wine that still has a fine future (1975).
[1990] 18

1947—Deep, dark color. Concentrated fruit in the nose with complexity and elegance. Mouth-filling with plenty of extract of fruit and other flavors. Great finesse with a delightful balance. Depth and earthiness linger in a long, velvety aftertaste. A classic (1977).
[1990] 20

1949—Dark color. Deep, concentrated Graves nose. Huge, rich wine loaded with fruit, concentration and intense flavors. Round and elegant. Some useful tannin is still present. A beautiful wine with some youth, it will last long (1980).
[2000] 19

1953—Deep, dark brown color. Rich, intense bouquet. Medium to full on the palate. Soft, elegant, and round. Well balanced with a fine finish. Should be consumed now (1978).
[1985] 18

1955—A wine with great character, finesse, and elegance. Intense fruit and fragrant aroma. Good tannin, subtle balance, and long on the palate. It has all of the attributes of a long-lived wine (1978).
[1999] 19

1959—Color is not too deep. Impressive fragrance of ripe, concentrated cabernet laced with an earthy Graves overtone. It has fruit and a lot of tannin. Medium-to-full body. A bit austere for the moment but should make a great wine (1976).
[2009] 18+

1961—Surely one of the best wines made of this vintage in Bordeaux. We had the pleasure and honor to try this wine at several double-blind tastings, and it has always been very impressive. Marvelous, rich, concentrated nose with cassis, spice, and tobacco. Excellent flavors of ripe fruit. Full-bodied and mouth-filling. Great depth, huge and fleshy, yet velvety and elegant. Loaded with rounded tannin. Very long on the palate. A magnificent wine! (1981)
[2010] 20

1962—Lovely Graves character but does not have the depth and intensity that wines of this château normally achieve. Still an excellent wine that is graceful and exhibits a lovely balance. Good bouquet, delightful flavors, and medium

La-Mission-Haut-Brion

Appellation Contrôlée: Graves

Principal Owner: Domaine Clarence Dillon

Average Production: 8,000 cases

Vineyard Area: 18.5 hectares, 46 acres

Grape Varieties: 60% CS, 5% CF, 35% M

Average Vine Age: 27 years

Average Yield: 38 hectolitres per hectare

Classified Graves Cru Classé

Yves's Classification: First growth

Food Complements: (6 to 8 years old) game pâté, (12 years or older) breast of duck confit

weight. This is a wine that is charming, easy, and open, and should be consumed within a few years (1978).

[1983] 17

1964—Without doubt, one of the best wines made in 1964. Deep, earthy nose with a hint of roses. An impressive bouquet. On the palate, even more impressive. Full-bodied, voluptuous concentration of fruit, oak, and extract. Great texture, almost chewy. Finishes long with a lusty, powerful aftertaste (1984).

[1994] 18-1/2+

1966—Very dark color. Deep bouquet showing ripe fruit, cassis, cedar, and earthiness along with some spicy elements. Full-bodied, rich cedar/cassis/ tobacco flavors. Hefty structure loaded with robust tannin. A bit firm and tight, and, perhaps, lacking the generosity of the '64 vintage (1986).

[2006] 18

1967—I tasted many bottles of this wine. The bouquet is charming and characteristic of a graceful Graves (which is a rare occurrence in this appellation). Light-to-medium body, soft, and stylish. Savory berry/tobacco flavor. Lacks intensity and concentration. Nevertheless, one of the most attractive '67s. Easy to drink. Should be consumed by now (1981).

[1987] 17

1970—An outstanding big nose with deep, concentrated fruit and cedar undertones. A huge mouthful of wine with ripe black currant flavors enhanced by smoky oak. Round, rich, and fleshy with great elegance and character.

Superb balance. Long, lingering finish. A classic! Can be consumed now but will continue to improve for many years (1987).

[2010] 19+

1971—Nice dark color for the vintage. Elegant, tobacco/fruity cabernet aroma. Medium body. Finesse and balance are the main points here. An extremely flavorful and charming wine that might still improve a little (1982).

[1991] 17-1/2

1973—Soft, floral aroma of berry fruit and earthy iron. Attractive old wine-cellar/mushroom taste. Medium-to-light body with soft, gentle texture. Balanced but a little acidic. Long aftertaste with ripe cassis and cedar wood. A well-made wine (1987).

[1988] 15-1/2+

1975—A magnificent, opulent, and generous wine. Dark color with no amber edge. Abundant aroma of cassis, baked cherries, and tobacco. Mouth-filling, beautiful texture and hefty structure. Harmoniously well balanced. Succulent cassis/cherry/cigar box flavors. Concentrated backbone of tannin. Long, intense finish (1987).

[1990/2010] 19

1976—Lacks the intensity and mouth-filling quality that one expects from La Mission (we are spoiled). A very well-made wine, however, in a smaller style. Gentle tannin that needs to dissolve a bit. The nose is deliciously fruity, almost sweet. Mellow and complex on the palate. Delicately balanced. Appetizing cassis and tobacco flavors. Graceful finish (1981).

[1996] 17

1978—Sweet cassis fruit with ironlike, mineral scents, tobacco, smoky oak, and that gravelly *terroir* of Graves. The aroma is fragrant and deep. I love this powerful nose. Huge, full body. Forward and generous with great concentration. Loaded with oodles of fruit and rounded tannin, *gout de terroir* (hot pebbly, earthy flavor). Outstanding, luscious finish. Perhaps it joins Château Margaux in being the best Bordeaux of the vintage. Bravo! (1983)

[1990/2028] 19

1979— Tasting '79 just after the '78 shows it to be a lighter edition of La Mission but with all the same exquisite components. Lovely flavors with a soft, round texture and balance. Good tannin and fairly concentrated. This charming wine will mature earlier than the '75 or '78 and will make a delicious wine (1983).

[2006] 17

1980—Soft, unyielding vanilla and cedar aroma. Light-to- medium body, good texture and flavor. Balanced with some tannin. Harmonious and well proportioned. Not a biggy but quite good for this vintage (1983).

[1988] 15+

1981—Although Haut-Brion is already round and supple, La Mission is still closed and tannic. Nevertheless, this wine has some hidden qualities which forecast a better and brighter future. The color is very dark. The wine is mouth-filling, has great concentration and depth. The flavors piercing through are cherry, cassis, vanillin oak. Not a pleasure to drink now. Another wine we will have to wait for a long time (1984).

[1995/2021] 18

1982—Dark purple color. The nose is deep and concentrated with oak, truffle and tobacco scents coming through. Delicious flavors of cassis and cedar with a tobacco aftertaste. Rich, opulent, full-bodied wine. Chewy, yet silky texture. Powerful finish. A great amount of rounded tannins prepare this wine for a long life. After 64 years, the Woltners could not have left a better witness of

their accomplishment. Jim Gaby and I salute the Woltner family and pay tribute to their precious nectar. We shall miss them (1985).
[1992/2015] 19

1983—The first vintage produced by the Dillon family since the Woltners sold out and moved to California, although the wine may have been made prior to the change of ownership. In any case, the style is a bit restrained, less generous, and smaller than we are accustomed to. It is not in the first-growth league this time. Soft, cedar/fruity nose. Attractive flavors of vanilla, cedar, and fruit. Medium body, round and supple texture. Elegantly balanced. The wine finishes well with a cedar taste lingering in the mouth. All of this is very enjoyable due to good rounded tannins (1986).
[1992/2003] 16-1/2

1984—More restrained and also more concentrated than '84 Haut-Brion. Dark in color. Subdued aroma. Rich yet tannic on the palate. Vigorously structured yet balanced and fairly supple (1987).
[1990/2000] 17

Montrose

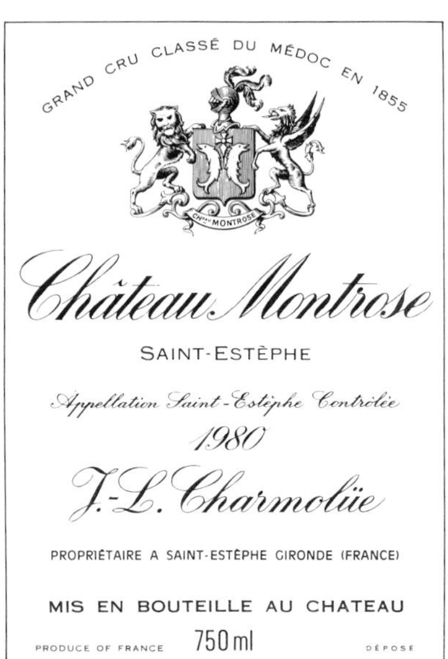

1945—Medium brick color. Old wine-cellar aroma of humus, mushrooms, and damp forest soil. Gentle and elegant on the palate, long with a smooth finish. A charmer! (1986)
[1995] 17

1953—Excellent nose. Rich and lasting with a refined, fruity aroma. Elegant and subtle on the palate. Full-bodied with good fruit that is quite flavorful. Still some tannin (1979).
[1990] 18

1955—Quite austere when young, it has developed into a big, powerful, and magnificent wine with depth and concentration. Beautiful on the palate, flavorful, with a long finish (1981). Concentrated, deep, sweet cassis/bing cherry aroma. Generous, ripe berry flavor laced with penetrating oak. Full-bodied, mouth-filling texture. Rounded tannins. Excellent, full finish (1986).
[1995] 18-1/2

1959—Another great wine. Bravo, Mr. Charmolüe! These powerful Montroses take a very long time to come around. In their youth they are so austere and tannic there is little pleasure in drinking them. Waiting, however, pays off. This vintage is now mature, though it will live for a long time. Beautiful, elegant nose. Big and rich on the palate. Robust and round, almost velvety. A good example of this property (1980).
[2005] 18-1/2

1961—A very robust wine! Powerful nose, fruity and very spicy. On the palate, the wine is still tannic and very concentrated. It is still a bit austere and the fruit is not showing well yet. Needs more time. Please wait (1981). Opaque color. Subdued aroma of mushrooms and forest soil. Mouth-filling, full-bodied wine. Robust, hefty tannins not yet dissolved, rendering the wine austere. Intense and deep concentration with a chewy texture. Fruity flavors restrained by a dry, oaky component. Dry finish (1985).
[2009] 17

1962—The 1962 vintage, following the great [illegible] and '59, was underrated by the trade. Those of us who bought some were [illegible]nate indeed for [illegible] prices were low and the quality was high. This '62 Montrose has a fine bouquet. On the palate, it is round and firm with weak flavors. The finish is austere and tannic. A virile wine lacking charm and generosity (1986).
[1995] 14-1/2

more forward La Mission. The nose is closed and austere with a hint of cedar and vanilla. Good flavor, character, and balance. Lingering aftertaste. Full-bodied. Tannic and backward. A sleeper. Needs more time. Superior quality (1983). Dark color. Subdued aroma of cherries, black currants, and nuts. On the palate, the wine is intensely concentrated and loaded with a lot of rounded tannin. A multitude of complex flavors including cassis and cherries. Aristocratic style. Long-lasting, majestic finish. Needs more time to blossom to its fullest (1987).

[1990/2015] 18-1/2

1971—It's been said that the '71s were made to drink while we wait for the '70s. This wine has depth, fairly good concentration, and is more forward than the '70. It is round, full of fruit, delicate, and elegant. Quite attractive to drink now, but can be kept without fear to the end of this century. A well-made Mouton (1977). Dark color. Older cabernet aroma, concentrated but no lilacs or fruit. Medium-to-full body with fairly good depth. Well built but the fruit is not there (1983).

[1995] 17

1973—The vintage with the Picasso label. Extremely austere for a '73. It has concentration but no fruit. Too much tannin and acid. I did not particularly enjoy drinking it. The price was inflated due to the label (1981).

[1990] 14

1975—At a premiers grands crus horizontal-blind tasting, beautiful aroma with cedar and concentrated, earthy, cabernet nose laced with cassis and lilacs. Chewy texture with plenty of hefty tannin. Restrained cassis flavor. Dense and powerful. Vigorous, yet has breed. Some acid in the aftertaste. Be patient for this *vin de garde* (1986).

[1992/2025] 18

1976—Dark color. Ripe cabernet nose with cedar, cassis and lilacs. Silky texture. Oaky, cassis flavor restrained by some powerful tannin. Robust, stale aftertaste lacking complexity (1987).

[1990/2010] 17

1978—At a horizontal-blind tasting, the Mouton's challengers were Ducru, Chevalier, Latour, and La Mission. On the nose, it seemed at first a St-Julien with its graceful cedar aroma. Then the fruit came forth and was reminiscent of a rich California cabernet. It finally revealed its identity through its unmistakable rose and lilac fragrance of Mouton. Smooth and silky on the palate. Concentrated, full-bodied, and still restrained (1987)

[1990/2010] 18+

1979—Less depth and concentration than usual. Cedar and fruit in the nose. Complex and attractive on the palate with good fruit and cedar. Lots of tannin. For the price, there are better wines from this vintage (1983).

[1988/1997] 16

1980—A light year that produced an attractive, soft, and round Mouton. Good fruit with vanilla flavor. Well balanced but on the light side. A restaurant wine, not to be kept long (1983).

[1990] 15-1/2

1981—Unyielding and austere, it is in a stage which makes it hard to assess. Dark color. Not much out of the nose. Medium body with rounded tannins. Some cherry and oak flavors are trying to push through. Well structured but unrevealing. It has length and depth. A wine of great breed for which we shall have to wait another several years (1984). Medium-dark, ruby color. Young, peppery, clovey nose enhanced by some light, berry fruit. Medium-to-full body. Abundant cassis/cherry/oaky flavors. Supple, complex, and multifac-

eted. Soft, silky texture, rounded structure, distinguished elegance. Most of all, it achieves a complex balance, having now acquired gentle and mellow tannins (1987).
[1989-2005] 17-1/2

1982—Very dark purple color. Deep, elegant, multi-scented aroma teases your nostrils. A mixture of ripe black currants, cherries, spices, raspberries, smoked oak, and more. Very rich and concentrated, yet elegant and complex with opulent flavors. Huge and powerful, mouth-filling elixir. Beautiful rounded tannin followed by great depth and delicious, almost sweet after-taste. A fantastic Mouton (1985).
[1995/2025] 19+

1983—Dark- to medium-dark color. Deep cedar/cassis/rose nose, not yet very forward. Mouth-filling with depth and good concentration. Well-structured, beautiful texture, exquisite floral flavor reminiscent of roses. Great rounded tannins. Supple. Perfect balance. It has breed and character, is long in the mouth. The only negative is a shade of herbaceousness which I hope will disappear in a few years. A first- class wine (1986).
[1991/2008] 18

1984—Medium-dark ruby color. Cherrywood/cassis aroma. Full-bodied, fairly concentrated, with cassis/bell pepper/cherry flavors. Good backbone and almost a bit austere due to some hefty tannins. A wine made of cabernet, lacking, at least in its youth, the fleshy roundness of merlot (even though Mouton uses very little merlot in a normal year). This is a wine that will improve with age, and in time will show us its true breed, finesse and complexity (1987).
[1992/2005] 17-1/2+

Palmer

1953—Advanced brick color. Undeveloped nose, not what one would expect of a '53. On the palate, rich, concentrated, and balanced. It has a smooth elegance laced with attractive flavors (1976).
[1985] 16-1/2

1959— During the past few years, I have had this wine more than a dozen times in double-blind tastings. It has a beautiful bouquet, soft and concentrated with old-cedar overtones and a hint of earthiness. Rich, deep, and concentrated on the palate and extremely flavorful with a good savory taste of an old wine laced with sweet cassis. Great silky texture. It achieves a majestic elegance that continues in a long, lingering finish (1985).
[1999] 18-1/2

1961—A superlative wine. One of the best Margaux ever made! Deep, soft, elegant mulberry aroma. Loaded with ripe, red berry fruit. Voluptuous, smooth, and generous on the palate. Opulent, velvety texture with great concentration and a perfect balance of cassis, coffee, tobacco, and oak flavors. An outstanding wine that has style, grace, and elegance. This mouth-filling wine is ready but will last for many more years (1986).
[1995] 20

1962—Another rich, voluptuous wine! The nose is full of violets with a hint of cedar, blossoming to an intense bouquet. Medium body, soft and rich. Silky texture and sweet berry fruit. Finishes smoothly (1983).
[1988] 18

1964—I have had this wine also some two dozen times during recent years in double-blind tastings and it has always scored well. The last time was against the '61 and '66 Palmer. Soft, elegant nose with cassis overtones. On the palate, medium-bodied, good texture with breed and character. Silky but lacks a certain fullness. Attractive finish. This is a very good wine for a '64 and should be enjoyed without delay while it still retains its wonderful balance (1983).

🍷 [1984] 17-1/2

1966—An exceptionally successful vintage at Palmer. Very deep, extraordinary aroma of ripe berry fruit with a hint of earthiness. Smooth and bountiful. On the palate, full, soft, velvety, rich, and concentrated. Extremely flavorful, great depth, elegance, and breed. Outstanding balance as a great Margaux should have. Long, long lingering finish. A classic! Comparing it with the '61, I prefer the latter, but they are very close in quality and both ready to drink (1983).

🍷 [1993] 19-1/2

1967—Has reached a plateau now and should be consumed without delay. It still has a beautiful forward bouquet with a hint of cassis. Round and soft on the palate. Medium-bodied with attractive flavors, charming complexity, and style (1981).

🍷 [1982] 17

1970—Another great wine from this property. It is more open and forward than most of the '70s from the Left Bank. In a double-blind tasting, the contestants were '59 and '66 Palmer, '62 Margaux, and '61 Rauzan-Gassies.

Appellation Contrôlée: Margaux

Principal Owner: Société Civile du Château Palmer

Administrator: B. Bouteiller

Average Production: 11,000 cases

Vineyard Area: 35 hectares, 86 acres

Grape Varieties: 45% CS, 5% CF, 40% M, 10% PV

Average Vine Age: 23 years

Average Yield: 31 hectolitres per hectare

Classified Third Growth in 1855

Yves's Classification: Second growth

Food Complements: (5 to 8 years old) rabbit with prunes, (12 years or older) roast pork loin

Palmer

Intense, deep aroma with a touch of earthiness. Loaded with a berrylike fragrance. On the palate, very concentrated, full-bodied, rich, and flavorful with great texture and depth. Still some tannin which promises a long life. Well balanced with a long, lingering finish. One of the best wines of the vintage (1984).

[2005] 19

1971—Dark brick color with amber edge. The nose is open and gentle, with deep cassis and flowery components. Delicious ripe berry flavors, velvety, and feminine in style. Medium weight. Elegant, silky texture. Mouth-filling, rounded tannin, generous and graceful. Should improve for a few more years (1985).

[1995] 17

1973—There are many other '73s more attractive than this one. It has a good bouquet, if a bit simple. Light-to-medium body, it lacks depth and finishes short (1981).

[1985] 14

1975—Magnificent floral bouquet full of sweet mulberry fruit and vanillin oak. Rich, powerful, and concentrated on the palate. Ripe cabernet and merlot grapes give the wine a generous, round, silky texture backed by a load of rounded tannin. Long in the mouth and very elegant. A winner in the class of the '61, '66, and '70 Palmers (1984).

[1988/2010] 19

1976—Shows an unattractive, strange fruity bouquet not usual for Palmer. Good fruit on the palate with some spice. Medium-bodied and well balanced. Finishes okay with a good aftertaste. Needs to be laid down (1980). Deep, concentrated nose with cassis. Some herbal and minty flavors. Fairly good concentration and depth for this vintage. Medium- to full-bodied. Well-textured, good amount of tannin. Round, excellent balance (1983).

[1988/1996] 16-1/2+

1978—Dark color. Big, deep, full bouquet. Fruity and spicy, loaded with fruit. Full-bodied. Luscious texture, soft, generous, and velvety. Some tannin and acid to lose. Rich, concentrated, and flavorful. Good future (1984).

[1988/2000] 17-1/2

1979—I prefer this vintage to the '78 because it has the outstanding bouquet characteristic of this property: ripe mulberry fruit, cassis, flower, laced with a touch of cedar. It is big, generous, forward, and enchanting. On the palate, it has the same succulent flavors with adequate depth and length. Good concentration and silky texture. Harmonious, elegant, and graceful. An outstanding balance. The complex finish makes this wine a great success (1982).

[1988/2000] 18

1980—Pleasant if small perfumed aroma. Vanilla and fruity nose. Light and soft on the palate. Flavors of fruit, cedar, and spices. Good balance. An attractive, small wine to be enjoyed soon. A trace of tannin will keep it lively for a few more years (1983).

[1986] 14-1/2

1981—Medium color. Aromatic flowery bouquet enhanced by ripe berries, quite forward. On the palate, the wine is very supple and round with a medium-to-light body. Delicious flavors make it very easy to taste and drink. Lacks flesh, concentration, depth, and perhaps some tannic structure. I would not expect this Palmer to become great (1984).

[1996] 16

1982—Medium dark with some amber already on the edge. The nose is nice but not much depth. Simple berry aroma with a hint of herbaceousness. Medium body, soft, supple, and harmonious on the palate. Quite precocious flavors of rich fruit enhanced by soft vanillin oak. Well balanced but in a lighter style. Elegant, attractive, and quaffable but lacks concentration and depth. Palmer could have done better in this vintage. A restaurant wine (1986).
[1989/1996] 16-1/2

1983—Medium-dark color with purple edge. Fragrant nose a bit vegetative but enhanced by appealing ripe fruit. Adequately concentrated with good flavors. Well balanced, it is long in the mouth but it lacks amplitude and a certain breed. This is a very good wine but not outstanding. I expect better from Palmer (1986).
[1991/2003] 17

1984—Medium ruby color. Abundant, expansive, perfumed and fruity bouquet and flavor. Yet the wine is light in structure and texture. It even finishes short, but it has, for the time being, the winsome attributes of youth. Enjoy this wine while it is relatively young (1987).
[1992] 15+

Pape-Clément

Appellation Contrôlée: Graves
Principal Owner: Montagne family
Average Production: 10,000 cases
Vineyard Area: 27 hectares, 67 acres
Grape Varieties: 67% CS, 33% M
Average Vine Age: 33 years
Average Yield: 33 hectolitres per hectare
Classified Graves Cru Classé
Yves's Classification: Third growth
Food Complements: (5 to 8 years old) herb-crusted roast loin of lamb, (12 years or older) baked ham

1959—Medium color with amber edge. Lovely nose with some earthy, mushroom undertones. Some good flavors but lacks finesse and, as in many vintages of Pape-Clément, it is austere and unbalanced by a little too much acid and dried-out tannins. Medium-to-light body. It does not have the opulent "peacock's tail" found in many of the great '59s (1978).
[1980] 14-1/2

1961—Medium-dark color. Attractive fragrance of fruit, spice, oak, and mushroom. Much more ready to drink than many other '61s. Loaded with ripe yet simple red fruit. Medium body, nicely structured, rich and round. Delicious aftertaste, well balanced with good finish (1984).
[1991] 17

1962—One of the best wines of this vintage, perhaps better even than La Mission. Deep, earthy bouquet, backed with roasted cabernet fruit. Good depth and delightful flavors from what was already found on the nose. Medium body, harmonious, supple, and round. Magnificent balance (1979).
[1992] 17+

1964—Dark color with amber edge. Great nose, deep and earthy. It has depth and excellent flavors of ripe cabernet, earthiness and truffles. It is concentrated, rich, and chewy. Full-bodied with long finish. A great Pape-Clement (1984).
[1994] 18

1966—Herbaceous, stemmy nose, one-dimensional and quite forward. Full and firm on the palate. Good texture but no finesse. Some acidity unbalances the wine with a dry and firm finish. Does not have the characteristics expected of a Graves (1979).
[1990] 15-1/2

1967—Light wine. Some good flavors but should be consumed by now (1978).
[1977] 13

1970—Medium dark color. Very advanced, powerful, roasted nose. Robust

Pape-Clément

and dry on the palate. Fair amount of fruit. Good tannin. Good structure but lacks softness and romance. Dry finish (1982).
[1996] 16+

1971—In the mid-'70s, this wine was very much like the '70 vintage but more elegant and round. Today it is lighter in body. Supple with some good flavors. Not a great wine but pleasant to drink (1982).
[1988] 15

1975—Medium-dark color. Soft, fruity nose uncharacteristic of a Graves. Medium body, well structured, good tannin and acid balance. Not too much fruit. Firm and dry aftertaste (1980).
[1995] 15

1976—Medium color with amber edge. Earthy and cherry aroma. Medium body, suppler than the '75. Still austere to my taste with some tannin to shed (1980).
[1991] 14

1978—Medium-to-dark purple color. Excessive mushroom and earthy bouquet, not to my liking. Medium-to-full body. Severe and harsh. Unattractive flavors. Tannic and firm aftertaste. Not pleasant (1981).
[1988/1998] 12-1/2

1979—Medium-dark color. Deep earthy and fruity aroma. Simple cassis and cherry flavors. Good tannin. Medium body, supple, and round. Lacks complexity and generosity. Finishes well but a bit firm (1983).
[1995] 15-1/2

1980—In the style of many Pape-Cléments, firm, unyielding, and austere. Fairly textured but lacks softness and breed. It has its share of tannin with some tar in the aftertaste (1983).
[1990] 14

1981—Medium color. Complex, fruity aroma develops in the glass after several minutes. Very attractive young cabernet flavors with pepper and clove. Medium body with fair concentration, yet the wine is round and soft. Excellent aftertaste of cedar, long and lingering. Overall, this is a medium-weight wine extremely well balanced with charming flavors and texture. Also very stylish (1985).
[1987/1993] 16-1/2+

1982—Medium ruby color. The nose is earthy, flowery, and a bit herbaceous. Mint, clove, stemmy, and herbal flavors. Medium body, lacks flesh and fat. Hard finish. Not much breed (1985).
[1990/2002] 14

1983—Medium color. Unappealing, dusty aroma and the taste is herbaceous and offensive. Unbalanced. Pape Clément must be turning in his grave since he cannot turn this Graves around! (1986)
9

Pavie

SAINT-ÉMILION 1er GRAND CRU CLASSÉ

Château Pavie

Appellation St-Emilion 1er Grand Cru Classé Contrôlée

1983

VALETTE
PROPRIÉTAIRES A St-ÉMILION (GIRONDE)
75 cl
PRODUCE OF FRANCE

1959—Medium brick color. Lovely bouquet. Good ripe merlot flavors with a cedar overtone. Medium body, well balanced and round. An enjoyable wine (1979).
[1989] 16-1/2

1961—Dark color with no amber. Beautiful, deep, cedary bouquet. Big on the palate with powerful yet silky flavors of cedar and sweet ripe merlot. Mouth-filling yet firmly structured, rich, round, and intensely concentrated. Great depth followed by inky finish and aftertaste, which is an omen of quality. Bravo! (1985)
[2011] 18

1962—Light fruit, light body. A mediocre wine (1976).
[1974] 13-1/2

1964—Not a biggy but has some charming and delicate attributes and a good balance (1976).
[1980] 15

1966—Round, soft, and delicate. Ready to drink (1978).
[1980] 14

1970—Light with some fruity components. Short finish. At best, a pleasant wine (1982).
[1982] 14

1971—Dark color. Delicate, restrained bouquet. Harmonious, subdued flavors with cassis and cedar overtones. Round, supple, and gentle on the palate. Elegant style and structure. A seductive and suave Pavie (1985).
[1991] 16-1/2

Pavie

Appellation Contrôlée: St-Emilion Grand Cru

Principal Owner: Consorts Valette

Administrator: Jean-Paul Valette

Average Production: 16,000 cases

Vineyard Area: 36 hectares, 89 acres

Grape Varieties: 20% CS, 25% CF, 55% M

Average Vine Age: 40 years

Average Yield: 40 hectolitres per hectare

Classified First Great Growth "B"

Yves's Classification: Third growth

Food Complements: (3 to 6 years old) filet of venison, (8 years or older) roast goose

1973—Pleasant bouquet, lean, and light (1977).
[1978] 12-1/2

1975—Deeper and more concentrated style than we are accustomed to. Excellent sweet flavors. Long on the palate. Good balance and finish. It has breed and backbone (1980).
[1995] 16+

1976—Medium color with amber edge. Light, simple, fruity aroma. Ordinary vinous taste, lacks depth and breed. Not very long in the mouth. Medium-to-light body. At best, pleasant for a small wine (1985).
[1987] 12

1978—Much like the '76 but with more character and style. The wine displays good fruit in a medium, concentrated body. Balanced and round, it is quite forward. The finish is fair. Attractive for lunch (1982).
[1991] 15

1979—Attractive but not very complex. Restrained nose with some fruit and cedar in the background. Subdued, roasted fruit, tobacco, and cedar flavors. Good concentration on the palate. Fair amount of tannin. Evolved well (1986).
[1987/1995] 15-1/2

1980—Pleasant, light, and simple. Some ripe merlot characteristics make this wine attractively tasty (1983).
[1986] 13

1981—Medium color. Soft, round, cedar nose with tobacco and coffee overtones. Quite forward and most attractive. Full-bodied, mouth-filling, very spicy, and concentrated. Loaded with rounded tannin. Dense yet harmonious and smooth. Long, velvety finish. Great prospects (1985).
[1991/2005] 17

1982—Dark color. Restrained aroma. Rich and huge on the palate. Loaded with tannin. Full-bodied and very concentrated. There is plenty of sweet ripe

fruit begging to blossom. The wine is heftily structured. A wine to lay down for a decade (1985).
[1995/2015] 17+

1983—Medium-dark ruby color. Soft, sweet raspberry aroma reminiscent of a Burgundy. Loaded with sweet red fruit flavors which I love. Well structured with good depth and balance. It is harmonious, supple, and graceful. Pavie is consistently better each year (1986).
[1990/2003] 17

Pétrus

Appellation Contrôlée: Pomerol

Principal Owners: Madame L.P. Lacoste and Jean-Pierre Moueix

Administrator: Christian Moueix

Average Production: 4,000 cases

Vineyard Area: 12 hectares, 30 acres

Grape Varieties: 95% M, 5% CF

Average Vine Age: 38 years

Average Yield: 31 hectolitres per hectare

Yves's Classification: First growth

Food Complements: (7 to 8 years old) veal steak sautéed with cream, (12 years or older) baby squab with foie gras

1952—The best wine made in Bordeaux in 1952. Rich, intense cedar bouquet enhanced by a graceful, earthy, iron and truffle aroma. Same voluptuous flavors, velvety texture and powerful on the palate. It has depth, complexity, impeccable balance, and an excellent, lingering finish (1985).
[2000] 19

1953—I first had this wine in a horizontal double-blind tasting in 1977. Among them was a '53 La Conseillante, which the members of our wine club rated very highly. Our host served this nectar wine as a comparison standard for Pétrus—a great idea! The Pétrus had a superbly rich cedar bouquet. Deep, concentrated and full on the palate. Velvety and round with outstanding balance and great depth. The finish lingered forever. A classic (1985).
[2000] 20

1955—Fully developed cedar bouquet enhanced by oodles of ripe fruit. Powerful fragrance. Rich, beefy, almost Burgundy-like on the palate. Marvelously savory and sensuously complex. This wine has been a sleeper (1980).
[2010] 18-1/2

1959—Excellent, enormous, rich wine. As with the '55, I find some similarity to the great growths of Burgundy. Massive aroma, full of flower, raspberries, and cedar. Full-bodied and deep on the palate. Extremely rich and velvety. A wine to remember (1978).
[2000] 19-1/2

1961—Very dark color. Deep, concentrated, powerful aroma of coffee, cassis, tobacco, and cedar overtones. Extremely rich, round, full, with succulent, luscious grape flavors. Full with great depth. A magnificent wine. Bravo! (1983)
[2025] 20+

1962—Complex, mellow, rich bouquet. Velvety, concentrated cassis, cedar, and tobacco flavors. Elegant, almost sweet and feminine. Well balanced (1983).
[2000] 18

1964—The best '64 made in Bordeaux. The abundant and generous fragrance almost jumps from the glass. The aroma is smooth, deep, and intoxicating with the mulberry, tobacco, and cedar components of a Right-Bank wine. Powerful, generous, and velvety with great texture. Another magnificent Pétrus with depth, length, and the same delicious flavors displayed on the nose (1983).
[2010] 20

1966—At a Pétrus vertical tasting, very dark color with an amber edge. Deep, complex aroma, full of sweet berries laced with a lovely cedar overtone still a bit subdued. Delicious flavors of ripe mulberries, truffles, and cedar. Concentrated, fleshy, and intense with good old tannin. Huge, mouth-filling, velvety, and generous. A wonderful wine with a powerful finish. Not quite at its peak. Will live long, getting better every day (1983).

🍷 [2025] 19-1/2

1967—Again, the best wine of the vintage. Very dark color. The aroma and flavors have the most graceful cedar qualities with a dash of earthiness and violets. It has character and style—big, full, and voluptuous. The wine has a delightful, velvety texture. A long-lasting, complex, and creamy, lingering finish. A splendid wine to enjoy now (but not with a fish course, my dear Madeline Triffon!) (1983).

🍷 [2000] 18+

1970—At a Pétrus vertical tasting, this wine had a medium-dark ruby color. Cedary mulberry bouquet not as forward or graceful as the '71. This is a massive and concentrated wine for long aging. Yet, in its own intense style, it is supple, round, and generous. Excellent balance followed by a sweet aftertaste of ripe cassis. This wine still needs to shed some tannin but is improving every day (1983).

🍷 [2015] 18-1/2

1971—Another superior wine of the vintage. More advanced than the '70 and a hundred times more graceful, harmonious, and delicious. It has a sensuously charming cedar aroma with exquisite finesse. Immense on the palate with outstanding flavors of cedar and sweet ripe berries. Creamy and mouth-filling. Elegant, long, luscious finish (1983).

🍷 [2000] 19

1973—Pétrus is not at the top in this vintage. I found some first and second growths better. Nose is closed and weak. Medium body, some wood and fruit. Great balance and velvety finish. Overall, a bit stern (1981). At the vertical tasting, this wine showed better than in 1981. The nose is open with a very attractive sweet cedar aroma. Soft and elegant. Medium body, delicious flavors, round, rich, and velvety. Excellent finish. It only lacks concentration (1983).

🍷 [1993] 17-1/2+

1975—Restrained and impenetrable aroma. Big and rich yet bashful tobacco and merlot fruit. The wine has great concentration but is too tannic and austere to be enjoyed fully. Finishes long on the palate. Lacks softness and romance. We might have to wait a long time (1981). Dark, young, ruby color. The nose is still closed and shows just a shed of young merlot fruit with a lot of cedar. On the palate, the wine is very concentrated, mouth-filling, extremely flavorful, elegant, and well balanced. Loaded with hefty tannin. Long and lingering finish (1983).

[1988/2020] 19

1976—Appealing spicy, clove, tobacco, and cedar nose. Enticing flavors of cassis and cedar. Medium body, soft, supple, and harmonious. Distinguished, with a delicate balance. Not a big Pétrus but a charming one (1986).

🍷 [2000] 17-1/2

1978—Pétrus is St. Peter's vineyard and I sometimes wonder if St. Peter himself doesn't take a leave of absence to come down at harvest time to help. The '78 vintage has a precocious aroma and flavor of high quality with rich, ripe fruit, cedar, and spice. It has concentration and depth with breed and intensity. It will age gracefully and improve for a few more years (1986).

🍷 [2003] 18+

1979—I cannot see much difference between the '78 and '79 Pétrus at this young age. They both have great fruit, cedar, spice, and depth. They are

Pétrus

flavorful, well built, young, and blessed with a generous and velvety texture (1983).

🍷 [2010] 18

1980—Well-made wine for the vintage. Open and attractive aroma. Plenty of fruit and savory cedar on the palate. Medium body. Of course, the best feature is its exquisite balance, even though some tannin is evident. Extremely long, delightful, creamy aftertaste (1983).

🍷 [1992] 17+

1981—Young, dark purple color. Spicy, cedar, raspberry nose. Great savory flavors of cedar, berries, and spice. Creamy and luscious texture. Full-bodied. Good extract, depth and, above all, perfect balance. The finish has a fair amount of tannin that guarantees a long life, but also indicates long cellaring (1983).

[1993/2021] 19

1983—Medium color. Beautiful, elegant, soft cedar aroma. The nose is quite forward. A typical great Pomerol. Generous cedar, fruit, sweet flavors. Long and lingering on the palate. Silky, distinguished, creamy, and savory. Magnificent balance. A fantastic wine (1986).
[1991/2010] 18-1/2

1984—Medium-dark color. Beautiful floral nose followed by a soft oak bouquet—very classy! On the palate, the wine is majestically silky, generous with delicious, sweet ripe berry and oak flavors, velvety texture, and balance. Long, complex, and graceful aftertaste. A distinguished and sensuous wine! (1987)
[1989/1995] 17-1/2+

Pichon-Longueville-Baron

1945—Old wine-cellar nose of mushrooms and oak. Good depth and rather full on the palate. Very flavorful, and good finish but getting old (1975).
[1975] 16

1949—Thick wine, almost chewy. Rich with cedar and old wine-cellar flavors of mushrooms and oak. A big wine that should continue to age well (1975).
[1989] 16-1/2

1955—Lusty aroma. On the palate, a bit austere and sturdy but good earthy aftertaste (1975).
[1980] 15

1959—Oaky and Pauillac-like on the nose. Earthy and beautiful mushroom aroma and flavor. Big on the palate but with a hole in the middle. A short finish. The taste does not keep the promise of the nose, being a bit austere with some dried-out tannins (1983).
[1989] 14-1/2

1961—Dark color. Enormous oaky, mushroom nose. Powerful, one-dimensional flavor of damp earth and oak. Chewy texture full of extract. Still plenty of tannin to dissolve. Full and long, firm finish. A wine of *longue garde* that is just opening up. Lacks a certain charm (1983).
[2011] 17

1962—Austere for lack of fruit. Medium-to-full body. Fairly good concentration and texture. Lacks grace and charm (1978).
[1982] 14-1/2

1966—Tasted in several horizontal double-blind tastings. A very dense wine which was hard to assess due to its concentration, tannin, and restrained flavor. I am afraid that this wine (young or old) will never achieve the right balance. By the time it sheds some of its tannins, the fruit will be long gone (1984).
[1996] 16-1/2

1967—I had this wine many times, but only once in a blind tasting from a magnum brought by Jim Gaby. Medium dark brick color. Very pleasant, old-wood aroma. Medium body and an enjoyable flavor. Soft and elegant with a little sharp aftertaste. Good balance of acid and tannin. At its peak (1983).
[1987] 15

1970—Medium-dark color. Deep mushroom aroma with a hint of cassis. Medium-to-full body. Enjoyable, mouth-filling texture. Long-lasting on the palate with earthy, oaky, mushroom flavors laced with some red fruit. A bit austere in style with some dried-out tannin but appealing nevertheless

Pichon-Longueville-Baron

Appellation Contrôlée: Pauillac

Principal Owner: AXA Insurance Co.

Administrator/Co-Proprietor: Jean-Michel Cazes

Average Production: 11,000 cases

Vineyard Area: 30 hectares, 74 acres

Grape Varieties: 75% CS, 23% M, 2% Malbec

Average Vine Age: 22 years

Average Yield: 35 hectolitres per hectare

Classified Second Growth in 1855

Yves's Classification: Third growth

Food Complements: (4 to 6 years old) steak tartare, (10 years or older) civet of rabbit

(1985). Medium-dark brick color with amber edge. Deep oaky/mushroom aroma. Deep, silky concentration on the palate. All astringency is gone now and the wine is very round and supple. Full-bodied, discreet oaky/berry flavors. Long and deep. Well balanced. Gentle finish. Could use more outgoing flavors and complexity. Nevertheless, this is a good wine (1987).

[2005] 16-1/2

1971—Astringent, unbalanced wine. Deep red with tawny edge. The nose is closed with a slightly oxidized, metallic smell. It opens up after a while and becomes better. Very little fruit. Very astringent, acidic finish (1980).

[1983] 11

1975—Medium-dark ruby color. Pauillac style on the nose with very little cassis followed by a touch of oak. Medium-to-light body. It has some style and a certain elegance. Lightly structured with some tannin. Should develop quickly (1979).

[1988] 14

1976—The nose has fruit with some cedar, creating a subdued but attractive fragrance. On the palate, medium body with fair ripe cabernet and oak flavors. It lacks the depth of a classified second-growth Pauillac. It has a little bit of tannin to ensure a certain longevity (1985).

[1990] 14

1978—Dark color. The nose is a bit unyielding but shows ripe cabernet and cedar aroma. Medium-to-full body. Lots of tannin hides a huge amount of fruit just piercing through. It lacks complexity. We will have to wait a long time for this wine (1982).
[1990/2000] 15-1/2

1979—About the same as the '78 vintage which I tasted side by side. The '79 has a bit less tannin, is more supple, and a bit less austere. It has some mellow merlot flavor. A good wine that should mature earlier (1982).
[1988/1996] 16-1/2

1981—Dark color. Concentrated nose but a disturbing herbaceous bouquet. Concentrated fruity flavors, generous, warm and well balanced. Medium-to-full body. Unfortunately, the herbaceousness kept me from enjoying this wine (1984).
[1991/2011] 14-1/2

1982—Dark ruby color with amber edge. Deep earthy, fruity nose is quite attractive and precocious. On the palate, this Pichon-Baron is fleshier and rounder than most vintages of this property. It does not have the usual austerity. On the palate, it is medium-to-full-bodied and fairly concentrated with excellent texture and structure. A wine with style and class not often seen at this château (1985).
[1990/2010] 17+

1983—Medium-dark color. Very interesting perfumed nose composed of a multitude of scents—jasmine, bell pepper, eucalyptus, and coffee. Mouth-filling, deep, and concentrated. Excellent, warm, appetizing flavors so complex as to offer coffee, sweet cassis, chocolate, earthiness, and bell peppers. Jim Gaby pointed out with good reason, "It reminds one of a Mayacamas cabernet." Long and lingering, it is an intense, generous, and voluptuous wine. A superb Pichon-Baron. Probably their greatest ever (1986).
[1991/2005] 18-1/2

1984—Hard, lean, austere and tannic (1987).
[1989-1993] 13

Pichon-Longueville-Comtesse-de-Lalande

1945—Oaky, mushroom aroma. Austere on the palate. Lacks suppleness and romance because of a lack of fruit. Oaky flavors. Dry, tannic finish (1986).
🍷 [2000] 15

1952—Very dark color. Deep, powerful cedar aroma. Full-bodied, rich, and flavorful. Well structured with depth. A good tannic backbone, yet elegant and stylish. Tasted at an elegant dinner, it was a perfect accompaniment to wild duck perigourdine (1976).
🍷 [1992] 18-1/2

1953—Dark color. Beautiful bouquet, soft and round. Rich and velvety on the palate. Luscious balance with a cedar flavor in the aftertaste. Its concentration and texture lead me to expect a good longevity (1975).
🍷 [1995] 18-1/2

1959—A gentle, elegant, feminine wine. Flavorful and well balanced. Not yet showing its full potential (1977).
🍷 [1995] 18

1961—Outstanding, intense bouquet. Very concentrated, earthy, rich, ripe cassis/cedar aroma. Huge and powerful on the palate. Great concentrated extract of cabernet flavors. Excellent balance and a marvelous finish. Could be consumed now, but not at its peak yet, for the tannin is not completely rounded (1981).

🍷 [2010] 19

1962—Cassis, cedar, and cloves on the nose. Rather intense fragrance. Appetizing flavors, stylish and elegant. Medium body. Nice texture and structure. A very charming wine at its peak (1981).

🍷 [1988] 17

1964—Picked before the devastating rain, confirmed by the dark ruby color. On the nose, fruity, cedar bouquet. Gentle and elegant texture with good cabernet and merlot flavors. Medium body. A charmer. Perhaps slightly short on the finish. At its peak now (1979).

🍷 [1986] 17

1966—As with many of the '66s, this is a slow-maturing wine. Earthy bouquet, not too forward, deep and concentrated. Flavorful taste. Still a lot of tannin. Lacks greatness (1979). Dark ruby color. Deep, intense earthy aroma mixed with cassis and a hint of cedar. A typical Pauillac nose. A wine of high quality on the palate, full-bodied, great concentration and depth. Well structured with plenty of good tannin to be dissolved. A great wine but not ready yet (1983).

🍷 [2010] 18

1967—Tasted against Pichon-Baron of the same year. Lalande was a bit better, but the styles were different. The Lalande was smoother and more feminine than the austere Baron. The Lalande lacked fullness and length on

Appellation Contrôlée: Pauillac

Principal Owner: Madame de Lencquesaing

Chef de Culture: Mr. Gaudin

Average Production: 18,000 cases

Vineyard Area: 55 hectares, 136 acres

Grape Varieties: 45% CS, 12% CF, 35% M, 8% PV

Average Vine Age: 18 years

Average Yield: 33 hectolitres per hectare

Classified Second Growth in 1855

Yves's Classification: Second growth

Food Complements: (4 to 6 years old) wild boar, (10 years or older) roast pheasant

Second Label: Reserve de la Comtesse

Pichon-Longueville-Comtesse-de-Lelande

the palate. Fruit and other flavors were present but did not have intensity or grandeur (1980).

🍷 [1981] 15-1/2

1970—Compared to the '66, this wine is more ready to drink than its older brother. Dark color. The nose is predominantly ripe cabernet sauvignon laced with black currants and earthy scents. On the palate, deep and full, letting you rediscover the delightful ripe cabernet flavor. Peppery, silky, almost sweet aftertaste. Can be consumed now or cherished for many more years (1983). Dark brick color. Deep, forward, floral bouquet. Full-bodied coffee and tobacco flavors. Very concentrated, round, and elegant. Complex balance and a generous finish (1986).

🍷 [2015] 18-1/2+

1971—Deep ruby color. Fine, rich, chunky nose. Rather forward on the palate. Attractive velvety balance. Medium, supple body. Might not live long (1976).

🍷 [1986] 14-1/2

1973—Medium-light color with amber edge. Soft, cedar aroma. Medium-light body. Very supple and round, and also very ready. Appealing, creamy cedar flavor. Charmingly balanced with a gentle elegance. Unfortunately, there is a slightly bitter aftertaste. Overall, a typical, well-made '73 that is frail and delicate. Drink up now! (1984)

🍷 [1983] 16

1975—One of the ten best Bordeaux made in 1975 and the best at this property since 1961. Remarkable intensity on the nose with its classic bouquet of cassis, cedar, cloves, and earth. Huge on the palate with great depth and concentrated texture. Still tannic. Should make a splendid bottle in a few years, for this is a complete wine (1983).

[1987/2005] 18-1/2+

1976—Almost without fail, Pichon-Lalande reflects the precise characteristics of each vintage. While this wine does not have the concentration or intensity of fruit and tannin of the '75s, it still has redeeming qualities. Medium ruby color. The nose is fruity, reminiscent of black currants with some vanilla and oaky overtones. Medium- to full-bodied, loaded with fruit. Very flavorful, rich, nicely balanced with a lingering finish. A very good wine with some useful tannin, it should be at its peak when ten years old (1984).

🍷 [1996] 17-1/2

1978—In this vintage, Pichon-Lalande outdid itself. It is the best of the second growths along with Ducru-Beaucaillou. In several blind tastings, it has equaled first growths in quality. Bravo! Dark ruby color. Deep, concentrated nose with a cassis, cedar bouquet with oak and vanilla undertones. Full-bodied, very rich, with depth and great concentration. Lovely extract of fruit. Marvelously balanced even with its substantial amount of tannin. Finishes long in the mouth. A superbly vinified wine. A bargain compared to Lafite or Petrus at three to five times the price (1983).

[1990/2010] 18-1/2

1979—Another big success from this property. For the price, it was certainly a bargain. Dark ruby color. Deep fragrance of black currants, cedar, and oak—most impressive! Full, concentrated body, rich and luscious. Delightfully forward flavors which stay in a long, lingering aftertaste. A great wine that is also well balanced with good tannin and acid. Generous and already enjoyable, but good evolution predicted (1983).

[1989/2000] 18

1980—Like the vintage, this wine is light but extremely pleasant for today's

drinking. It does not have the concentration nor the structure of a great vintage year, but all the other components are there in good balance. Gentle violet, cedar nose. Soft and round on the palate. Extremely flavorful, complex, elegant, and silky. Would be perfect with a roast chicken (1983).
Y [1988] 16-1/2

1981—Dark ruby color. Deep, aromatic nose with cherry, cassis, and cedar perfumes. Full-bodied, luscious with generous flavors of ripe fruit. Round, fleshy texture. Concentrated and extremely well balanced. Long in the mouth. Easy-drinking wine due to its rounded tannins. What a wine! (1984)
[1988/2008] 18+

1982—Extremely dark color. Outstanding, soft, rich nose. Aromas of sweet black currants, coffee, and tobacco explode out of the glass. The wine on the palate is simply fantastic! Full-bodied and extremely concentrated. It has a velvety texture and savory flavors of very ripe sweet cassis laced with coffee and tobacco. The wine is unctuous, generous, elegant, deep, and powerful with a perfect balance. A dream of a wine. *Bravo les de Lencquesaing* and *merci* for this elixir (1986).
[1990/2015] 19-1/2

1983—Dark color. Outstanding, deep cedar, rose, and cassis aroma. Mouth-filling, full of rich, savory flavors of ripe cabernet laced with oak, violets, and a hint of cedar. The taste lingers in the mouth and finishes in a "peacock's tail." It has great generosity and amplitude. Huge, rich, and concentrated (1986).
[1993/2010] 19+

1984—Mrs. de Lencquesaing did not lie or brag when she told me on Christmas 1984 that she had made the best wine of the vintage. Medium-dark ruby color. Distinguished, graceful, cassis and toasty oak aroma and bouquet. Full body, excellent ripe black currant flavors, creamy texture, rounded tannins. Rich and concentrated yet mellow and luscious. Achieves a stylish, harmonious balance. Long, voluptuous, lingering finish (1987).
[1990/2004] 18-1/2

Pontet-Canet

GRAND CRU CLASSÉ EN 1855

SPECIMEN

CHATEAU
PONTET-CANET
PAUILLAC

APPELLATION PAUILLAC CONTRÔLÉE
RED BORDEAUX WINE PRODUCED IN FRANCE
750 ML (25.4 FL. OZ.) ALC. 11.5 % BY VOLUME
STE CIVILE DU CHATEAU PONTET-CANET
ADM. GUY TESSERON, PROPRIETAIRE A PAUILLAC (GIRONDE) FRANCE

1959—Medium color with amber edge. Attractive and sweet bouquet. This sweetness is also found in the taste. Round, supple, and nicely balanced with good acid and tannin. Finishes harmoniously (1979).
[1993] 16-1/2

1961—Very dark color. Powerful, deep, earthy, oaky nose loaded with ripe, sweet cassis fruit. Full-bodied, mouth-filling with rich, opulent black currant flavors. It has depth and a meaty round texture. Good tannin, slightly too much acid. Finishes long in the mouth. An outstanding wine (1983).
[1999] 18

1962—Though it has good flavor, I find it unbalanced and a bit acidic. Does not have the fruity sweetness of the '59 or '61 vintages. The wine is, therefore, firmer and more austere (1978).
[1982] 14-1/2

1964—Medium color with amber edge. Nice bouquet, quite advanced and forward. Rounder and fruitier than the '62. Medium-light body. Lacks concentration and breed, but charming. Drink without delay (1979).
[1980] 15

1966—When young, it was unyielding and tannic. Now opened up but still

Appellation Contrôlée: Pauillac

Principal Owner: Guy Tesseron

Average Production: 35,000 cases

Vineyard Area: 72 hectares, 180 acres

Grape Varieties: 70% CS, 8% CF, 20% M, 2% Malbec

Average Vine Age: 30 years

Average Yield: 38 hectolitres per hectare

Classified Fifth Growth in 1855

Yves's Classification: Third growth

Food Complements: (4 to 6 years old) beef bourguignon, (10 years or older) sweetbreads in red wine

Pontet-Canet

austere. Fairly good body and concentration. Subdued fruit with some dried-out tannins. It didn't evolve too well, but it's not too bad (1985).
[2000] 16

1967—A very light wine that should be finished by now (1977).
[1977] 13

1970—As many others of this vintage, needs more time. Should evolve well if it does not lose its fruit (1979). Served with lunch by Mr. Pierre Cordier at the Martell's Château in Cognac. Much rounder and suppler with medium body. Well-structured, well-developed flavors. Good length in the mouth. Extremely well balanced. The tannins have softened and the wine is most attractive. A perfect match to the tenderloin of veal chasseur served with it (1984).
[1999] 16

1971—Unimpressive, light, and very little fruit. Lacks depth, concentration, and complexity. A *vin de qualité ordinaire* with too much acidity (1979).
[1981] 12

1973—Medium color. Nice soft, attractive aroma. Charming, savory flavors.

Light-to-medium body. Well balanced, easy to drink. A little short on the finish (1979)

🍷 [1983] 14

1975—Big earthy and stern aroma. Full-bodied, loaded with tannin. Lacks fruit and roundness. Good texture. Immature and a bit rough, needs more time. Should have a good future (1983).

[1988/2005] 15-1/2

1976—This vintage seems to have been made in a different style than all the Pontet-Canets I have tasted before. This new style is more supple and round. The aroma is soft and generous, reminiscent of ripe merlot and cabernet sauvignon grapes. Mouth-filling with a delightful texture. Smooth, round, and supple. A delicious flavor of fruit and cedar. Smooth tannin. Lingering finish (1980).

🍷 [1996] 16-1/2

1978—Dark ruby color. Deep earthy, fruity nose. Medium-to-full body. Harmonious and rich flavors of ripe fruit and oak. Well balanced with tannin and acid. Fairly deep and long in the mouth (1982).

[1988/2000] 16-1/2

1979—Dark color. Deep but unyielding nose, still a bit stern. A well-structured wine that shows some fruit. Unfortunately, overshadowed by a harsh, austere, tannic taste. Should mellow up in a few years (1982)

[1988/1995] 15-1/2

1981—Medium-to-dark color. Attractive young Pauillac nose with cherry, cassis, and vanillin oak. Medium body. The entrance is charmingly flavorful with good texture. The wine is hard and tannic now but it should develop into a good bottle (1984).

[1991/2001] 15-1/2

1982—Medium-dark purple color. Restrained cherry, spicy, earthy bouquet. On the palate, the wine is light and unyielding, even austere. Lacks flesh and suppleness. Hard and tannic now, will mellow down in a few years, but I do not expect wonders (1985).

[1995/2010] 15-1/2

1983—Medium-dark color. Deep, concentrated nose with a most attractive sweet, candy aroma reminiscent of pinot noir. Atypical but the quality is there. Smooth, round entrance with medium concentration. Spicy clove taste (good sign) followed by sweet cherry flavors. It has length and style, even though it lacks a certain finesse due to rough tannins and high alcohol which, at this point, unbalance the wine (1986).

[1993/2005] 16

1984—Hard, lean, simple and austere (1987).

[1989/1992] 13

Rausan-Ségla

1959—Medium brick color with amber edge. Sweet, raisin nose. Medium body with soft, round texture. Sweet, ripe fruit and oaky flavors. Deep and long in the mouth (1978).

🍷 [1989] 16

1961—Dark color. Attractive fragrance of fruit and oak. Big and chunky on the palate. Lovely fruity flavors. Still some tannin to lose. Long, deep finish. Not a typical-style Margaux but distinguished nevertheless (1981).

🍷 [2005] 17+

PRODUCE
OF FRANCE
2e CRU CLASSÉ
EN 1855
N° 76215
1982
château
RAUSAN-SÉGLA
GRAND CRU CLASSÉ
MARGAUX
APPELLATION MARGAUX CONTRÔLÉE
75 cl
HOLT FRÈRES ET FILS, PROPRIÉTAIRES A MARGAUX - GIRONDE
DISTRIBUTEUR EXCLUSIF LOUIS ESCHENAUER S. A. BORDEAUX (GIRONDE)
SHIPPED BY ARMAND DEJEAN & Cie, BORDEAUX
IMPORTED BY
CHATEAU & ESTATE
WINES COMPANY
NEW YORK, N.Y.
Red Bordeaux Wine - Contents 750 ml - Alcohol 12% by Volume

Appellation Contrôlée: Margaux

Principal Owner: Holts (British firm)

Average Production: 14,000 cases

Vineyard Area: 42 hectares, 104 acres

Grape Varieties: 51% CS, 11% CF, 36% M, 2% PV

Average Vine Age: 23 years

Average Yield: 30 hectolitres per hectare

Classified Second Growth in 1855

Yves's Classification: Third growth

Food Complements: (5 to 8 years old) meat loaf, (12 years or older) chicken à la Périgourdine

1962—Lean, firm, and austere. Lacks fruit. Needs to round up a bit to be attractive (1978).
[1992] 14

1966—The nose develops into a deep fragrance of cabernet and oak. Concentrated and firmly structured on the palate. It has depth and good sturdy tannin. Firm aftertaste (1979).
[1985/2000] 16

1967—Lean and lively with some attractive flavors. A good claret for lunch or picnic. Drink without delay (1977).
[1978] 13-1/2

1970—Slow-maturing wine. Dark color. Unyielding nose and spicy bouquet. Medium-to-full body. Plenty of tannin and acid still to shed. Hefty structure. Good concentration of rich cassis and an abundance of oak (1985).
[2005] 16

1971—Deeply colored. Lovely perfume with some spice. Lots of fruit on the palate. Velvety, supple, and elegant. Light-to- medium body. Pleasant to drink (1977).
[1988] 15

1973—Soft, cedar aroma, quite attractive. On the palate, it is not big but keeping with the promise of the nose, very harmonious. The wine is gentle, round, velvety, and very flavorful. Drink it now. This wine is a charmer (1980).
[1985] 15-1/2

1975—I found this wine light for a '75. It is also more advanced and forward than others of the vintage. The bouquet is perfumed and loaded with flowers. Medium body, nicely textured. Cedar, cassis and violet flavors. Nice balance and smooth aftertaste (1980).
[1990] 16

1976—Light color. Interesting floral aroma. Medium-to-light body. Delicious flavors, elegant and supple. Not much backbone but easy-drinking, quick-maturing wine for early consumption (1980).
[1986] 15-1/2

1978—Dark color. Beautiful, aromatic, flowery nose. Medium-to-full body. Mouth-filling with good depth. Cassis and cedar flavors well balanced with good tannin and acid. Pleasant finish. One of the best Rausan-Séglas in years (1983).
[1988/2000] 17

1979—Very much in the style of their successful '78. Less concentration and depth, but suppler and rounder. More advanced for present drinking (1983).
[1993] 16

1981—Medium-dark color. Light body but elegant, soft texture with oak complexity. Simple flavors. Lacks breed, depth, and concentration (1984).
[1994] 14

1982—Good effort, better than usual for this property. Medium- dark ruby color. Ripe, sweet, gooseberry aroma laced with vanillin oak. Quite forward and most pleasant. Medium body, supple, round, and flavorful with a velvety finish. A precocious and gentle wine to drink (1985).
[1989/1998] 15-1/2

1983—Outstanding effort, in keeping with its classification. Very dark color. Deep, concentrated nose not showing much yet. Mouth-filling, full of extracts,

Rausan-Ségla

with rich, beautiful flavors of ripe cabernet sauvignon. Loaded with tannin. A great wine. I am happy to welcome Rausan-Ségla back to its true rank (1986).
[1993/2008] 17-1/2

1984—Medium-dark color. Dominant, spicy aroma with some berry overtones. Young, vivacious entrance with mild, spicy/fruity flavors. Unfortunately, there is a hole in the middle. The wine lacks sap, length, and depth (1987).
[1992] 14

Rauzan-Gassies

1961—Tasted in two double-blind tastings. Beautiful, deep aroma, forward, concentrated, and spicy. Big on the palate. Good concentration and depth. Long, flavorful, lingering finish. Excellent wine at its peak (1983). Medium brick color. Fragrant, oaky, mushroom aroma with a hint of violets. Soft and gentle with feminine characteristics. Elegant and long-lasting on the palate (1986).
[1990] 17+

1962—Good color. A bit too acidic but shows some redeeming, attractive flavors (1976).
[1986] 14-1/2

1966—Light brick red. Old wine-cellar aroma. Medium body. Attractive fruit, oak, and mushroom flavors. Well balanced but a bit light. Overall, a nice wine that has breed and a good finish (1986).
[1990] 16-1/2

1967—Light and lean. Good bouquet and flavors. Should be consumed now (1978).
[1977] 14-1/2

Rauzan-Gassies

Appellation Contrôlée: Margaux

Principal Owners: Madame Paul Quié and J.M. Quié

Average Production: 12,000 cases

Vineyard Area: 30 hectares, 74 acres

Grape Varieties: 40% CS, 23% CF, 35% M, 2% PV

Average Vine Age: 32 years

Average Yield: 36 hectolitres per hectare

Classified Second Growth in 1855

Yves's Classification: Third growth

Food Complements: (5 to 8 years old) shish kebab, (10 years or older) chicken Kiev

1970—Unyielding, tannic, hard, and concentrated (1975). Not much complexity or character. It has the concentration of many '70s but like a few others, it fails to express its attributes, which is acceptable in a young wine but not an old one (1986).

🍷 [1990] 13

1971—Refreshing, lively wine. A bit too much acid to my liking or for long cellaring. Dry, astringent finish. It does have some redeeming flavors. A luncheon wine to be served with green onions and prosciutto (1977).

🍷 [1979] 14

1975—A delightful surprise! I expected another innocuous Rauzan-Gassies and got instead a wine with a dark ruby color, cassis and violets in the nose. A deep and mouth-filling silky, chewy texture followed by a rich berry, oaky flavor. Long, lingering, concentrated finish. A great effort from this property (1986).

[1989/2005] 17-1/2

1976—Another light, easy-drinking wine. Not, however, in the class of a second or third growth. Lean body and vinous flavors. A *vin de qualité ordinaire* (1980).

🍷 [1983] 13

1978—Medium ruby color. Charming aroma of flowers and wood. Medium-light body, lean texture, and lovely flavors. An overdose of acid unbalances this wine (1982).

🍷 [1990] 14-1/2

1979—Medium color. The nose has the flowery fragrance often found in Rauzan-Gassies. The same qualities are found in the taste. Better balanced than the '78, this wine is much more attractive. It is medium light in body and finishes well (1982).

🍷 [1991] 16

1981—Light and attractive. Charming aroma and flavors. The little tannin is well in balance with the light structure and depth of the wine. Should come around soon. Not a *vin de longue garde* (1984).

[1987/1995] 14-1/2

1982—The medium-light color and amber edge tell me this wine should be consumed rather soon. Lovely, quite forward berry nose. Medium-light body, soft, round, and velvety. Appealing fruit flavors. Well balanced. Elegant and charming aftertaste. Leaves a good, soft impression on the palate. Not a *vin de longue garde*, but already enjoyable today (1985).
[1988/1995] 15-1/2

1983—A big, powerful, straightforward wine. I would never have guessed it a Margaux from its style. The untamed tannins are quite rough and coarse, hiding behind them the simple but attractive black cherry flavor. Mouth-filling with a chewy texture. Long and very concentrated. We will have to wait a while for this one (1986).
[1995/2010] 17

1984—A very light, thin, insipid little wine. Should not have been bottled under its own name—it can only hurt Rauzan-Gassies's image (1987).
[1988] 11

Talbot

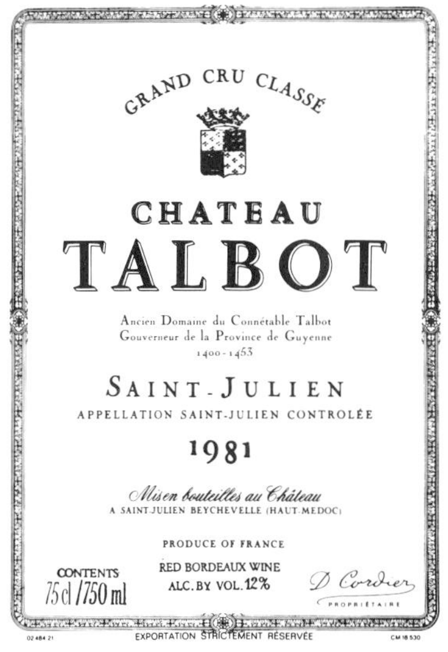

1959—Brick color with amber edge. Soft cedar aroma. Medium body and elegant, velvety texture. Complex, rich, and round. Delicious cedar flavor laced with sweet ripe fruit. Good tannin and velvety finish (1979).
Y [1990] 17

1961—Very dark color with amber edge. Powerful, deep nose with a fruity cedar aroma. Mouth-filling, rich, sweet cabernet flavors. Good balance and good tannin (1979).
[1991] 17

1962—Medium-dark color with amber edge. Typical St-Julien nose with round, cedar aromas. Quite powerful and elegant. Medium body on the palate with the same attributes found in the nose. Lacks softness and warmth due to some excess acidity. Nevertheless, it is a lively and charming wine (1979).
[1987] 15-1/2

1964—Reddish-purple when it was young, now a nice, medium-dark brick red with amber edge. Lovely fruity bouquet. On the palate, not too concentrated, even a bit diluted. Lacks depth and backbone. Some attractive fruity flavors. Drink now (1983).
[1983] 14

1966—Firm, unyielding, and uncompromising. Tough, dry tannins. This wine will never come around (1986).
[2000] 13

1967—Pleasant wine with an attractive nose. Much more palatable than the '66 vintage at all stages. Light body with good balance. Charming fruity, cedar flavors (1978). Should be consumed by now (1987).
[1981] 15

1970—Lean, austere, and unyielding (1980). Another '70 loaded with harsh tannin, not coming around. It is restrained on the nose and the palate. Dry finish. Lacks suppleness, flesh, and romance (1986).
[2000] 14

1971—Dark color. Superb velvety bouquet of cassis and cedar. Well structured on the palate, round and velvety. Quite big for a '71. Good concentration,

Talbot

Appellation Contrôlée: St-Julien

Principal Owner: Jean Cordier

Average Production: 38,000 cases

Vineyard Area: 87 hectares, 215 acres

Grape Varieties: 70% CS, 5% CF, 20% M, 5% PV

Average Vine Age: 25 years

Average Yield: 40 hectolitres per hectare

Classified Fourth Growth in 1855

Yves's Classification: Third growth

Food Complements: (4 to 6 years) coq au vin, (10 years or older) cèpes à la Bordelaise

Second Label: Connetable-Talbot

long in the mouth, with excellent, soft cedar and sweet fruity flavors. Harmonious balance. Bravo Talbot! (1982)

[1995] 17-1/2

1973—Light color. The nose is not too forward and the fruit is subdued. Light body. Some elegance and softness on the palate. A little off-balance but finishes okay. Average wine (1980).

[1981] 13

1975—Very dark, deep color. Underdeveloped, young, peppery, fruity, cedar bouquet. Medium-to-full body. Mouth-filling, concentrated, chewy texture. Extremely pleasant flavors of sweet cassis and cedar. The wine is rich, elegant, soft, and round. Beautiful balance followed by a delicious aftertaste (1985).

[1995] 17-1/2

1976—Unusually dark color. Deep, concentrated nose with a textbook St-Julien bouquet of ripe, soft, sweet cassis and cedar. The same exciting attributes are found in the taste with a touch of distracting herbaceousness. The wine is fairly concentrated. Soft, mouth-filling texture. It has breed and style but it is getting old (1985).

[1990] 16

1978—Dark color. Fruity, cedar bouquet with some herbaceous undertones. Big and complex on the palate. Great texture, round and elegant. Delicious

flavors of blackberries laced with cedar. Great warm, cedar aftertaste. Well balanced. I preferred it to the '78 Gruaud-Larose from the same proprietor (1982).
[1998] 17+

1979—Dark color. Deep, concentrated, ripe berry aroma. Full-bodied, powerful, delicious flavors of chocolate, cassis, and oak with a hint of cedar. Sensuously structured. This wine has depth and a graceful balance. Full of extracts and rounded tannin. Long-lasting finish (1986).
[1995] 17

1980—Very successfully made. This wine not only has an attractive, soft, round, St.Julien-like cedar bouquet, but has good depth for the vintage. Well balanced with medium tannin and acid (1983).
[1989] 15

1981—A great Talbot, powerful yet elegant. Medium-to-dark color. Rich, deep, black currant, tobacco leaf bouquet. Mouth-filling, full of extract and rich, complex flavors of cassis and powerful cedar. Silky texture. Long in the mouth, deep and lingering. Good rounded tannins. *Un vin de garde*! (1986)
[1991/2021] 17-1/2+

1982—Very dark purple color. Deep cedar, earthy, black currant aroma. Humongous on the palate, chewy and concentrated. Delicious, sweet, ripe red fruit flavor. Well structured and good depth. Rounded tannins as in many of the '82s. Velvety and long in the mouth. A pleasure to taste at this young age (1985).
[1989/2012] 18+

1983—Dark color. Deep, concentrated, fruity nose not yet fully developed. Very good wine, nicely flavored with ample concentration and depth. Very rich with abundant fruitiness. Lacking a bit in style and breed to deserve second-growth status. A very good wine (1986).
[1991/2003] 17

1984—Dark ruby color. Deeply scented, rich concentration of ripe cassis and chocolate aroma and flavors. Full-bodied, opulent and abundant cassis flavors. Generous, intense, saturated extract. Harmonious balance. Long and lingering. A very successful wine atypical of this vintage (1987).
[1990/2004] 17-1/2

Trotanoy

APPELLATION POMEROL CONTROLÉE

CHÂTEAU TROTANOY
POMEROL
1980
SOCIÉTÉ CIVILE DU CHATEAU TROTANOY
PROPRIÉTAIRE A POMEROL · GIRONDE · FRANCE
75cl
MIS EN BOUTEILLES A LA PROPRIÉTÉ PAR JEAN-PIERRE MOUEIX VITICULTEUR A LIBOURNE

1945—A charmer! Not in the style one expects of a '45 (concentration and depth). This atypical wine is smooth, subtle, and soft. Very elegant, perfumed bouquet and a sensuous, graceful balance (1986).
[1990] 17-1/2

1959—Medium-to-dark color with amber edge. Mushroom, truffle, and cedar nose. Well knit but a trifle lacking in fruit. Cedar flavors. Long, delightful aftertaste. A very good, firm wine, but somewhat "unromantic" (1981).
[1989] 17

1961—Very dark color. Deep iron/earthy nose enhanced by a fruity, truffle bouquet. Big and rich on the palate. Delicious flavors, chewy texture, round and very well balanced. Some tannin still in evidence. Long in the mouth with a great finish. A marvelous Pomerol (1983).
[2000] 19+

Trotanoy

Appellation Contrôlée: Pomerol

Principal Owner: Jean-Pierre Moueix

Average Production: 3,000 cases

Vineyard Area: 9 hectares, 22 acres

Grape Varieties: 85% M, 15% CF

Average Vine Age: 36 years

Average Yield: 30 hectolitres per hectare

Yves's Classification: Second growth

Food Complements: (3 to 6 years old) rillette of duck, (10 years or older) mignonette of beef

1962—I preferred this wine to the '62 Pétrus when tasted side by side in 1976. Now when it is twenty years old, it has a deep, huge, cedar bouquet with some mushrooms and truffles. Round, rich, generous, and velvety on the palate. Beautiful texture and delicious tobacco/cedar taste. Long, lingering finish (1982).

[1990] 18

1964—Deep-roasted aroma with some earthy undertones. Medium-to-full body. Excellent flavor. Good backbone of tannin and an agreeable finish (1978).

[1989] 16-1/2+

1966—Still very backward. Roasted aroma of ripe fruit, cassis, and cedar. Full-bodied and very concentrated. Austere and tannic. Needs more time but very good prospects (1981). Still tannic and austere (1984).

[1988/2006] 18

1967—A splendid wine from this average vintage. A very forward and powerful bouquet of cedar, fruit, and mushrooms laced with an iron, earthy bouquet. Velvety, concentrated wine. Rich, round flavor with great aftertaste and balance. Bravo! (1979)

[1987] 18

1970—Another very big wine. Still far from maturity even though the amber edge would lead you to think otherwise. The nose is subdued but has very ripe, roasted, fruity fragrances with overtones of truffles. Mouth-filling, rich, and fleshy. Delicious flavors hiding behind a good amount of tannin. Long on the palate. Let it sleep for another few years and it will become a jewel in your cellar (1980).

[2005] 18-1/2

1971—While we wait for the '66 and '70 to mature, enjoy this heavenly nectar. Great, huge nose of ripe berries, leather, iron, earth, and spice with a hint of cedar. Outstanding, luscious flavors. Medium-to-full body, extremely elegant. Velvety, long lingering finish. A marvelous wine, second to Pétrus in this vintage (1981).

[1991] 18+

1973—Not a *vin de garde*. For today's drinking, it is a charming and savory wine. Supple and harmonious. Good texture and, most of all, some delicious flavors (1981).

[1986] 16

1975—When I first had this wine in 1979, I knew it was going to be a great wine. It has even surpassed my expectations, having developed a deep, powerful aroma of cassis, vanilla, oak, tobacco, and truffles. It is mouth-filling, rich, luscious, and well structured. Chewy texture and a ripe, soft, mulberry, coffee taste. Very long on the palate with an outstanding, lingering finish (1983).

[1988/2000] 19

1976—A very good wine but not up to its class or reputation. Medium-dark color. Iron, earthy nose with good fruit. On the palate, the wine is still closed but shows some berrylike flavors with some overtones of spice and leather. A bothersome herbaceousness in the taste that will probably dissipate. Mild depth and gentle tannin (1982)

[1988/2000] 16

1978—Dark ruby color. Deep aroma of ripe merlot with truffles. Full, huge body on the palate. Powerful, fruity flavor. Well balanced with plenty of tannin still to lose. It has depth and is long in the mouth (1982).

[1988/2005] 18

1979—Medium-to-dark color. Very open and attractive nose with a blackberry, cedar bouquet. Medium-to-full body, round and well balanced. Good tannin. Charming flavors of cedar, fruit, and oak. Should be delicious in a few years (1983).

[1993] 17

1980—A very well-made wine for this vintage. Surprisingly, it is rather subdued and tannic. I wonder how this wine will develop in terms of balance, taste, and texture when the tannin dissipates (1983).

[1990] 15

1981—Medium color. Very fragrant aroma of rich, ripe fruit laced with cedar. Flavorful and luscious on the palate. Medium body, well balanced. A well-made, medium-weight Trotanoy which should be ready to drink soon, although it will last until the end of the century due to its great load of rounded tannins (1984).

[1988/1999] 16-1/2+

1983—Medium-dark color. The nose is closed, with just a hint of sweet fruit in the background, overwhelmed by a certain amount of herbaceousness. Medium-to-full body, good concentration. Well structured and shows an appealing fruitiness somewhat hidden behind the tannin. Some stemmy flavors are a bit distracting. A bit hard and unbalanced. Something is lacking (1986).

[1993/2007] 15-1/2

1984—Medium-dark color. Reserved, spicy/berry/oaky bouquet. Full-bodied and mouth-filling, but the wine is still restrained and tight. Relatively good depth and concentration. The vigorous, forceful tannins overshadow the rich, ripe berry flavors. Firm finish. Needs time (1987).

[1992/2005] 17

Vieux-Château-Certan

Vieux Château Certan

Grand Vin

POMEROL

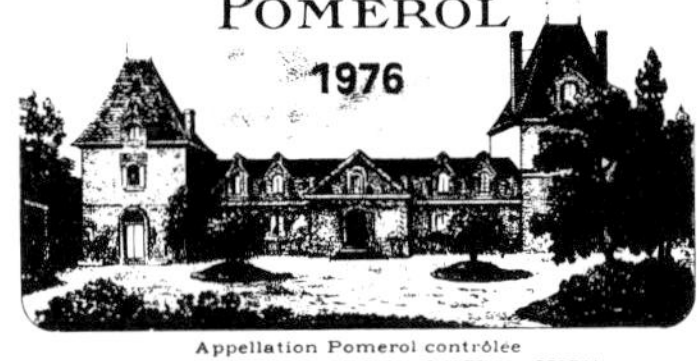

Appellation Pomerol contrôlee

SOCIETE CIVILE DU VIEUX CHATEAU CERTAN

Héritière de Mr et Mme Georges THIENPONT

PROPRIÉTAIRE A POMEROL - FRANCE 73cl

MIS EN BOUTEILLE AU CHÂTEAU

Appellation Contrôlée: Pomerol

Principal Owner: Héritiers Georges Thienpont

Average Production: 5,000 cases

Vineyard Area: 14 hectares, 35 acres

Grape Varieties: 50% M, 25% CF, 20% CS, 5% Malbec

Average Vine Age: 29 years

Average Yield: 33 hectolitres per hectare

Yves's Classification: Third growth

Food Complements: (3 to 6 years old) veal chop bourguignon, (10 years or older) lamb sweetbreads

1945—Tasted at a dinner party in St-Emilion. Very concentrated, opulent wine. Excellent texture and flavor. Deep and long in the mouth. Still has tannin to carry it for many more years (1978).

[2005] 18-1/2

1952—A very good wine for this vintage. Most of the wines of the Right Bank were more successful than those of the Médoc. Nice color. Deep, elegant bouquet. Round and soft on the palate. Medium body, harmoniously balanced. Fairly dry finish. At its peak right now and should be consumed within a few years (1979).

[1984] 17

1953—Deep, concentrated, earthy nose. Medium body. Good flavor of fruit and cedar. Nicely balanced, long and round with elegant finish. Tasted against '53 La Conseillante which was richer (1983).

[1986] 17-1/2

1959—Nice, dark brick color. Attractive cedar and blackberry bouquet with a hint of vanilla and sweetness. Round with rich flavors. Nicely structured with good texture, which makes this wine a pleasure to drink (1979).

[1989] 17+

1961—Deep, dark color with amber edge. Very fine bouquet of cassis and cedar. On the palate, it has finesse and elegance, is round and fat. Savory ripe flavor and a long finish. There is still some aggressive tannin (1985).

[1998] 17-1/2

1964—Medium-dark color. Deep, earthy nose with very ripe fruit, roses, lilacs and oak bouquet. Medium-to-full body, round and well structured. Loaded with ripe fruity flavors. Elegant and refined. At its peak (1983).

[1984] 16-1/2+

1966—I did not like it when it was young because of a bothersome jasminelike nose and taste. Now, however, it has a soft, round nose of roses and lilacs. It is full, elegant, and concentrated. The taste has an eccentric flavor. The wine is still tannic and needs more time (1983). The tannins have mellowed and I did not find the odd jasmine taste (1984).

[2006] 17

1967—Soft and weak cedar aroma. Medium-light body. Extremely pleasant and forward flavors of fruit and cedar. Round and soft with good balance and finish. Lacks only depth and amplitude (1986).

[1987] 16

1970—Dark color. Deep, unyielding nose of an earthy, fruity character.

Vieux-Château-Certan

Round and soft. Medium-to-full body. Lovely flavors, good tannin, and well balanced. Needs more time (1978).

[1995] 16-1/2

1971—Elegant, round, and supple wine. Very charming as are many well-made '71s. It has finesse and good fruity, cedar flavors. Well structured and balanced (1979).

[1988] 17

1975—Undeveloped. Good dark color. It shows concentration and depth on the palate but is also austere and tannic. Should mellow in a few years. I shall wait (1980). Dark ruby color. Deep, powerful aroma of cedar, truffles, and coffee enhanced by a sweet berry fragrance. Intensely concentrated, full-bodied, delicious cedar and berry flavors. A wine with complexity and very harmonious balance. Rounded tannins not quite dissolved. Long-lasting, generous aftertaste (1987).

[2005] 18

1976—Light color. The nose is vinous with a hint of fruit. Small flavor of cedar.

Light-to-medium body. Tannic finish. Too lean, not in its class in this vintage (1980).

🍷 [1990] 14

1978—Small, vinous wine. Disappointing for this property and price. Only the dark color is exciting. Otherwise, lacks concentration and depth. Small, fruity flavors and short finish (1982).

🍷 [1986] 13-1/2

1979—Better and more forward than the '78 vintage. Nice ruby color, already with an amber edge, which is a sign of age. Medium body. Attractive flavors of ripe fruit and cedar. Round and supple with no complexity. Lacks amplitude, depth, and generosity (1982).

[1987/1990] 15

1981—Medium purple color. Soft, round nose with cedar, cherry, and earth. Medium-to-full body, well structured, and an excellent silky texture. Long and creamy cedar flavors. Good rounded tannin and good depth. Long, elegant, creamy finish. A great Vieux-Certan already enjoyable (1984).

[1986/2001] 17

1982—When I tasted this wine from the barrel in 1984 just a few days before bottling, it was full-bodied and concentrated. Now I find the wine lighter in structure with less concentration of fruit. Still a very enjoyable wine, refined and elegant. Good ripe black cherry flavors laced with oak, cedar, and iron earthiness. Its rounded tannin gives an attractive backbone. The wine is long in the mouth with enough good depth to carry it a decade or more (1986).

[1989/1997] 17

1983—One of the best Vieux-Château-Certans in years, probably the very best. When I tasted this wine I thought it was Pétrus. Bravo *les Belges*! You deserve it. Medium color. Most attractive, subtle, cedar bouquet. Outstanding cedar, tobacco, coffee flavors. Great concentration, luscious, harmonious, long and lingering. Exquisite balance. Great breed. A magnificent wine (1986).

[1990/2003] 18-1/2

1984—In this bad merlot year, Vieux-Certan is lean, lacking flesh and romance. Its only redeeming attribute is its youth with all that it contributes: vivacity of flavors, spiciness, and young, simple, fresh berry flavors (1987).

🍷 [1992] 14

APPENDIX

A. General Vintage Evaluation

In order to evaluate my tasting notes and ratings, it is wise to keep in mind a generalized assessment of the overall vintages. Consider these guidelines to tell you which of the vintages since 1900 merit an outstanding rating (20 points), an excellent rating ($19^1/_2$-to-19 points), great ($18^1/_2$ points), very good (18-to-17 points), good ($16^1/_2$-to-$14^1/_2$ points), fair (14-to-12 points), mediocre ($11^1/_2$-to-10 points), or disastrous (below 10 points). This should help you remember the great red Bordeaux vintages so that you know when to take advantage of an offer to purchase or taste these wines.

Outstanding (20)

1900—If well kept, they can still be outstanding.

1929—Drink up. They are aging rapidly.

1945—Many approaching their peak, but a few are still young.

1961—The top-classified wines were ready to drink in the late '70s and early '80s. A few will last until 2025 or longer.

Excellent (19–$19^1/_2$)

1928—Well structured, big, concentrated, and ripe. *Vin de longue garde.* Some are still excellent today (1987).

1947—Round, rich, and ripe wines which matured early. Still great today, if a bit old (1987).

1949—Round, rich, and concentrated ripe flavors. Very much like the 1947.

1953—Savory, concentrated, and generous. Drink up now (1987).

1959—Concentrated, rich, flavorful, and generous. Some will last until the end of this century.

1982—This much-heralded vintage has oodles of fruit and concentration. The wines are uniformly excellent, and should be ready by 1992.

Great (18 ½)

1920—Aged very well. Now past their peak (1987).

1926—Concentrated and aged gracefully. A few are still great (1987).

1955—Harmonious and concentrated. Supple with nice fragrance and flavors. Drink soon (1987).

1964—Balanced, supple, and rich, but exercise extreme caution. The wines of the Médoc harvested after the rains are detestable. The other wines reached their peak between '80 and '84.

1966—Very concentrated, tannic, and hard when young. Just opening up in '84 for the wines of the Médoc. Stylish with great depth and elegance from St-Emilion, Graves, and Pomerol, which are more mature and advanced.

1970—Fleshy, severe, deep, and concentrated. Start drinking the first and second growths by 1988. *Vin de longue garde.*

1975—Concentrated, deep, and complete wine. Will live a long time, but will be drinkable relatively early (10 to 12 years after vintage). This is similar to the '29 and '47 vintages.

1978—Fleshy, generous, and well-balanced wines. They will mature early, '86 to '88, and should have a reasonable longevity thereafter.

1983—Powerful, concentrated, and harmonious. Should mature by '90 to'95 and have adequate longevity.

1985—Uniformly consistent with lots of fruit and backbone. Start drinking in 1993.

Very Good (17–18)

1906—Hearty and of good quality.

1921—Very concentrated, high sugar and tannin. *Vin de longue garde.*

1924—Much flavor, full, and round. Fading by now.

1948—Medium-bodied and distinguished wines. Its reputation suffers for being between two excellent vintages.

1952—Much better in St-Emilion and Pomerol (18) than in the Médoc (17), where the wines lack romance and sap. Drink now.

1962—Medium bodied, lots of finesse, extremely flavorful and well balanced. At their peak right now, perhaps until 1990 for the first growths.

1971—Charming and delicious wines. Medium bodied. Very attractive when young, will provide great pleasure through 1990 (some of the great growths will last longer).

1976—Very much like the '71s. But beware of quality inconsistencies.

1979—Fleshy, generous, and well balanced. Will mature early (1986-89). There will continue to be discussions as to which is better, '78 or '79.

1981—Qualitatively similar to the '78 and '79 vintages. Will not mature as fast. Medium-bodied style.

Good (14 ½–16 ½)

1905—Light with some elegance.

1911—Good quality.

1918—Good quality and a bit hard.

1919—Good and light.

1923—Light, soft, and round.

1934—Deep, vigorous, and tannic.

1943—Fruity and well structured. Lacks finesse.

1950—Medium-to-light body. Agreeable flavors with good balance.

1958—Round, soft, and charming flavors. Drink up.

1967—Drink up. They are losing the appeal of their youth. There are a few exceptions.

1973—Charming, very supple, and quite flavorful when young and from a great château. Some others can be coarse and austere. Most have passed their prime. Drink up by now (1987).

1980—Not a *vin de longue garde* but a wine that is supple, balanced, and light. To be drunk during the '80s while you wait for your other treasures.

1984—Wines without flesh and generosity. A disaster in St-Emilion and Pomerol. Some of the top Médoc wines are excellent; others lack structure and grace. Drink by 1990 to 2000.

Fair (12–14)

1904—Did not age well.

1907—Light with some elegance. Probably dead by now.

1908—Light and a bit hard.

1909—Light.

1912—Light.

1916—Full, but with no finesse.

1917—Light, round, and aromatic.

1925—Pleasant. Drink it up—it is fading.

1933—Light but with good flavor. Drink up.

1937—Good when young. Today, unbalanced and raw. Drink up.

1940—Light with nice fragrance. Pleasant.

1944—Light and agreeable. Aged well. Drink up.

1954—Light and healthy, but without maturity. Some can be nice.

1957—Light and uneven. Drink up.

1960—Light and pleasant.

1969—Promising at first, then disappointing after a few years. Drink up.

1974—Some pleasant and attractive wines and some not so good. Test and taste. If the price is right, it could be worth the gamble, but many are already dead.

Mediocre (10–11½)

1902	1935	1946
1914	1936	1956
1915	1938	1963
1922	1939	1972
1927	1941	1977
1931	1942	

Disastrous (below 10)

1901	1913	1951
1903	1930	1965
1910	1932	1968

B. The 1855 Médoc Classification

The following is the list of the 1855 classified growths of the Médoc. The wines are listed in alphabetical order within their class ranks. The only non-Médoc included in the classification is Château Haut-Brion from the Graves district. Since 1855, some châteaux have divided their estates through inheritance, combined their properties, changed their names, partially or completely. One château no longer exists, and one (Château Mouton-Rothschild) has been upgraded from second to first growth in 1973. The left column indicates how each château was named and spelled under Napoleon III. The right column is the list of the present names. The middle column is the appellation contrôlée in which the château is located.

The 1855 Médoc Classification

(57 in 1855)		(61 today)
	PREMIERS CRUS (First Growths)	
(4 in 1855)		(5 today)
Château Lafite	Pauillac	Château Lafite-Rothschild
Château Latour	Pauillac	Château Latour
Château Margaux	Margaux	Château Margaux
	Pauillac	Château Mouton-Rothschild
Château Haut-Brion	Graves	Château Haut-Brion
	DEUXIÈMES CRUS (Second Growths)	
(11 in 1855)		(14 today)
Château Brane	Margaux	Château Brane-Cantenac
Château Cos-Destournel	St-Estèphe	Château Cos-d'Estournel
Château Ducru-Beau-Caillou	St-Julien	Château Ducru-Beaucaillou
Château Vivens-Durfort	Margaux	Château Durfort-Vivens
Château Gruau-Laroze	St-Julien	Château Gruaud-Larose
Château Lascombe	Margaux	Château Lascombes
Château Léoville	St-Julien	Château Léoville-Barton Château Léoville-Las-Cases Château Léoville-Poyferré
Château Montrose	St-Estèphe	Château Montrose
Château Mouton	Pauillac	
Château Pichon-Longueville	Pauillac	Château Pichon-Longueville Baron Château Pichon-Longueville Comtesse de Lalande
Château Rauzan	Margaux	Château Rausan-Ségla Château Rauzan-Gassies

TROISIEMES CRUS (Third Growths)

(14 in 1855)		(14 today)
Château Boyd	Margaux	Château Boyd-Cantenac
		Château Cantenac-Brown
Château Calon	St-Estèphe	Château Calon-Ségur
Château Desmirail	Margaux	Château Desmirail
Château Dubignon	Margaux	(No longer exists)
Château Ferriere	Margaux	Château Ferriere
Château Giscours	Margaux	Château Giscours
Château d'Issan	Margaux	Château d'Issan
Château Kirwan	Margaux	Château Kirwan
Château Lagrange	St-Julien	Château Lagrange
Château Lalagune	Haut-Médoc	Château La Lagune
Château Langoa	St-Julien	Château Langoa-Barton
Château Saint-Exupery	Margaux	Château Malescot-Saint-Exupery
Château Becker	Margaux	Château Marquis d'Alesme-Becker
Château Palmer	Margaux	Château Palmer

QUATRIÈMES CRUS (Fourth Growths)

(11 in 1855)		(10 today)
Château de Beychevelle	St-Julien	Château Beychevelle
Château Du-Luc	St-Julien	Château Branaire-Ducru
Château Duhart	Pauillac	Château Duhart-Milon-Rothschild
Château Rochet	St-Estèphe	Château Lafon-Rochet
Château Marquis-de-Thermes	Margaux	Château Marquis-de-Terme
Château Poujet-Lassale	Margaux	Château Pouget
Château Poujet	Margaux	
Château Le Prieuré	St-Julien	Château Prieuré-Lichine
Château Saint-Pierre	Margaux	Château Saint-Pierre
Château Talbot	St-Julien	Château Talbot
Château Carnet	Haut-Médoc	Château La Tour-Carnet

CINQUIÈMES CRUS (Fifth Growths)

(17 in 1855)		(18 today)
Château Batailley	Pauillac	Château Batailley
		Château Haut-Batailley
Château Coutenceau	Haut-Médoc	Château Belgrave
Château Camensac	Haut-Médoc	Château de Camensac
Château Cantemerle	Haut-Médoc	Château Cantemerle
Château Clerc-Milon	Pauillac	Château Clerc-Milon
Château Cos-Labory	St-Estèphe	Château Cos-Labory
Château Croizet-Bages	Pauillac	Château Croizet-Bages
Château Dauzac	Margaux	Château Dauzac
Château Artigues-Arnaud	Pauillac	Château Grand-Puy-Ducasse
Château Grand-Puy	Pauillac	Château Grand-Puy-Lacoste
Château Haut-Bages	Pauillac	Château Haut-Bages-Libéral
Château Lynch	Pauillac	Château Lynch-Bages
Château Lynch-Moussas	Pauillac	Château Lynch-Moussas
Château Darmailhac	Pauillac	Château Mouton-Baronne-Philippe
Château Pedescleaux	Pauillac	Château Pédesclaux
Château Canet	Pauillac	Château Pontet-Canet
Château Le Tertre	Margaux	Château du Tertre

C. The 1855 Sauternes and Barsac Classification

The 1855 classification of the wines of Sauternes and Barsac comprises three categories, as opposed to the five categories in the Médoc. The following classified growths are listed in alphabetical order, within their own ranking class.

Since 1855, some châteaux have divided their estates through inheritance; one has combined two properties; many have changed their names partly or completely; one has uprooted its vineyard and no longer exists. The left column lists the châteaux as they were known under Napoleon III. The right column lists the present names of these same properties. The middle column is the appellation and the commune in which the château is located.

(21 in 1855)		(26 today)
(1 in 1855)	**PREMIER CRU SUPERIEUR**	(1 today)
Château Yquem	Sauternes	Château d'Yquem
(9 in 1855)	**PREMIERS CRUS**	(11 today)
Château Climens	Barsac	Château Climens
Château Coutet	Barsac	Château Coutet
Château Bayle	Sauternes	Château Guiraud
Château Peyraguey	Sauternes (Bommes)	Château Lafaurie-Peyraguey Clos Haut-Peyraguey
Château Vigneau	Sauternes (Bommes)	Château Rayne-Vigneau
Château Rabeaud	Sauternes (Bommes)	Château Rabaud-Promis Château Sigalas-Rabaud
Château Rieussec	Sauternes (Fargues)	Château Rieussec
Château Suduiraut	Sauternes (Preignac)	Château Suduiraut
Château Latour-Blanche	Sauternes (Bommes)	Château La Tour-Blanche
(11 in 1855)	**DEUXIÈMES CRUS**	(14 today)
Château d'Arche	Sauternes	Château d'Arche
Château Broustet-Nérac	Barsac	Château Broustet Château Nairac
Château Caillou	Barsac	Château Caillou
Château Doisy	Barsac	Château Doisy-Daene Château Doisy-Dubroca Château Doisy-Védrines
Château Filhot	Sauternes	Château Filhot
Château Lamothe	Sauternes	Château Lamothe (Despujols) Château Lamothe (Guignard)
Château de Malle	Sauternes (Preignac)	Château de Malle
Château Mirat	Barsac	Château Myrat (uprooted after the 1975 harvest)
Château Pexoto	Sauternes (Bommes)	Château Rabaud-Promis
Château Romer	Sauternes (Fargues)	Château Romer (*) Château Romer-du-Hayot
Château Suau	Barsac	Château Suau

(*) Château Romer's sweet wine is currently bottled by Château Romer-du-Hayot.

D. The St-Emilion Classifications

St-Emilion is composed of five distinct geographical zones. Each wine has a character of its own, according to its area of origin. For your information, I have defined the five areas and included them in this listing (see map also):

1. Limestone plateau (Plateau),
2. Hills (Côte),
3. Ancient gravely sands (Graves),
4. Ancient sands (Sable), and
5. New sandy gravely soils (Sablo-Graveleux).

The 1969 St-Emilion Classification

PREMIERS GRANDS CRUS CLASSÉS (12)

A. Château Ausone	Côte & Plateau
Château Cheval-Blanc	Graves
B. Château Beauséjour (Becot)	Plateau & Côte
Château Beauséjour (Duffau-Lagarrosse)	Côte
Château Belair	Plateau & Côte
Château Canon	Plateau & Côte
Château Figeac	Graves
Clos Fourtet	Plateau & Sable
Château La Gaffelière	Côte
Château Magdelaine	Plateau & Côte
Château Pavie	Plateau & Côte
Château Trottevielle	Plateau

GRAND CRUS CLASSÉS (72)

Château L'Angélus	Côte & Sable
Château L'Arrosée	Côte
Château Baleau	Côte & Sable
Château Balestard-La-Tonnelle	Plateau
Château Bellevue	Plateau & Côte
Château Bergat	Plateau & Côte
Château Cadet-Bon	Plateau & Côte
Château Cadet-Piola	Plateau & Côte
Château Canon La Gaffelière	Côte
Château Cap-de-Mourlin (Jean Capdemourlin)	Côte & Sable
Château Cap-de-Mourlin (G.F.A. Capdemourlin)	Côte & Sable
Château La Carte	Plateau & Sable
Château Chapelle Madeleine	Plateau & Côte
Château Le Chatelet	Côte & Sable
Château Chauvin	Sable

Château La Clotte	Côte
Château La Clusière	Côte
Château Corbin (Giraud)	Sable
Château Corbin-Michotte	Sable
Château La Couspaude	Plateau
Château Coutet	Côte
Château Le Couvent	Plateau
Château Couvent des Jacobins	Sable
Château Croque-Michotte	Sable & Graves
Château Curé-Bon	Plateau & Côte
Château Dassault	Sable
Château La Dominique	Sable & Graves
Château Faurie-de-Souchard	Côte
Château Fonplégade	Côte
Château Fonroque	Côte & Sable
Château Franc-Mayne	Côte
Château Grand-Barrail-Lamarzelle-Figeac	Sable
Château Grand-Corbin (Pecresse)	Sable
Château Grand-Corbin-Despagne	Sable
Château Grand-Mayne	Côte & Sable
Château Grand-Pontet	Côte & Sable
Château Grandes-Murailles	Côte & Sable
Château Guadet-Saint-Julien	Plateau
Château Haut-Corbin	Sable
Château Haut-Sarpe	Plateau & Côte
Clos des Jacobins	Côte & Sable
Château Jean-Faure	Sable
Château Lamarzelle	Sable & Graves
Château Laniote	Sable
Château Larcis-Ducasse	Côte
Château Larmande	Sable
Château Laroze	Sable
Clos La Madeleine	Plateau & Côte
Château Matras	Côte
Château Mauvezin	Plateau & Côte
Château Moulin-du-Cadet	Côte & Sable
Clos de L'Oratoire	Côte
Château Pavie-Decesse	Plateau & Côte
Château Pavie-Macquin	Plateau & Côte
Château Pavillon-Cadet	Côte & Sable
Château Petit-Faurie-de-Soutard	Sable & Côte
Château Le Prieuré	Plateau & Côte
Château Ripeau	Sable
Château Saint-Georges-Côte-Pavie	Côte
Clos Saint-Martin	Côte & Sable
Château Sansonnet	Plateau
Château La Serre	Plateau
Château Soutard	Plateau & Côte
Château Tertre-Daugay	Plateau & Côte
Château La Tour Figeac	Sable & Graves
Château La Tour-du-Pin-Figeac (Giraud)	Sable & Graves
Château La Tour-du-Pin-Figeac-Moueix	Sable & Graves
Château Trimoulet	Sable
Château Trois-Moulins	Plateau & Côte
Château Troplong-Mondot	Plateau
Château Villemaurine	Plateau
Château Yon-Figeac	Sable

The 1985 St-Emilion Classification

PREMIERS GRANDS CRUS CLASSÉS (11)

A. Château Ausone
Château Cheval-Blanc
B. Château Beauséjour (Duffau-Lagarrosse)
Château Belair
Château Canon
Château Figeac
Clos Fourtet
Château La Gaffèlière
Château Magdelaine
Château Pavie
Château Trottevielle

GRAND CRUS CLASSÉS (63)

Château L'Angélus
Château L'Arrosée
Château Balestard La Tonnelle
Château Beauséjour (Becot) (*)
Château Bellevue
Château Bergat
Château Berliquet (**)
Château Cadet Piola
Château Canon La Gaffelière
Château Cap-de-Mourlin
Château Le Chatelet
Château Chauvin
Château La Clotte
Château La Clusière
Château Corbin (Giraud)
Château Corbin-Michotte
Château Couvent des Jacobins
Château Croque-Michotte
Château Curé-Bon la Madeleine
Château Dassault
Château La Dominique
Château Faurie-de-Souchard
Château Fonplégade
Château Fonroque
Château Franc-Mayne
Château Grand-Barrail-Lamarzelle-Figeac
Château Grand-Corbin (Pecresse)
Château Grand-Corbin-Despagne
Château Grand-Mayne
Château Grand-Pontet
Château Guadet-Saint-Julien
Château Haut-Corbin
Château Haut-Sarpe
Château Clos des Jacobins
Château Lamarzelle
Château Laniote
Château Larcis-Ducasse
Château Larmande
Château Laroze
Clos La Madeleine
Château Matras
Château Mauvezin
Château Moulin-du-Cadet
Clos de L'Oratoire
Château Pavie-Decesse
Château Pavie-Macquin
Château Pavillon-Cadet
Château Petit-Faurie-de-Soutard
Château Le Prieuré
Château Ripeau
Château Saint-Georges-Côte-Pavie
Clos Saint-Martin
Château Sannonnet
Château La Serre
Château Soutard
Château Tertre-Daugay
Château La Tour Figeac
Château La Tour-du-Pin-Figeac (Giraud)
Château La Tour-du-Pin-Figeac-Moueix
Château Trimoulet
Château Troplong-Mondot
Château Villemaurine
Château Yon-Figeac

DECLASSIFIED (10)

Château Baleau
Château Cadet-Bon
Château La Carte
Château Chapelle Madeleine
Château La Couspaude
Château Coutet
Château Le Couvent
Château Grandes-Murailles
Château Jean-Faure
Château Trois-Moulins

(*) Declassified from Premier Grand Cru Classé to Grand Cru Classé.
(**) New classified château

The 1959 Graves Classification

Contrary to the Médoc, St-Emilion, and Pomerol districts, which can only make red wines under their respective appellations, Graves can make red and white wines under its appellation. Therefore, I have included both the red and white classifications in alphabetical order.

CRUS CLASSÉS (13 Red Wines)

Château Bouscaut
Château Carbonnieux
Domaine de Chevalier
Château de Fieuzal
Château Haut-Bailly
Château Haut-Brion
Château Malartic-Lagravière
Château La Mission-Haut-Brion
Château Olivier
Château Pape-Clément
Château Smith-Haut-Lafitte
Château La Tour-Haut-Brion
Château La Tour-Martillac

CRUS CLASSÉS (9 White Wines)

Château Bouscaut
Château Carbonnieux
Domaine de Chevalier
Château Couhins
Château Couhins-Lurton
Château Laville Haut-Brion
Château Malartic-Lagravière
Château Olivier
Château La Tour-Martillac

E. The 1932 Classification of Crus Bourgeois

The three levels of this official classification are:

Crus Bourgeois Superieurs Exceptionnels (BSE)
Crus Bourgeois Superieurs (BS)
Crus Bourgeois (B)

The initials "NL" indicate that the property no longer exists. In that case, the vineyards were either acquired by another property or uprooted.

CHÂTEAUX	CRUS	COMMUNES
Domaine de l'Abbaye-Skinner (NL)	B	Vertheuil
Château Abbé-Gorsse-de-Gorsse	BS	Margaux
Château Abel-Laurent (NL)	BS	Margaux
Château d'Agassac	BS	Ludon
Château Andron (NL)	B	Civrac
Domaine Andron (NL)	B	St-Seurin-de-Cadourne
Château Andron-Blanquet	B	St-Estèphe
Château d'Aneillan (NL)	BS	Pauillac
Château Aney	B	Cussac
Château d'Angludet	BSE	Cantenac
Château Anthonic	BS	Moulis
Château d'Arche	BS	Ludon
Château d'Arcins	B	Arcins
Château Arnauld	B	Arcins
Château d'Arsac	B	Arsac
Château d'Avensan (NL)	B	Avensan
Château Bages (NL)	B	Pauillac
Domaine de Bages (NL)	B	Pauillac
Château Balac	B	St-Laurent
Château Balogues (NL)	B	Pauillac
Cru La Banna (NL)	B	Bégadan
Château Barateau	B	St-Laurent
Château Le Barrail	B	Bégadan
Château Barreyres	B	Arcins
Château La Batisse (NL)	B	St-Sauveur
Château Beaulieu (NL)	B	St-Germain-d'Esteuil
Château Beaumont	BS	Cussac
Château Beauséjour (NL)	B	Listrac
Château Beauséjour	B	St-Estèphe
Château Beau-Site	B	St-Estèphe
Château Beau-Site-Haut-Vignoble (NL)	BS	St-Estèphe
Château La Bécade	B	Listrac
Château La Bécade de Veyrin (NL)	B	Listrac
Château La Begadanet	B	Bégadan
Château Bel-Air (NL)	B	Blanquefort

CHÂTEAUX	CRUS	COMMUNES
Château Bel-Air-Arsac (NL)	B	Arsac
Château Bel-Air-Lagrave	B	Moulis
Château Bel-Air-Marquis-d'Aligre	B	Soussans
Château Bellegrave	B	Pauillac
Château Bellegrave	B	Valeyrac
Château Bellegrave	B	Listrac
Château Bellegrave-du-Poujeau (NL)	B	Pian
Château Bellerive-Clos-Valeyrac	B	Valeyrac
Château Belle Rose	B	Pauillac
Château des Belles-Graves	B	Ordonnac
Château Bellevue	B	Macau
Château Bellevue-Cordeillan-Bages (NL)	B	Pauillac
Château Bellevue-Ferchaud (NL)	BS	Pauillac
Château Belmont-Puyastruc (NL)	B	Blanquefort
Château Bel-Orme-Tronquoy-de-Lalande	B	St-Seurin-de-Cadourne
Château Bergeron (NL)	B	Moulis
Château Bernones	B	Cussac
Cru de Bert (NL)	B	Couqueques
Château des Bertins	B	Bégadan
Château Bessan-Ségur	B	Civrac
Château Beyzac (NL)	B	Vertheuil
Château Bichon-Bages	B	Pauillac
Château Biston-Brillette (M. Barburin)	B	Moulis
Cru de Bizeaudun (NL)	B	Ludon
Château Blaignan	B	Blaignan
Château Bonneau-Livran	B	St-Seurin-de-Cadourne
Château Bontemps-Dubarry (NL)	BS	St-Julien
Château Le Bosq	B	St-Christoly
Château Le Bosq	BS	St-Estèphe
Château Bouqueyran	B	Moulis
Château Le Bourdieu (NL)	B	Valeyrac
Château Le Bourdieu	B	Vertheuil
Château Bourgade-la-Chapelle (NL)	BS	Labarde
Château du Breuil	B	Cissac
Château Brillette	BS	Moulis
Château Brun (NL)	B	Taillan
Château Buzaguet (NL)	B	Taillan
Château de By	B	Bégadan
Château de Cach	B	St-Laurent
Château Cambon-la-Pelouse	BS	Macau
Château Camino-Salva	B	Cussac
Château Cantegric (NL)	B	Listrac
Château Canteloup (NL)	BS	St-Estèphe
Château Capbern-Gasqueton	BS	St-Estèphe
Château Cap-de-Haut	BS	Lamarque
Château Capdeville (NL)	B	Lamarque
Château Cap-Léon-Veyrin	B	Listrac
Château La Cardonne	B	Blaignan
Château Caronne-Sainte-Gemme	BS	St-Laurent
Cru-Carrasset (NL)	B	Lamarque
Grand Cru des Carruades (Moulin des Carruades)	B	Pauillac
Château du Cartillon	B	Lamarque
Château du Castera	BV	St-Germain-d'Esteuil
Château Caussan	B	Blaignan
Château Les Chalets	B	St-Christoly
Château Chambert-Marbuzet	B	St-Estèphe
Château Charmail	B	St-Seurin-de-Cadourne
Château Chasse-Spleen	BSE	Moulis
Cru de La Chatolle (NL)	B	St-Laurent
Château La Chesnavy-Sainte-Gemme	BS	Cussac

CHÂTEAUX	CRUS	COMMUNES
Château Chollet (NL)	B	Blanquefort
Clos des Cimbats (NL)	B	Blanquefort
Château Cissac	B	Cissac
Château Citran	BS	Avensan
Château La Clare	B	Bégadan
Château Clarke	BS	Listrac
Château Clauzet	B	St-Estèphe
Château La Closerie-Grand-Poujeaux	B	Moulis
Château Colombier-Mompelou	BS	Pauillac
Château La Colonilla (NL)	B	Margaux
Château La Commanderie	B	St-Estèphe
Château Conseillant (NL)	B	Labarde
Château Constant-Bages-Monpélou (NL)	BS	Pauillac
Château Constant-Lesquireau	B	Vertheuil
Château Constant-Trois-Moulins (NL)	BS	Macau
Château Corbeil (NL)	B	Blanquefort
Cru Le Coteau	B	Arsac
Château Coufran	B	St-Seurin-de-Cadourne
Château La Couronne	BSE	Pauillac
Château Coutelin-Merville	B	St-Estèphe
Château Le Crock	BS	St-Estèphe
Château Croizet-Touchant-Latour (NL)	B	Pauillac
Château Cujac (NL)	B	Moulis
Château Cujac-Langlois (NL)	B	St-Aubin
Château Daubos (NL)	B	Pauillac
Château Dehez (NL)	B	Blanquefort
Château Deyrem-Valentin	B	Soussans
Château Dillon	B	Blanquefort
Château Donissan	B	Listrac
Cru Douat-Sénot (NL)	B	Soussans
Château Doumens (NL)	B	Margaux
Château Dubignon-Talbot (NL)	BS	Margaux
Château Ducluzeau	B	Listrac
Château Dulamon (NL)	B	Blanquefort
Château Duplessis-Fabre	BS	Moulis
Château Duplessis-Hauchecorne	BS	Moulis
Château Duroc-Milon (NL)	B	Pauillac
Château Duthil-Haut-Cressan	B	Pian
Château Dutruch-Grand-Poujeaux	BS	Moulis
Château d'Egmont (NL)	BS	Ludon
Château d'Escot	B	Lesparre
Château Faget	B	St-Estèphe
Château Fatin	BS	St-Estèphe
Château Felletin (NL)	B	Lamarque
Château Felloneau (NL)	B	Macau
Château Fleurennes (NL)	B	Blanquefort
Château La Fleur-Milon	B	Pauillac
Château Fonbadet	BS	Pauillac
Château Fongravey (NL)	B	Blanquefort
Château Fonpetite (NL)	BS	St-Estèphe
Château Fonpiqueyre	B	St-Sauveur
Château Fonreaud	BS	Listrac
Château Fontanet	B	Taillan
Château Fontbonne-Agassac (NL)	B	Ludon
Château Fontesteau	B	St-Sauveur
Château Fourcas-Dupré	BS	Listrac
Château Fourcas-Hostens	BS	Listrac
Château Fourcas-Loubaney	B	Listrac
Château La France	B	Blaignan
La Fuie-Saint-Bonnet	B	Couquèques

CHÂTEAUX	CRUS	COMMUNES
Château Galan (NL)	B	St-Laurent
Château Gallais-Bellevue	B	Ordonnac
Château La Garosse (NL)	B	St-Sauveur
Château Gastebois (NL)	BS	Moulis
Château de Germignan (NL)	B	Taillan
Château Gironville (NL)	B	Macau
Château du Glana	BS	St-Julien
Château Gloria	B	St-Julien
Château La Gorce	B	Blaignan
Château Grand-Clapeau-Olivier	B	Blanquefort
Cru Grand Duroc (Ardilley) (NL)	B	Pauillac
Château Grand-Duroc-Milon	B	Pauillac
Château Grand-Médoc (NL)	B	Vertheuil
Château Grand-Pontet-Ludon (NL)	B	Ludon
Château Grand-Saint-Julien (NL)	BS	St-Julien
Château Grand-Saint-Lambert (NL)	B	Pauillac
Cru Grand-Saint-Lambert (NL)	B	Pauillac
Château du Grand-Soussans (NL)	B	Soussans
Château Grandis	B	St-Seurin-de-Cadourne
Grange de Heby (NL)	B	Castelnau
Château Granges d'Or	B	Blaignan
Château Granins (NL)	B	Moulis
Graves de By (NL)	B	Bégadan
Graves des Quatre-Moulins (NL)	B	St-Christoly
Graves de Guitignan (NL)	B	Moulis
Cru La Gravette (NL)	B	Lamarque
Château La Gravière-Couerbe (NL)	B	Vertheuil
Château Gressier-Grand-Poujeaux	BS	Moulis
Cru Guiraud-Grach (NL)	B	St-Christoly
Château de Guitignan	B	Moulis
Cru de Guitignan (NL)	B	Moulis
Domaine des Gunes (NL)	B	Cissac
Château La Gurgue	BS	Margaux
Château Hanteillan	B	Cissac
Château Haut-Bages-Averous	B	Pauillac
Cru Haut-Bages-Drouillet (NL)	B	Pauillac
Château Haut-Breton-Larigaudiere	B	Soussans
Château Haut-Brignays (NL)	B	Vertheuil
Château Haut-Canteloup (J. Sarrazy)	B	Couquèques
Château Haut-Canteloup (C. Vilas-Samica)	B	Couquèques
Château Haut-Carmail (NL)	B	St-Seurin-de-Cadourne
Cru Haut-Cenot (NL)	B	Soussans
Clos Haut-Duras (NL)	B	Blanquefort
Château du Haut-Galan (NL)	B	Avensan
Château Haut-Marbuzet	B	St-Estèphe
Château Haut-Myles (NL)	B	Blaignan
Château Haut-Saint-Estèphe (NL)	B	St-Estèphe
Château Haut-Saint-Julien-Marian (NL)	BS	St-Julien
Château Haut-Tayac	B	Soussans
Cru Haut-Vignoble-Seguin (NL)	B	St-Estèphe
Château Hauterive	B	St-Germain-d'Esteuil
Château La Haye	BS	St-Estèphe
Château La Haye (NL)	B	Taillan
Domaine de l'Hermitage-Lamourous (NL)	B	Pian
Château L'Hopital	B	St-Estèphe
Château Houissant	BS	St-Estèphe
Château La Houringue (NL)	BS	Macau
Château Hourtin-Ducasse	B	St-Sauveur
Château Jautard (NL)	B	Listrac
Château Labadie	B	Bégadan

CHÂTEAUX	CRUS	COMMUNES
Château Labarde (NL)	B	Labarde
Château Labégorce	BS	Margaux
Château Labégorce-Zédé	B	Soussans
Cru Lacaussade-Milon (NL)	B	Pauillac
Château Ladouys	B	St-Estèphe
Château Laffitte-Carcasset-Padirac	B	St-Estèphe
Château Laffitte-Laujac (NL)	B	Bégadan
Château Lafitte-Canteloup	B	Ludon
Château Lafitte-Cantegric (NL)	B	Listrac
Château Lafon	BS	Listrac
Cru Lafontaine (NL)	B	St-Christoly
Domaine de Lagorce (NL)	B	Taillan
Château Lalande	B	Listrac
Château Lalande-Borie	BS	St-Julien
Château de Lamarque	BS	Lamarque
Château Lamothe-De-Bergeron	B	Cussac
Château Lamothe-Cissac	B	Cissac
Château Lamorere (NL)	B	Moulis
Château Lamouroux	BS	Margaux
Château Lancien-Brillete (NL)	B	Moulis
Château Landon (NL)	B	Bégadan
Château Lanessan	BS	Cussac
Château Laride	B	Vertheuil
Château Larose-Trintaudon	BS	St-Laurent
Château Larrieu-Terrefort	BS	Macau
Château Larrivaux (NL)	B	Cissac
Château Lartigue	B	Valeyrac
Château Lartigue-de-Brochon	B	St-Seurin-de-Cadourne
Château Lassus	B	Bégadan
Château Laudère (NL)	BS	Avensan
Château Laujac	B	Bégadan
Château Lemoine-Lafont-Rochet	B	Ludon
Château Les Lesques (NL)	B	Lesparre
Château Lestage	BS	Listrac
Château Lestage-Darquier-Grand-Poujeaux	BS	Moulis
Château Lestage-Simon	B	St-Seurin-de-Cadourne
Château Leyssac	B	St-Estèphe
Château Leyssac-Morange (NL)	B	St-Estèphe
Cru Lhereteyre (NL)	B	St-Estèphe
Château Liouner	B	Listrac
Château Listrac-Savy (NL)	B	Listrac
Château Liversan	BS	St-Sauveur
Château Livran	B	St-Germain-d'Esteuil
Château Loudenne	B	St-Yzan
Château Lousteauneuf	B	Valeyrac
Château Lugagnac	B	Vertheuil
Château La Luzette (NL)	B	Listrac
Château Mac-Carthy (Raymond)	B	St-Estèphe
Château Mac-Carthy-Moula	B	St-Estèphe
Château Maison-Blanche (NL)	B	St-Yzan
Château Malecot-Desse (NL)	BS	Pauillac
Château Malescasse	B	Lamarque
Château de Malleret	BS	Pian
Château de Marbuzet	BS	St-Estèphe
Château Marsac-Séguineau	B	Soussans
Château Martinens (NL)	BS	Cantenac
Château Maucaillou	B	Moulis
Château Maucamps	BS	Macau
Château Maurac	B	St-Seurin-de-Cadourne
Château Maurian (NL)	B	Blanquefort

CHÂTEAUX	CRUS	COMMUNES
Château Mauvesin	BS	Moulis
Clos de May (NL)	B	Macau
Château Mazails	B	St-Yzan
Château Meyney	BS	St-Estèphe
Château Meyre-Estèbe (NL)	B	Avensan
Château Mayre-Rabot (NL)	B	Avensan
Château Meyre-Vieux-Clos (NL)	B	Avensan
Château de Monbrison	BS	Arsac
Château du Mont (NL)	B	St-Seurin-de-Cadourne
Château Montbrun	B	Cantenac
Cru le Monteil-Arsac (NL)	BS	Arsac
Domaine de Montgiraud (NL)	B	Blanquefort
Château du Monthil	B	Bégadan
Château Morin	B	St-Estèphe
Clos du Moulin	B	St-Christoly
Moulin-de-Boucheau (NL)	B	Pian
Château de Moulin-du-Bourg	B	Listrac
Moulin-Neuf (NL)	B	St-Julien
Château Moulin-Riche	BSE	St-Julien
Château Moulin de La Rose	B	St-Julien
Moulin de Soubeyran (NL)	B	Pian
Château Moulin à Vent	BS	Moulis
Château La Mouline	B	Moulis
Château Moulis	BS	Moulis
Château Nexon	BS	Ludon
Château Nodris (NL)	B	Vertheuil
Château Notton-Baury	B	Arsac
Château les Ormes-de-Pez	B	St-Estèphe
Château Pabeau	B	St-Seurin-de-Cadourne
Château Padarnac (NL)	B	Pauillac
Château Paloumey (NL)	BS	Ludon
Château Panigon	B	Civrac
Château de Parempuyre (Dominique Pichon)	BS	Parempuyre
Château Patache-d'Aux	B	Bégadan
Château Paveil de Luze	B	Soussans
Château du Perier (NL)	B	St-Christoly
Château Peris de Courcelles (NL)	B	Vertheuil
Cru Perrichonne (de Courcelles) (NL)	B	St-Sauveur
Château Pey-de-Pont	B	Civrac
Château Peyrabon	B	St-Sauveur
Château Peyrat (NL)	B	St-Laurent
Château Peyrelebade (NL)	B	Listrac
Château de Pez	BS	St-Estèphe
Château Phélan-Ségur	BS	St-Estèphe
Château Pian-Geneste (NL)	B	Pian
Château Pibran (NL)	BS	Macau
Château Pibran	B	Pauillac
Château Picard	B	St-Estèphe
Château Picourneau	B	Vertheuil
Château Pierre-Bibian	BS	Listrac
Château La Pigotte (NL)	B	Blaignan
Château Plagnac	B	Bégadan
Château Plantier-Rose	B	St-Estèphe
Château Pomeys	BS	Moulis
Château Pomys	BS	St-Estèphe
Château Pontac-Lynch	B	Cantenac
Château Pontoise-Cabarrus-Brochon	B	St-Seurin-de-Cadourne
Château Pontensac	B	Ordonnac
Château Poujeaux	BS	Moulis
Château Preuillac	B	Lesparre

CHÂTEAUX	CRUS	COMMUNES
Château Privera	B	St-Christoly
Château Quimper	B	St-Seurin-de-Cadourne
Château Ramage-la-Batisse	B	St-Sauveur
Château du Raux	B	Cussac
Château la Raze-Taffard (NL)	B	Civrac
Château Real (NL)	B	St-Seurin-de-Cadourne
Château Renouil-Franquet (NL)	B	Moulis
Château du Retout	B	Cussac
Château Reverdi (NL)	B	Lamarque
Château Ricaudet-Troussas (NL)	B	Valeyrac
Château Robert-Franquet	B	Moulis
Château Le Roc	BS	St-Estèphe
Cru du Roc (NL)	B	St-Christoly
Château Roche (NL)	BS	St-Estèphe
Château Romefort (NL)	B	Blaignan
Château Romefort (NL)	B	Cussac
Cru Romefort (NL)	B	Avensan
Château Roquegrave-Haut-Valeyrac	B	Valeyrac
Château Rose la Biche (NL)	BS	Macau
Château Rosemont (NL)	BS	Labarde
Château Ruat	B	Moulis
Château Saint-Bonnet	B	St-Christoly
Château Saint-Christoly	B	St-Christoly
Château Saint-Christophe	B	St-Christoly
Château Saint-Estèphe	B	St-Estèphe
Château Saint-Julien (NL)	BS	St-Julien
Château Saint-Lambert (NL)	B	Pauillac
Château Saint-Laurent (NL)	B	St-Laurent
Cru Saint-Pierre (NL)	BS	St-Julien
Château Saint-Saturnin	B	Bégadan
Château Sainte-Anne (NL)	B	St-Christoly
Château la Salle-de-Breillan (NL)	B	Blanquefort
Château Saransot-Dupré	BS	Listrac
Château Ségur	BS	Parempuyre
Château Ségur-Fillon	BS	Parempuyre
Château Semeillan	BS	Listrac
Château Semeillan-Mazeau	BS	Listrac
Château Sénéjac	BS	Pian
Château Senilhac	B	St-Seurin-de-Cadourne
Cru Servant-Ainé (NL)	B	St-Christoly
Château Sigognac	B	St-Yzan
Château Sipian (NL)	B	Valeyrac
Château Siran	BS	Labarde
Château Sociando-Mallet	B	St-Seurin-de-Cadourne
Château Souley-Sainte-Croix	B	Vertheuil
Château Taffard-La-Raze (NL)	B	Civrac
Château du Taillan	B	Taillan
Château Tanais-Clapaud (NL)	B	Blanquefort
Château Tayac	B	Soussans
Château Le Temple (Alibert) (NL)	B	Valeyrac
Château Le Temple (Pourreau) (NL)	B	Valeyrac
Château de Testeron (NL)	B	Moulis
Cru La Tour-L'Aspic (NL)	B	Pauillac
Château La Tour-Blanche	B	St-Christoly
Château La Tour-du-Breuil (NL)	B	St-Christoly
Château La Tour de By	B	Bégadan
Clos La Tour du Camp (NL)	B	Blanquefort
Château La Tour-Castillon	B	St-Christoly
La Tour du Haut-Carmail (NL)	B	St-Seurin-de Cadourne
Château La Tour-Haut-Caussan	B	Blaignan

CHÂTEAUX	CRUS	COMMUNES
Château Tour-du-Haut-Vignoble	B	St-Estèphe
Cru La Tour-Haut-Vignoble (Signoret) (NL)	B	St-Estèphe
Château de La Tour-de-Marbuzet	B	St-Estèphe
Château La Tour-Marcillanet	B	St-Laurent
Château La Tour Massac (NL)	B	Cantenac
Château La Tour-Milon (NL)	B	Pauillac
Château la Tour du Mirail	B	Cissac
Château La Tour de Mons	B	Soussans
La Tour du Mont (NL)	B	St-Seurin-de-Cadourne
La Tour Négrier (NL)	B	Couquèques
Château La Tour-Pibran	B	Pauillac
Cru La Tour-Pineau (NL)	B	St-Estèphe
Château Tour-Prignac	B	Prignac
La Tour du Roc	B	Arcins
Château La Tour-du-Roc-Milon (NL)	B	Pauillac
Château La Tour-Saint-Bonnet	B	St-Christoly
Château La Tour-Saint-Joseph	B	Cissac
La Tour-Seran	B	St-Christoly
Château La Tour-Sieujan (NL)	B	St-Laurent
Château Tour-des-Termes	B	St-Estèphe
La Tour des Termes (Bernard) (NL)	B	Vertheuil
La Tour des Termes (Faugeras) (NL)	B	Vertheuil
Château Tourteran	B	St-Sauveur
Château Tramont	B	Arcins
Cru Triomphant (NL)	B	St-Christoly
Château des Trois-Moulins (NL)	BS	Macau
Château Tronquoy-Lalande	BS	St-Estèphe
Château Troussas (NL)	B	Valeyrac
Château Tujean (NL)	B	Blanquefort
Domaine de Verdasse (NL)	B	Valeyrac
Château Verdignan	B	St-Seurin-de-Cadourne
Cru de Verdun (NL)	B	Valeyrac
Château Verdus	B	St-Seurin-de-Cadourne
Château Vernous	B	Lesparre
Château de Vertheuil (NL)	B	Vertheuil
Château Victoria	B	Vertheuil
Château de Villambis (NL)	B	Cissac
Château Villegeorge	BSE	Avensan
Château Vincent	B	Cantenac

The Appellation d'Origine Contrôlée of each commune of the Médoc is as follows:

A.O.C.'s	Communes
St-Estèphe:	St-Estèphe
Pauillac:	Pauillac
St-Julien:	St-Julien
Listrac:	Listrac
Moulis:	Moulis
Margaux:	Cantenac, Margaux, Soussans, Arsac, and Labarde
Haut-Médoc:	All of the above, if they do desire, in addition to the following: Blanquefort, Le Taillan, St-Aubin, St-Hélène, St-Médart-en-Jalles, Parempuyre, La Pian, Ludon, Macau, Avensan, Castelnau, Arcins, Lamargue, Cussac, St-Laurent, St-Sauveur, Cissac, Vertheuil, and St-Seurin-de-Cardourne
Médoc:	All of the above, if they so desire, in addition to the following: Vensac, Jau-Dignac-et-Loirac, St-Vivien, Valeyrac, Queyrac, Bégadan, St-Christoly, Couquèques, Civrac, Prignac, Gaillan, Blaignan, St-Yzans, Lesparre, Ordonnac, and St-Germain-

F. The 1978 Syndicates Classification of Crus Bourgeois

CRUS GRANDS BOUREGOIS EXCEPTIONNELS (18)

D'Agassac (Ludon)
Andron-Blanquet (St-Estèphe)
Beau-Site (St-Estèphe)
Capbern Gasqueton (St-Estèphe)
Caronne-Sainte-Gemme (St-Laurent)
Chasse-Spleen (Moulis)
Cissac (Cissac)
Citran (Avensan)
Le Crock (St-Estèphe)
Dutruch-Grand-Poujeaux (Moulis)
Fourcas-Dupré (Listrac)
Fourcas-Hosten (Listrac)
Du Glana (St-Julien)
Haut-Marbuzet (St-Estèphe)
De Marbuzet (St-Estèphe)
Meyney (St-Estèphe)
Phélan-Ségur (St-Estèphe)
Poujeaux (Moulis)

CRUS GRANDS BOURGEOIS (41)

Beaumont (Cussac)
Bel-Orme (St-Seurin-de-Cadourne)
Brillette (Moulis)
La Cardonne (Blaignan)
Colombier-Monpelou (Pauillac)
Coufran (St-Seurin-de-Cadourne)
Coutelin-Merville (St-Estèphe)
Duplessis-Hauchecorne (Moulis)
La Fleur Milon (Pauillac)
Fontesteau (St-Sauveur)
Greysac (Bégadan)
Hanteillan (Cissac)
Lafon (Listrac)
De Lamarque (Lamarque)
Lamothe-Cissac (Cissac)
Larose-Trintaudon (St-Laurent)
Laujac (Bégadan)
Liversan (St-Sauveur)
Loudenne (St-Yzans-de-Médoc)
Mac-Carthy (St-Estèphe)
De Malleret (Le Pian)
Martinens (Margaux)
Morin (St-Estèphe)
Moulin à Vent (Moulis)
Le Meynieu (Vertheuil)
Les Ormes de Pez (St-Estèphe)
Les Ormes Sorbet (Conquèques)
Patache d'Aux (Bégadan)
Paveil de Luze (Soussans)
Peyrabon (St-Sauveur)
Pontoise-Cabarrus (St-Seurin de Cadourne)
Potensac (Potensac)
Reysson (Vertheuil)
Ségur (Parempuyre)
Sigognac (St-Yzans-de-Médoc)
Sociando-Mallet (St-Seurin-de-Cadourne)
Du Taillan (Le Taillan)
La Tour-de-By (Bégadan)
La Tour-du-Haut-Moulin (Cussac)
Tronquoy-Lalande (St-Estèphe)
Verdignan (St-Seurin-de-Cadourne)

CRUS BOUREGOIS (64)

Aney (Cussac
Balac (St-Laurent)
La Becade (Listrac)
Bellerive (Valeyrac)
Bellerose (Pauillac)
Les Bertins (Valeyrac)
Bonneau (St-Seurin-de-Cadourne)
Le Boscq (St-Christoly)
du Breuil (Cissac)
La Bridane (St-Julien)
De By (Bégadan)
Cap-Léon-Veyrin (Listrac)

CRUS BOURGEOIS (64) continued

Carcanieux (Queyrac)
Puy Castera (Cissac)
Chambert (St-Estèphe)
La Clare (Bégadan)
Clarke (Listrac)
La Closerie-Grand-Poujeaux (Moulis)
Duplessis-Fabre (Moulis)
Fonpiqueyre (St-Sauveur)
Fonreaud (Listrac)
Fort Vauban (Cussac)
La France (Blaignan)
Gallais-Bellevue (Potensac)
Grand-Duroc-Moulin (Pauillac)
Grand-Moulin (St-Seurin-de-Cadourne)
Haut-Bages-Monpelou (Pauillac)
Haut-Canteloup (Couquèques)
Haut-Garin (Bégadan)
Haut-Padarnac (Pauillac)
Hourbanon (Prignac)
Hourtin-Ducasse (St-Sauveur)
De Labat (St-Laurent)
Lamothe-Bergeron (Cussac)
Landat (Cissac)
Landon (Bégadan)
Larivière (Blaignan)
Lartigue-de-Brochon (St-Seurin-de-Cadourne)
Lassalle (Potensac)
Lestage (Listrac)
Mac-Carthy-Moula (St-Estèphe)
Monthil (Bégadan)
Moulin Rouge (Cussac)
Panigon (Civrac)
Pibran (Pauillac)
Plantey-de-la-Croix (St-Seurin-de-Cadourne)
Pontet (Blaignan)
Ramage-la-Batisse (St-Sauveur)
Romefort (Cussac)
La Roque de By (Bégadan)
De la Rose Maréchal (St-Seurin-de-Cadourne)
St. Bonnet (St-Christoly)
St. Roch (St-Estèphe)
Soudars (St-Seurin-de-Cadourne)
Tayac (Soussans)
La Tour Blanche (St-Christoly)
La Tour du Haut-Caussan (Blaignan)
La Tour du Mirail (Cissac)
La Tour Saint-Bonnet (St-Christoly)
La Tour Saint-Joseph (Cissac)
Des Tourelles (Blaignan)
La Valière (St-Christoly)
Vernous (Lesparre)
Vieux-Robin (Bégadan)

NEW MEMBERS FOR CLASSIFICATION

Château Bellevue (Valeyrac)
Château Canuet (Margaux)
Château l'Estruelle (Ordonnac)
Château Hauterive (St-Germain-d'Esteuil)
Château Lestage-Simon (St-Seurin-de-Cadourne)
Domaine Magnol-Dehez (Blanquefort)
Château Malescasse (Lamarque)
Château Maucaillou (Moulis)
Château Malmaison (Listrac)
Château Monbrison (Arsac)
Château Pey-Martin (Ordonnac)
Château Tour-du-Roc (Arcins)
Château Cailloux de By (Bégadan)
Château de Conques (St-Christoly)
Château Moulin-de-la-Roque (Bégadan)
Château Saransot-Dupré (Listrac)

G. Yves Durand's Sauternes Wine Ratings

	1959	1961	1962	1966	1967	1970	1971	1975	1976	1978	1979	1980	1981	1982	1983	1984
Average Vintage Rating	19	16	18	16	18	17	17h	18	17h	15h	16	17	17	16	19	14
PREMIER CRU SUPERIEUR (1)																
Château d'Yquem	19	17	18	17	19	18h	18	19h	18h	17	17h	18h	18			
PREMIERS CRUS (5)																
Château Climens	19	16h	18+	16	17	16h	17h	18	16h	15	16	17h		16	18	
Château de Fargues*					18		17h	17h	18		17	18	17h			
Château Raymond-Lafon*								18		17h		18	17h+	17h	18h	
Château Rieussec	13	14h	17h	15h	17	17	18	17h	18	16	17+	17	18	17	19	
Château Suduiraut	18	17	18	12	18h	16h	14	17	18	15	16h	15	17	17h	17+	
DEUXIEMES CRUS (10)																
Château Bastor-Lamontagne*								16h	16h			16		16h	17	
Château Broustet			16h	13	16h	16h	16h	15	none	14	15h	16h				
Château Coutet	19	16	18	14	13	15	17h	17h+	17	15h	16	17	16h	17+		
Château Doisy-Daene		16	15			15	15h	16	15h	16+	16h	16+	16	16+	17h	
Château Doisy-Dubroca					16	16	17	16h	14							
Château Doisy-Védrines		14	16h			17h	14h	16h	16h	15	15	16h				
Château Guiraud	14h	15h	11	13	17	14h	12	15	15h	14	15h	14	15h	14	16h	
Château Lafaurie-Peyraguey	18	15	15	14	17h	14	14	14h	15h	14	16	16h	17h	17	18	
Château Nairac								17	17+		15h	17	16	16h		
Château Sigalas-Rabaud		16		12	17h	13	16	15	16	11	14h	15	16	15	17h	
TROISIEMES CRUS (5)																
Château d'Arche		15	15	10	16	13	16	16+	12	13	13	16h			17h+	
Château Caillou					15	16	14	16	15		14h	15	15h			
Château Filhot			15	8	13	16h	15h	14	16h	13	15h	14h	16h			
Château Rayne-Vigneau			16h	12	16h	11	14h	14h	14h	12	14	14	14h	14	16+	
Château Romer-du-Hayot					16h	16h	15	15h	16h	14	16				17	

QUATRIÈMES CRUS (3)

Château Lamothe (Despujols)	12	11	12	14h	13h	13h	15	14h	14	14h				
Château de Malle	16	16h	12	12h	14	14	15	14	13	14	14h	14	13	16
Château La Tour Blanche	16	14	12h	16h	16h	15h	15	16		14				

CINQUIÈMES CRUS (3)

Clos Haut-Peyraguey	12	13	14	14h	13	13h	14h	15	13	13h				
Château Rabaud-Promis			13	15	12	13	16	15	13	14h				
Château Suau				15	14h	15	14	13	14	15	13			

*Property not classified in 1855, which made it to my classification.

NOTES:
Château Lamothe (Guignard): proprietors Phillippe et Jacques Guignard had their first vintage in 1981. I have not tasted any of their wines yet. This property was classified as a second growth in 1855 when it was part of one estate. Today, the other half of that property is owned by the Despujols family.

Château Romer: Its wines are being commercialized by Mr. du Hayot and labeled under Château Romer-du-Hayot. The last Château Romer I tasted was the 1970 vintage.

H. Food and Bordeaux Wine Harmony

Is it better to match wine with food or food with wine?

It is important to be able to do both. If you want to enhance a special or favorite food, you must choose a wine that will complement it in the best possible way. On the other hand, you may want to serve an old vintage of wine that you have kept for two decades in your cellar. In that case, the taste, texture, and type of food should accentuate every positive aspect of the wine. A dish which goes perfectly well with a certain young Médoc vintage will probably not be very harmonious with this same wine ten years later. Great Médocs are living things. As they mature, their tannins round up, they acquire great elegance, and display many subtle flavors. The following suggestions are my favorite combinations of foods with Bordeaux wines.

Médoc Wines

ST-ESTÈPHE

When these wines are from three to eight years old, they can be very tannic and austere. If you insist on opening one, choose one of the following châteaux: Montrose, Cos d'Estournel, Calon-Ségur, Lafon-Rochet, Meyney, Cos-Labory, de Marbuzet, Haut-Marbuzet, de Pez, Les Ormes-de-Pez, Capbern-Gasqueton, Le Boscq, and Phélan-Ségur, recommended with the following dishes:

Red Meats

Beef bourguignon, beef stroganoff, hamburgers (with little or no ketchup), pot roast, prime rib of beef, roast beef, charcoal-grilled steak, meat loaf, steak tartare, shish kebab, venison, leg of lamb

Cheeses

Goat cheese and other mild-to-fairly strong cheeses

Pasta

Lasagna with meat sauce

Miscellaneous

Cassoulet, calf liver, *pâté de Campagne*

The St-Estèphe wines that were made in the '60s and early '70s are still austere for lack of fruit and heavy tannins. (This will not be the case for most of these wines produced in recent years.) When reaching twelve years of age, these better-made wines will show more generosity, more sweet fruit, better balance, and even some elegance. Here are my food recommendations for those older wines before the mid-'70s.

Red Meats

Beef Wellington, crown roast of lamb, sautéed lamb chops, sautéed steak (never grilled over charcoal because the taste could overwhelm the old wine). The sauces and spices for each dish should be mild and delicate enough to complement the wine.

Cheeses

Brie, Gruyère, and almost any mild cheese (without herbs, garlic or peppercorns)

Poultry

Coq-au-vin, Peking duck, roast duck, squab

Miscellaneous

Baked ham, veal cordon-bleu, *pâté-en-croute*, mousse of duck liver

PAUILLAC

When young (three to eight years old) these wines show much better than their St-Estèphe counterpart. Pauillacs display more fruit, better flavors, less astringency, and are well structured without being severe. Although they are fleshier and more quaffable when young, it is a pity to pull the cork too early. Most of them age gracefully, and, of course, the first-growth wines age majestically. Here are a few of my recommendations for the following châteaux: Lynch-Bages, Pichon-Lalande, Duhart-Milon-Rothschild, Grand-Puy-Lacoste, Pichon-Baron, Pontet-Canet, Batailley, Grand-Puy-Ducasse, Haut-Bages-Liberal, Haut-Batailley, Clerc-Milon, Croizet-Bages, Fonbadet, Lynch-Moussas, Mouton-Baronne-Philippe, Pédesclaux, La Couronne, La Fleur-Milon, Belle-Rose.

Red Meats

Lamb chops, leg of lamb; game such as bison, young venison (known as "Bambi"), wild boar; pan-fried rib-eye or New York strip steak, filet mignon with a Bordelaise sauce; coq-au-vin, kidneys, rabbit

Cheeses

Mild-to-fairly-strong cheeses

Pasta

Any pasta with cheese or a light, spicy stuffing. Never use a sauce with tomatoes, clams or carbonara.

Miscellaneous

Rib-eye *Marchand-de-vin, lamprey à la Bordelaise; pâté de Campagne,* and all other pâtés made with meat (duck, lamb, pheasant, etc.).

When Pauillac wines are matured and have acquired delicacy, subtlety, and softness, they have to be treated with the utmost respect. The food and the spices complementing these exquisite wines have to be very mild and delicate so as to never overwhelm the different flavors of the wine, and should enhance all of the subtleties of the distinguished nectar. When twelve years or older, I recommend the wines listed in the previous category in addition to the following first-growth properties. Lafite-Rothschild, Latour, and Mouton-Rothschild.

Red Meats

Tenderloin of beef sautéed and served with a béarnaise sauce and a hint of tarragon, mildly spiced venison (especially with a Latour), beef Wellington, roast beef, châteaubriand

Poultry

Oven-roasted chicken is probably the best accompaniment with a mature Pauillac (particularly with a Lafite), game poultry, duck with a mild and unctuous sauce (not orange, cherry or green peppercorn), pheasant under glass, quail, roast turkey (without cranberry sauce) with mild trimmings

Pasta

Fettuccini

Cheeses

Very mild cheeses, Havarti, 60 percent butterfat brie

Miscellaneous

Mild pâtés, foie gras, sweetbread prepared with a mild red wine sauce (make the sauce with the same Pauillac you are going to serve it with—but don't use a '59 Mouton. Rabbit chasseur, any veal dish provided the ingredients do not disturb the subtleties of the wine. Pork chops or pork loin as long as it is not charcoal grilled.

ST-JULIEN

When three to six years old they are perhaps the most charming and savory wines of the Haut-Médoc. Their soft, rounded, cedar flavors laced with sweet ripe black currants is often gorgeous. Even though many St-Juliens are not fully mature at this young age, one has to be very careful in the way one matches food with their precious, complex, and elegant flavors. The following are my recommendations should you serve one of these wines: Beychevelle, Ducru-Beaucaillou, Léoville-Las-Cases, Léoville-Poyferré, Branaire, Langoa-Barton (softer than its stable mate—Léoville-Barton, which is vinified in the old style), Gloria (very precocious since it is aged in very large old oak vats instead of new barrels), St. Pierre, Lagrange, du Glana, Hortevie, Lalande-Borie, Moulin-de-la-Rose. Gruaud-Larose and Talbot at that young age should be treated more as a Pauillac and aged a little longer than other St-Juliens.

Red Meats

Beef Wellington, prime rib of beef; leg of lamb,

NOTES

NOTES

NOTES